AN ACCOUNT OF THE PRIMITIVE TRIBES AND MONUMENTS OF THE NILAGIRIS

JAMES WILKINSON BREEKS

GYAN

Published by

GYAN

Gyan Publishing House
5, Ansari Road
Daryaganj, New Delhi-110002
Phone: 011-47034999, 9811692060
E-mail: books@gyanbooks.com

Distribution Network
gyanbooks.com
India, USA, Canada, UK, Australia

ISBN: 978-93-3304-175-1 (PB)

First Published, 1873

2nd Impression 2025

Printed at: Gyan Press, Delhi.

AN ACCOUNT OF THE PRIMITIVE TRIBES AND MONUMENTS OF THE NILAGIRIS
Author: JAMES WILKINSON BREEKS

AN ACCOUNT

OF THE

PRIMITIVE TRIBES AND MONUMENTS

OF THE

NILAGIRIS.

JAMES WILKINSON BREEKS,

OF THE MADRAS CIVIL SERVICE, COMMISSIONER OF THE NĪLAGIRIS;

EDITED BY

HIS WIDOW.

LONDON:

INDIA MUSEUM,

1873.

Wm H. ALLEN AND CO., 13, WATERLOO PLACE, S.W.

Publishers to the India Office.

PREFACE.

THE subjoined letters, and the orders passed thereon by the Government of Madras, will explain the circumstances under which this account of the Primitive Tribes and Monumental Remains of the Nīlagiris was written.

It was not originally designed for publication in its present form. Mr. Breeks's intention was to print only twelve or fifteen copies for the Madras Government, and the present extended edition is published by their orders. Mr. Breeks hoped to have completed the work in the Autumn of 1872. Almost all the necessary information had been obtained, and the greater part of the rough draft written, before his death on the 6th June. Hardly any revision, however, had been attempted, and to this any omissions (or perhaps errors in minor points) which may occur in the book, are attributable. Corrections made in England by another hand, and under all the disadvantages of distance, can never supply the place of the author's immediate revision. Considerable delay in the publication was also unavoidable under these altered circumstances. I hope, nevertheless, that this description of the jungle tribes and the rude monuments of the Nīlagiris will be found valuable. Its accuracy may be relied on. No pains were spared to verify every statement, in cases where actual seeing or hearing at first hand was impossible; and the few pages that follow, represent a very small part of the labour expended in extracting and comparing the incoherent statements of half-savage people, utterly unused to describing their own habits and practices, and often very suspicious of interrogations.

The illustrations, unfortunately, are for the most part indifferently executed. Mr. Breeks's object was to furnish the Government with the information they desired in as perfect a form as possible, without any great expense; and he therefore intended to have a few copies of a very complete set of photographs. No good photographer, however, was willing to supply these at a reasonable rate; and, as the expense of the excavations left little to spare for illustrations, Mr. Breeks was obliged to engage a photographer from the School of Arts at Madras, whose performances were by no means satisfactory.

Captain Sargeaunt of the Madras Revenue Survey Department kindly supplied the plans of cromlechs (Plates XLIV and XLIV (a)) from Mr. Breeks's drawings.

It will be observed that they are not drawn to scale, the object being rather to show the construction and arrangement of each group of cromlechs than their comparative size.

A collection of the utensils, ornaments, &c. in use among the different tribes, was made in accordance with the Government order subjoined, and Appendix B. contains a list of these. Appendix C. is a list of articles found in cairns and cromlechs. In most cases any assistance given has been acknowledged in the text; but for kind help afforded since Mr. Breeks's death, I have to thank Mr. Metz, Mr. Broughton, Dr. Cornish, Sir Walter Elliot, K.C.S.I., and most of all Sir Alexander Arbuthnot, K.C.S.I.

Edengate, Warcop,
November 1873.

S. M. Breeks.

PROCEEDINGS OF THE MADRAS GOVERNMENT, PUBLIC DEPARTMENT, 14th JUNE 1871.

Read the following Letter from the Honorary Secretary, Trustees Indian Museum, Calcutta, to the Secretary to Government, Fort St. George, dated Calcutta, 27th May 1871, No. 577.

1. The attention of the Trustees has recently been directed to the importance of devoting a section of the Indian Museum to illustrations of the state of the arts among the aboriginal and other jungle races in India and its Dependencies. With this view, it is desired to obtain collections of their arms, ornaments, dresses, household utensils, tools, agricultural implements, musical instruments, and indeed all objects that are the products of their own manufacturing skill, and that will serve to illustrate the habits and modes of life of those indigenous races that have remained but little affected by foreign civilization. It is unnecessary to dilate upon the interest that would attach to such a collection, both as leading to a knowledge of the habits of the less-known tribes in this part of Her Majesty's dominions, and as affording materials for a comparative study of the arts practised by races in an early stage of social development. It is desired at the same time to bring together a similar collection of the objects found in the ancient burial places, frequently associated with stone circles, which are known to exist abundantly in Central, Western, and Southern India, and may yet be met with elsewhere. Those, as at present known, consist chiefly of pottery, ornaments, and iron weapons. The stone flakes and celts, both of the chipped and polished types, and hatchets of copper, and perhaps bronze, which have been found in many parts of India, since attention has been prominently directed to such objects, are also desired for this collection.

2. In order to carry out these objects, I am desired to solicit through you the assistance of the officers under your Government, who, being employed among, or in the neighbourhood of, aboriginal tribes, or in places where ancient cairns and burial places are known to exist, may enjoy facilities for obtaining objects of the kinds enumerated. Objects of the former classes may probably be obtained by purchase for very moderate sums. It is, of course, not intended that any expense that may be incurred in their purchase, or transmission, should fall on the officers, to whose good offices the Trustees may be indebted for procuring the specimens. Objects of the latter class will probably only be obtainable under conditions where labour is easily and cheaply procurable for the purpose of excavating; and although the Trustees will be willing to purchase objects thus obtained at any moderate cost, they cannot undertake the responsibility of guaranteeing beforehand the cost of exploration.

3. In conclusion, I am desired to solicit His Excellency's personal support and co-operation in making known the Trustees' object to such officers as may be in a position to afford assistance in its practical accomplishment.

ORDER THEREON, 14th June 1871, No. 831.

His Excellency the Governor in Council considers that such a collection as that suggested by the Trustees of the Indian Museum, in the foregoing letter, would be very interesting and useful in the Madras Central Museum as well as in the Indian Museum, and he resolves, therefore, to request the Superintendent of the Central Museum, the Collectors of the several Districts in the Provinces, and the Commissioner of the Nilagiris, to report what can be done to procure the desired collections, and the probable cost of doing so.

Proceedings of the Madras Government, Public Department, 19th July 1871.

Read the following Letter from the Commissioner of the Nīlagiris, to the Chief Secretary to Government, Fort St. George, dated Ootacamund, 3rd July 1871, No. 57.

1. I have the honour to acknowledge Proceedings of Government, No. 92, Public Department, 14th June 1871, calling upon me to report what can be done to procure a collection * of arms, ornaments, dresses, manufactures, &c., that will serve to illustrate the habits and modes of life of the jungle tribes of the Nīlagiris, as well as a collection of objects found in ancient cairns and burial places, and to state the probable cost.

2. I am glad the matter is receiving attention, late in the day as it is, for year by year the Nīlagiri tribes at any rate are abandoning their distinctive customs. For example, among the Todas infanticide has been put a stop to; polyandry is on the decline; their buffalo sacrifices at the dry funeral are curtailed, and create comparatively little interest. Some few of the rising generation take service on plantations, and one or two have even asked for a school. With all the tribes, I believe, drink and disease are on the increase. Amongst a people in so low a state of civilization, a very few years serve to efface all trace of a custom that has been given up; whilst a careful examination into their existing condition and habits, affords the only hope of arriving at their origin and past history.

3. I am afraid that the time has passed for making a *complete* collection of the objects contained in the Nīlagiri cairns and cromlechs. Most of them have been opened by private individuals, and their contents are now dispersed far and wide.

Mr. Metz, however, who takes great interest in Nīlagiri antiquities, has promised me his assistance. He knows of some cairns and cromlechs still unopened, and some of them are built of stones ornamented with sculptures, of which copies ought to be made.

4. Considering the interest excited, and the speculations that have been advanced with regard to the history of the Nīlagiri tribes, especially the Todas, it seems to me desirable that the present inquiry under the auspices of Government should be as exhaustive as possible. I propose, therefore, if approved, to pursue the following course with each of the four† Nīlagiri, so-called, jungle tribes, viz.:

The Todas. | The Kurumbas.
The Kotas. | The Irulas.

I.—To make a collection of their dresses, weapons, implements, musical instruments, ornaments, utensils, and manufactures.

II.—To obtain photographs or drawings of each of the tribes and of their houses.

III.—To record all the facts I can collect with regard to their language, their present habits, ceremonies, and modes of life.

IV.—To inquire if they have any traditions or legends illustrative of their history.

V.—To collect objects that I may find in cairns, cromlechs, barrows, and stone circles still existing.

VI.—To obtain drawings of all ancient sculptures to be found on the hills.

5. It is impossible to say what the probable cost may be, but I think Rs. 1,000 would be ample.

6. I cannot promise any satisfactory results under at least a year.

Order thereon, 19th July 1871, No. 1,097.

1. The Government entirely approve the Commissioner's proposals, and beg him to take steps at once towards carrying them out. For the present he is authorised to incur expenditure not exceeding Rs. 1,000 for the purpose, and will report when further funds are required.

2. The Commissioner's attention is directed to the records of previous labours in this field, which will be found in the Journal of the Madras Literary Society, and probably in those of the Asiatic Society.

---

* One collection for the Calcutta Indian Museum, and one for the Madras Central Museum.

† The Badagas cannot be called an aboriginal or jungle race. *See* Plate I.

CONTENTS.

CHAPTER I.

CHAPTER II.

The Todas.

CHAPTER III.

The Kotas.

CHAPTER IV.

The Kurumbas.

CHAPTER V.

The Irulas.

CHAPTER VI.

Cairns and Cromlechs.

APPENDIX A.

APPENDIX B.

APPENDIX C.

LIST OF PLATES.

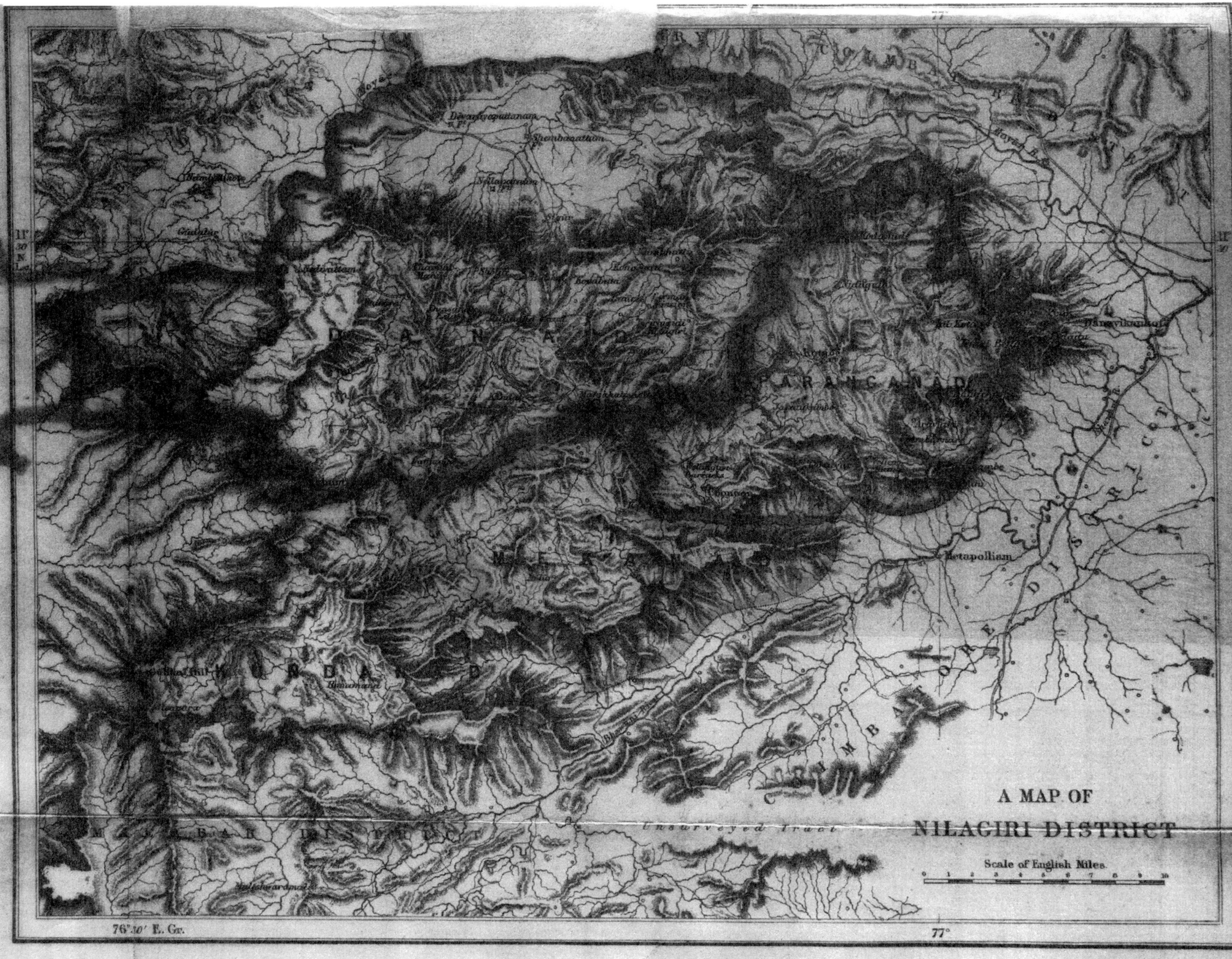

A MAP OF
NILAGIRI DISTRICT
Scale of English Miles
0 1 2 3 4 5 6 7 8 9 10
76°30′ E. Gr.
77°
11°30′ N.
PARANGANAD
MEKANAD
KUNDAH
MALABAR DISTRICT
COIMBATORE DISTRICT
Unsurveyed Tract
Metapolliam
Dévaráyaputtanam
Shembanattam
Nillapatnam
Bhavani R.
Moyar R.

THE PRIMITIVE TRIBES OF THE NĪLAGIRIS.

CHAPTER I.

GEOGRAPHICAL POSITION OF THE NĪLAGIRIS—ALTITUDE AND GENERAL CHARACTER—SCENERY.—CLIMATE.—RAINFALL.—RECOGNISED GEOGRAPHICAL DIVISIONS.—FIVE NATIVE TRIBES.—THE BADAGAS NOT ONE OF THE PRIMITIVE TRIBES.

The Nīlagiris* are a lofty range of mountains in Southern India situated between 11° 10′ and 11° 32′ North latitude and 76° 59′ and 77° 31′ East longitude.

They may be said to form an abutment on the great belt of mountains, which, under the name of the Western Ghâts, runs down the western side of the Peninsula, from the River Tapti to Cape Comorin. They are bounded on the north, partly by the territory of the native kingdom of Mysore, partly by Wainâd, the upland division of the Madras

---

* Nīlagiris means blue mountains, from *nīla*, blue, and *giri*, a mountain or hill; the common, but corrupt, spelling is Neilgherries. Accounts of these mountains and their inhabitants will be found in the following works:—

1826. *Letter to the Calcutta Harkaru, by Rev. James Hough.*
1827. *General and Medical Topography of the Neilgherries, by Dr. Young.*
1832. *The Todas, by Captain Harkness.*
1834. *Notes through Malabar and among the Neilgherries, by Captain Mignon.*
„ *Falls of Cauvery and Neilgherries, by Lieutenant Jervis.*
„ *Neilgherries, by Dr. Baikie.*
1835. *Geological Sketch of the Neilgherries, by Dr. P. M. Benza.*
1838. *Topographical Report of the Neilgherries, by Dr. De Burgh Birch.*
1844. *Antiquities of Neilgherries, by Captain Congreve. Vol. XIV., Madras Journal of Literature and Science.*
1847. *Memoir of the Neilgherries, by Captain J. Ouchterlony. Vol. XV., Part II., Madras Journal of Literature and Science,* 1848.
1851. *Goa and the Blue Mountains, by Lieutenant Burton.*
„ *Neilgherry Letters, by Captain Sir Francis Ford.*
1864. *The Tribes inhabiting the Neilgherry Hills, by Rev. F. Metz.*
1868. *An Account of the Tribes inhabiting the Neilgherries, by J. Shortt, Esq., M.D.; also Hill Ranges of Southern India, Part I.*
1870. *The Aboriginal Tribes of the Neilgherry Hills, by Lieut.-Colonel W. Ross King. Journal of Anthropology, No.* 1, *July* 1870.

Besides the above, notices may be found in different Literary and Scientific Journals.

Colonel W. Marshall has just published a book called *A Phrenologist among the Todas.*—ED.

district of Malabar; on the east by the district of Coimbatore; on the south partly by Coimbatore, and partly by Malabar; and on the west by Malabar.

The Nīlagiri plateau is from thirty to forty miles in length, and from ten to twenty-four in breadth. It contains several lofty peaks, the highest of which, Doddabett, is 8,642* feet above the sea.

The altitude of Coonoor is 5,886 feet; that of Ootacamund† 7,416 feet.

The mountains rise very abruptly to two-thirds of their total height, presenting from the plains below almost the aspect of a wall, unbroken by any lower ridges. Their base is covered with a belt of dense jungle, rising to a height of from 2500 to 3500 feet. This is succeeded by an open grassy space, one or two miles wide, nearly destitute of trees. Above this the vegetation is entirely different from that of the jungle below, and the forests assume more the appearance of those found in temperate climates. Along the edge the plateau is, in parts, especially on the western side, very precipitous, broken by wooded ravines, and exceedingly picturesque. The interior of the plateau consists chiefly of grassy undulating hills, divided by narrow valleys, which invariably contain a stream or a swamp. In the hollows of the hillsides nestle small beautiful woods, locally known as *sholas*.‡

It is seldom that so much variety of beauty is found in so small a compass. From the bleak heights of the Kūndahs, with their storm-beaten moss-hung woods and rank coarse grass, to the springy turf and many-coloured *sholas* of Ootacamund, and the tropical vegetation of the western slopes, every five or ten miles brings the traveller to a new climate, and new scenery. Even on the summit of the plateau the rainfall varies with each different aspect, and ranging from about 30 inches to 150 or more, produces a corresponding range of vegetation. It is, however, the views over the edges of the table land that are most singular and striking, from the extreme abruptness of the descent. Let a visitor take a short ride in almost any direction from almost any part of the plateau, and, passing along shady English-looking lanes, sheltered by thickets of blackberry and wild rose; across bare breezy downs, sometimes dotted with twisted, crimson-flowering rhododendron trees, and intersected by swampy valleys, where buffaloes wade and wallow; through dense woods carpeted with rare beautiful ferns and gorgeous in spring tints, beside which the colouring of an English autumn is faint and dull; by native villages, with their patches of cultivation and their magnificent single trees; he will find himself on some ridge or promontory, looking straight down from 4000 to 6000 feet, on a scene that changes like the figures in a kaleidoscope. In the morning a sea of clouds lies at his feet, and gradually rises round him. In the afternoon this has cleared away, and reveals, perhaps, a vast crimson plain, veined by dark lines

* According to a recent observation made by Colonel Saxton of the Trigonometrical Survey Department.

† Ootacamund, properly Utakamand, is the principal European settlement on the Nīlagiris; the others are Coonoor and Kotagherry. There is also a military sanatorium at Wellington. Of late years, Europeans have established themselves in various parts of the district, and opened out plantations of tea, coffee, and cinchona.

The names of the settlements above referred to are spelt according to the mode which long usage has assigned to them. The same course has been pursued in the case of other well-known names, such as Mysore, Coimbatore, &c. According to the system of spelling adopted in the vocabulary, Appendix A., Utakamand, Kūnur, and Kotagiri, would be substituted for Ootacamund, Coonoor, and Kotagherry.

‡ From the Kanarese *chōle*, a wood or forest.

of wood, dotted with isolated hummocks like giant ant-hills, and terminating in faint blue lines of mountains the furthest of which seems to hang half-way up the sky; perhaps on a tumbled mass of hills and valleys, a perfect dissolving view, for the eye has hardly traced the outline of some rocky ridge, glowing red in the sunlight, before a blue cloud-shadow blots it out, and a fresh series of crests and ravines starts into sight beyond. Broken peaks, hung with woods, frame the picture, and on all lies tropical sunlight, intensified by the keen thin mountain air.

The climate is temperate and equable. At Ootacamund, according to a series of observations, extending over seven years, the mean maximum temperature ranges from 60·06° in December to 68·76° in May. The hottest months of the year are April and May, the coldest, December and January. The hottest hours of the day in summer and winter do not vary more than nine degrees, and the extreme variation of temperature throughout the year is only 21·25°.

The climate of Coonoor and Kotagherry is warmer; no observations have been recorded for the Kūndahs. The average rainfall at Ootacamund is about 45 inches, but it is much greater on the Kūndahs, and generally on the western side of the plateau, which feels the full force of the S.W. monsoon.

Early in June this monsoon breaks with great violence on the western face of the mountains, but diminishes in violence as it extends eastward. At Ootacamund it is much milder than on the Kūndahs, and at Coonoor and Kotagherry it is but slightly felt. It lasts until about the middle of September. The north-east monsoon, which commences in the middle or end of October, bursts heavily on the north-east corner of the plateau, and the first fall usually extends over the whole of it. At Ootacamund, from December to May, the weather is dry and very bright; the winter nights bring sharp frosts in the swampy valleys, but on higher ground these are little felt, and English garden and greenhouse flowers may be had in profusion all the year round. The average number of days on which rain falls at Ootacamund in the course of the year is said to be 100, of cloudy days without rain 28, and of clear fine days 237.

The Nīlagiris are divided into four *nâds* or divisions, named respectively—

Todanâd.
Mekanâd.
Peranganâd.
Kūndanâd.

They are inhabited by five native tribes, viz. :—

Badagas.
Todas.
Kotas.
Kurumbas.
Irulas.

Of these, the Badagas, although far the most numerous, not being an aboriginal or jungle race, do not come within the scope of the following pages, which will be devoted to an account of the four primitive tribes, and of the rude stone monuments, of uncertain origin, which are found in various parts of the plateau.

The Badagas are Hindus, chiefly of the Saiva sect, and are supposed to have migrated to the Nilagiris from Mysore, about 300 years ago, after the breaking-up of the kingdom of Vijayanagar. According to the last Census they numbered 19,476. They are an agricultural race, and cultivate various cereals of rather a poor sort. They hold their lands under Government at very easy rates, and of late years many of them have acquired considerable wealth, and own large herds of cattle. They pay a sort of tribute, in grain, to the Todas. Their language is a corrupt form of Kanarese.

CHAPTER II.

THE TODAS.

Census.—Physical Characteristics.—Mode of Life.—Religion.—Rites and Ceremonies.—Funeral.—Language.—History and Traditions.

The Todas numbered 639 by the Census of the 15th November 1871. Considering the pains taken to ensure accuracy, we may accept this enumeration as approximately correct. *Census.*

List* of Toda Population in the Nîlagiri District according to the Final Census of 15th November 1871.

Village.	No. of Persons. Male.	Female.	Total.	Mands occupied.	Mands unoccupied.
Todanâd - -	319	212	531	30	38
Peranganâd - -	55	49	104	5	3
Mêkanâd - -	2	2	4	1	—
Koondahs - -	—	—	—	—	2
Total - -	376	263	639	36	43

* The foregoing list was taken from the original returns of the population of the Mands. When the returns were revised and tabulated, it was found that thirty-eight Todas, counted in the Ootacamund population, had been omitted, and that there were other slight inaccuracies. The revised list is as follows:—

Todanâd - - -	507
Peranganâd - - -	105
Mêkanâd - - -	33
Ootacamund Town - -	38
Total - -	683

—*Editor.*

The total number of Todas, male and female, in Todanâd and Mekanâd in 1835 was officially* reported to be 194, in 45 villages.

Todas are divided into two classes, which cannot intermarry, viz. :—

1. Dêvalyâl.
2. Tarserzhâl.

The first class consists of the Peiki clan, corresponding in some respects to Brahmans. The second of the four remaining clans, the Pekkan, Kuttan, Kenna, and Todi.

The Peikis eat apart; and a Peiki woman may not go to a village of the Tarserzhâl, although the women of the latter may visit Peikis.

The Peikis are not, however, like the Brahmans, recognised as superiors. On the contrary the other clans say, "Are they not our servants?"

Peiki women are called Kotti, those of the other clans Panni.

Physical characteristics.

For a description of the men and women I quote from Dr. Shortt's *Tribes of the Neilgherries*, page 4.

"ETHNOLOGY.—*Toda Tribe.*—In physique the Todas are by far the most pre-" possessing as a tribe, and it is this superiority in personal appearance, in conjunction " with their singular costume, peculiar mode of wearing their hair, their bold and " self-possessed deportment, and unique social and domestic institutions, that have " at all times attracted for them the greatest share of attention and interest from " Europeans. In complexion the Todas are of a dull copper hue,† not deeper or " darker in colour than most of the inhabitants of the plains; but they are darker than " the Badagas and many of the Kotas, a few of whom are met with fairer even than " the Badagas. The Kurumbas and Irulas are not only darker than the Todas, but " strikingly so to the eye. The Todas are tall in stature, well-proportioned, and in " features partake of the Caucasian type:—*Head*, slightly elongated like the Hindoos; " *forehead*, rather narrow and receding, measuring 2¼ inches from the root of the nose " to the growth of hair and scalp; *eyebrows*, thick and approaching each other; *eyes*, " moderately large, well formed, expressive, and often intelligent; *irides*, varying in " colour from hazel to brown;‡ *nose*, long, large, and well-formed, generally aquiline— " in some slightly rounded, arched, or what is termed Roman, in others cogitative— " measuring from root to tip 2½ inches, and height from base of alæ to ridge 1½ inches, " breadth of alæ from side to side 1½ inches; *upper lip*, narrow; *lower lip*, thick or " full—and face covered with a close thick moustache, whiskers, and beard, all of

---

* See letter from Principal Collector of Malabar, 9th February 1835.

Mr. Sullivan, referring to this letter in an official memorandum, dated 20th August 1835, says:—

"This does not tally with former returns, and is certainly incorrect. The Census of 1826 gave a " total of 326 for the whole Hills; and there is no doubt of their numbers having increased, since " Captain Harkness counted 300 men, nearly half that number of women, and about as many boys and " girls at a Toda funeral."

† Agreeing in this respect with Paul Brocas' Table, No. 28.

‡ The majority being intermediate with Nos. 1 & 2 of Paul Brocas' Tables.

"which are worn full; *ears*, of moderate size, and lying close to the skull; *teeth*, "white, clean, and regular; head well covered with black hair, of moderate "fineness, and worn in a peculiar fashion, combed smoothly around from the "crown, and cropped evenly in line with the eyebrows, and covering the head very "much like a natural skull-cap; body of the male, hirsute, especially on back and "chest; *figure and contour of person*, generally attractive, and carriage graceful. "Of 25 men, I found the average weight and measurements as follow:—Weight, "121·40 lbs.; height, 63 30 inches; circumference of head, 20·81 inches; neck, "12·81 inches; chest, 32·22 inches; arms, 9·36 inches; thighs, 16·64 inches; "length of arm from acromion process to tip of fingers, 32 inches; length of hand, "7·50 inches—breadth, 3·50 inches; lower extremities, well proportioned, with "moderate calves; feet, well formed and arched, length of foot, 11·50 inches— "width of sole, 4 inches.

"*Females of the Toda Tribe.*—The women of this tribe are generally tall and "stalwart; good-looking both in features and person, with a smooth, clear, and delicate "skin; fresh and rather fair in complexion. They have more of an aquiline nose "than the men, which, however, does not diminish from the strong feminine cast of "their features. The hair is of a lighter colour than in the male, parted in the "centre, and carefully combed around and thrown behind the ears, and left "hanging free over the shoulders and back, in a mass of flowing curls in some, "and in others, wavy. I have not seen any of the women with very long hair. "In those I met, it did not exceed 1½ or 2 feet in length, and was of moderate "fineness. The females, like the males, are self-possessed in a great degree, and "readily enter into conversation with strangers, be they white or black. It has "been averred that the Toda females, as a class, are strikingly handsome and comely "in features; but although many of them certainly possess charms in person of a "robust character, I cannot say that I met with even one with a handsome or "pretty face, much less any with features approaching in perfection or beauty to a "classical model.

"From an average of 25 the following weights and measurements were obtained:— "Height, 60·25 inches; weight, 110·80 lbs.; circumference of head, 20·8 inches; "neck, 11·11 inches; arm, 8·90 inches; chest, 30·11 inches; thighs, 14·6 inches; "length of arm, 27 inches; length of hand, 6·75 inches, breadth, 3 inches; forehead "from root of nose to growth of hair on scalp, 2 inches." (*Plates* III., IV., V., VI., VII.)

The facial peculiarities of the Todas are not so great as they at first sight appear. When they shave and wear turbans, which many now do, they are hardly to be distinguished from other natives. Their frank bold manners are, however, entirely peculiar to themselves, and very attractive. A Toda laughs without disguise or restraint at anything in an Englishman that strikes him as ludicrous, and generally seems to consider himself as an equal or superior. I suspected them of a little hoaxing sometimes. It is impossible not to like them, if only for their independence and good-humour.

They live in villages called *mands** (*Plates* VIII., IX.), of which the following description is given in Dr. Shortt's work:—

Mode of life. " A *mund* or *mott* is the term used to designate a hamlet or village by the Toda " tribe. Each mund or hamlet usually comprises about five buildings or huts, three " of which are used as dwellings, one as a dairy, and the other for sheltering the " calves at night. These huts or dwellings form a peculiar kind of oval pent-shaped " construction, usually 10 feet high, 18 feet long, and 9 feet broad. The entrance or " doorway into this building measures 32 inches in height and 18 in width, and is " not provided with any door or gate; but the entrance is closed by means of a solid " slab or plank of wood from 4 to 6 inches thick, and of sufficient dimensions to " entirely block up the entrance. This sliding door is inside the hut, and so " arranged and fixed on two stout stakes buried in the earth, and standing to the " height of $2\frac{1}{2}$ to 3 feet, as to be easily moved to and fro. There are no other " openings or outlets of any kind, either for the escape of smoke or for the free ingress " and egress of atmospheric air. The doorway itself is of such small dimensions, that, " to effect an entrance, one has to go down on all fours, and even then much wriggling " is necessary before an entrance can be effected. The houses are neat in appearance, " and are built of bamboo closely laid together, fastened with rattan, and covered with " thatch, which renders them water-tight. Each building has an end walling before " and behind, composed of solid blocks of wood, and the sides are covered in by the " pent-roofing which slopes down to the ground. The front wall or planking contains " the entrance or doorway. The inside of a hut is from 8 to 15 feet square, and is " sufficiently high in the middle to admit of a tall man moving about with comfort. " On one side there is a raised platform or pial formed of clay, about 2 feet high, " and covered with sambre or buffaloe skins, or sometimes with a mat. This platform " is used as a sleeping place. On the opposite side is a fireplace and a slight elevation " on which the cooking utensils are placed. In this part of the building faggots of " firewood are seen piled up from floor to roof, and secured in their place by loops " of rattan. Here also the rice-pounder or pestle is fixed. The mortar is formed by " a hole dug in the ground 7 to 9 inches deep, and rendered hard by constant use. " The other household goods consist of 3 or 4 brass dishes or plates, several bamboo " measures, and sometimes a hatchet. In one hut I found an old table knife, two " empty beer bottles, and a broken goglet.

" Each hut or dwelling is surrounded by an enclosure or wall formed of loose " stones piled up 2 to 3 feet high, and includes a space or yard measuring 13 × 10 " feet."

The inhabitants of a mand are generally related to one another, and consider themselves one family. The family will possess one or two, sometimes three mands in different parts of the hills, to which they resort periodically for grazing their buffaloes. Each mand has its acknowledged pasture ground, which is not encroached upon by

* Derived from *Manĕ,* Canarese for *House,* pronounced and commonly spelt *Mund.* The words *Mott* or *Mortt,* which so often appear in old records, seem also to be corruptions of *Manĕ.*

others. Each householder in the mand has his own cattle, which he can dispose of absolutely, and their milk is kept for his use; but the whole mand herd graze together, tended generally by the village *pūjāri* (priest), who milks them morning and evening in the monsoon months, and morning only at other times. The milk of all is kept in one dairy-house, which none may enter but the *pūjāri*.

Each family has a recognised head, in whose name the Government grazing *pattā** is made out. On the death of the head the eldest son generally succeeds. One old Toda, however, when I asked him which of his sons would take his place, replied, "the wisest." (Compare *Menu*, Chap. IX., Sec. 117:—"Let the eldest have a double "share, and the next born a share and a half, *if they clearly surpass the rest in virtue "and learning*." Sir W. Jones' translation of the *Institutes* shows that the saving clause of the above section is one of the numerous interpolations by which commentators have attempted to harmonise *Menu's* precepts with modern practice. It is curious to find the same qualification acknowledged by the Todas). The father's property is equally divided among all his sons, but the house goes to the youngest, upon whom falls the duty of supporting the females of the household.

The Todas are a purely pastoral people. They have large herds of buffaloes, and depend for support on their produce, with the addition of the *gūdu*,† which they levy in kind from Badagas and Kotas. Labour of any kind they hardly ever attempt; indeed so entirely incomprehensible is the notion to them, that when, on one occasion, an unlucky mistake about the ownership of some buffaloes committed an old Toda to jail, it was found impossible to induce him to work with the other convicts, and the authorities, unwilling to resort to harsh measures, were compelled to save appearances by making him an overseer.

Of late years one or two have taken contracts to fell wood,‡ but the result has not been satisfactory to the employers.

The women do a coarse kind of embroidery with blue and red thread procured from the low country, for ornament to some of their cloths. They use the Nīlagiri nettle for stitching their cloths, and English needles; formerly their needles were made by the Kotas. They also cook and fetch water, the men fetch firewood. Whether they live entirely on grain and milk seems doubtful. They admit that they at one time used to eat their male buffalo calves, but deny vehemently that they do so now, having apparently imbibed from their Hindu neighbours an idea that the practice is disgraceful. It is suspicious, however, that the skins of buffalo calves are found in their

* *Pattā*, commonly spelt *puttah* or *pottah*, is a document given by the Collector or Chief Revenue Officer of a district, however styled, to a landholder or other person having rights connected with the land, specifying the conditions on which the land is held, or the nature of the rights.

† *Gūdu.*—Name known among the Hill tribes for the annual gift of grain made by the cultivators to the Todas; said formerly to represent about $\frac{1}{10}$ or an $\frac{1}{8}$ or $\frac{1}{6}$ of the gross produce. *Gūdu*, Canarese for *basket, nest.* The Badagas, after threshing in their fields, bring the grain to the *Kēri* (terrace in front of their houses), and measure it off by baskets before they store it in the granary beneath the *Kēri*. One basket or *Gūdu* out of so many is set apart for the Todas.

‡ See letter to Government appended to Preface. It was said that some Todas worked on plantations, but on further inquiry this was found to be a mistake.—*Editor.*

houses, and I am informed by an officer who has been for many years on the Hills, that he has frequently found them in the woods cooking meat, which they appeared anxious to hide.

Polyandry is on the decline amongst them, and its practice depends now chiefly on the means of individuals. It is considered desirable for each man to have his own wife if he can afford it, and some few men have two; but in poor families two or more younger brothers have still but one wife; in this case the brothers generally live in separate houses and take the wife in turn.

The practice of female infanticide has, I believe, entirely ceased. Indeed I can hardly induce any Toda to acknowledge that it ever existed. The disproportion, however, between the number of men and women supports Mr. Metz's assertion that it was practised within the last thirty years.

Their pastimes are not numerous. They are expert at a game called *Iláta*, which is played as follows :—

A cylindrical piece of wood pointed at both ends is placed against the corner of a stone; a slight tap from a stick sends it flying into the air; as it comes down the batsman hits it away to a great distance, and scouts are posted to catch it as it falls. In fact *Iláta* is a variety of *tipcat.*

Another game is called *Nārthpimi* (*Plate* X.) Close to some mands a sort of stone table may be observed, consisting of two slabs stuck edgewise into the ground and another laid across them, leaving an opening just large enough for a man to drag himself through on his stomach. Two stones are fixed as starting posts, one at about thirty the other about sixty yards from the table. A man stands by each of these, and the nearer of the two runs to the table, and tries to wriggle under it, before the other, starting at the same time from the farther stone, can catch him. The rapidity with which they squeeze through the opening must be the result of long practice in crawling in and out of their house doors.

A third game, called *Kāriálapimi*, has some resemblance to puss in the corner.

Some of them, by way of a trial of strength, lift a large round stone (*Plate* X.), raising it first to the knee, and rolling it up the thigh and the chest on to the shoulder. The stone must be very heavy, for putting forth all my strength, I could not raise it more than two inches from the ground. The man I saw lifting it, was a fine athletic fellow, but he strained every nerve in the effort, and only one other man in the mand could do it at all.

For a list of Toda garments, ornaments, household utensils, &c., see Appendix B.

Major King, in his article in the *Journal of Anthropology* of July 1870, describes the Toda dress as follows :—

" The garment* in which the Toda envelopes himself is of a thick, coarse, " cotton cloth of native manufacture, white when clean, and having a red stripe or

* *Toda : Pútkuli.*

" border. It is hung over the left shoulder, brought across the back, and forward " under the right arm, the point being flung backwards over the left shoulder again, " leaving the right arm at liberty, and allowing the folds to fall gracefully about the " lower part of the person down to the knees." (*Plate* XI.)

* * * * *

" The female dress (*Plate* IV.) on ordinary occasions consists of a robe similar " to that of the men, though it is worn differently, being merely thrown over both " shoulders and clasped in front by the hand."

Singularly massive ornaments are worn by the women (*Plate* V.). A pair of brass armlets worn on one arm above the elbow weighed 6 lbs.

The *Būguri* (*Plate* XI.) is the only musical instrument they possess. It is a hollow bamboo with holes like a flute, and a piece of horn or wood at the lower end. The performer blows in at the top and produces a disagreeable sound, aggravated by the fluttering of a piece of paper inserted between the bamboo and the horn. They are fond of singing, that is, of chanting in a monotonous drone apparently without words. To a European ear, however,—

" their song is death "
" And makes destruction please."

like that of the Sirens, but for a different reason. They dance in circles with clubs (*Plate* XI.), holding hands or linking arms, and marking time with shouts of *Hoh, Hoh.*

They generally greet Europeans with a simple salaam; sometimes with a sort of bow or military salute made in a courteous and dignified manner. A Toda woman meeting a man salutes him by raising his feet one after the other to her forehead. An old woman, however, receives instead of paying this reverence. A Badaga meeting a Toda lays his hand on the head of the latter. This, and the title *Māv*, father-in-law,* which is assigned to the Badagas, seems to imply some belief in the superiority of the latter.

Tenure of land.

When Europeans came to the Hills under the auspices of Mr. Sullivan in 1820, to settle at Ootacamund and elsewhere, one of the first questions that arose, concerned the nature and extent of the Toda rights in the soil.

The subject was discussed for years, during which no attempt was made by Government to have these rights ascertained and defined. Ultimately, however, an inquiry took place, which, amidst a mass of correspondence, elicited the following noteworthy points:—

From as far back as our records extended, it appeared that the Todas had paid annually a light pasture tax for about 190 *Ballas* † of land, and 2 *Kantirâi fanams* ‡ for each buffalo, and had enjoyed the right of pasturing their herds over

* A Badaga house is sometimes called *Pâlthchi*, like the Todas' temples.

† A *Balla* = 4 acres nearly.

‡ *Kantirâi fanam* = 0r. 4a. 8p. of present money.

an undefined extent of land. Further, the Badaga and Kota cultivators had always given them annually a portion of their field produce under the name of *gūdu*, but, "*whether out of superstitious motives, or to induce the Todas not to " molest them, or in acknowledgment of their proprietary right in the land*,"* was uncertain.

This seems to be the case for the Todas.

On the other hand there is nothing in the Toda occupation which affects the universally acknowledged right of the Government to levy full assessment on all uncultivated land, when actually brought under tillage, a right which the Government had exercised without objection in the case of all lands cultivated by the Badagas and paying *gūdu* to the Todas.

The first step in the settlement of the matter was to declare in 1843 that the Todas had an absolute right in their mands or village sites and in the spots appropriated to religious rites, and had also a claim to compensation† for abridgment of their grazing privileges, but that purchasers from Todas could only buy the right of occupying the land for pasture. On this principle compensation was paid by Government for the area now forming the Ootacamund settlement. Subsequently, on further inquiry, in connexion with the survey of the Hills by Captain Ouchterlony, it was found that the Badagas generally were not disposed to admit the right of the Todas to demand *gūdu* from them at any specified rate, although they acknowledged the practice of giving *gūdu*, and their readiness still to give it "according to their own wants or fancy." It was found too that the Badagas had for some time past sold lands to Europeans and others without any mention of the *gūdu*, and that no claim had subsequently been urged by the Todas on the buyer. On inquiry into the extent of table land over which *gūdu* was claimable, it appeared that on the whole plateau of the Hills there were not more than about a hundred mands occupied and unoccupied, and that the pasturage rights of the Todas, in practice, only extended to the area surrounding each mand. Under these circumstances it was ruled that lands in the proximity of a mand or of spots appropriated to religious rites formed the grazing grounds of the Todas, but elsewhere unoccupied land might be given by Government on lease for building or agricultural purposes. Every lease, however, was to contain a stipulation that *gūdu* would be charged to the grantee, and added to the annual assessment, if it appeared to the satisfaction of the revenue authorities that *gūdu* was payable thereon. Subsequently, in 1863, sales by public auction were substituted for leases. Under orders from Government the revenue authorities have abstained from leasing, or putting up to public auction, land which could be said to be in inconvenient proximity to Toda

---

* *Despatch from the Court of Directors to Madras*, dated 21 June 1843, No. 13.

† Compensation equivalent to the *Gūdu* was to be given, and added to the assessment when the land was taken and tilled; and in case the land so taken was a portion of that for which the Todas paid the pasture tax, in proportionate share of the tax was to be remitted.

In *Minutes of Consultation*, dated 7 May 1852, the *Gūdu* equivalent was fixed at 1 anna per Kāni (cawny). A Cawny = 1·32 acres.

mands, and I cannot find that in a single instance has *gūdu* been claimed* for lands disposed of by Government.

Thus the rights of the Todas remain to the present day. They receive *gūdu* from the Badagas and Kotas, more or less according to the season and the means of the cultivator, and they retain possession of their village sites and the surrounding lands under grazing *pattās*, for which they pay two annas an acre in lieu of the taxes formerly levied.

They have an effective mode of extracting the *gūdu* from a refractory Badaga village without reference to law courts. Throughout the district, wherever Badaga cultivation has extended, the Todas have reserved the old sites of their mands and buffalo kraals,† and have persuaded the Badagas that these places, however long abandoned, and now surrounded with cultivation, are in some sense sacred. When a difficulty about the *gūdu* arises, the Todas, by way of an ultimatum, make ready the nearest abandoned mand for habitation. The prospect of having a herd of Toda buffaloes *kraaled* in the midst of their fields soon brings the Badagas to reason.

Religion, Rites and Ceremonies.

There are five kinds of priests, who rank as follows:—

I. *Pâlâls* (*Plate* XII.), who, according to the regular sequence of Toda ideas, are a mixture of ascetic and herdsman. They live at isolated mands called *Tiriaris*.

"No female is allowed to go near the mand, nor can any man hold converse with "the Pàlaul without special permission, and then only at a considerable distance.

* * * * *

"Great sanctity attaches to the person of the Pàlaul in the eyes of his Toda brethren, "and he therefore exerts a powerful influence over their minds. They believe that "God dwells in him, and makes known His will through him to those who come to him "for counsel."‡

There are about nineteen *Tiriaris* occupied at certain periods of the year by five *Pâlâls*; two, whose head quarters are near Mukkurti Peak (*Plate* XII.), two near Naujenâd, and one near Kodanâd. They have charge of sacred bells, which they carry from mand to mand. The *Pâlâls* must be Peikis; the *Tiriaris*, however, belong to certain Tarserzhâl mands, the inhabitants of which elect the *Pâlâls*, and furnish each with an attendant called a *Kavilâl*, who may be either a Peiki or Pekkan, and gets six rupees a year, his food, and a cloth, which however he may not wear when in immediate attendance on the *Pâlâl*.

The latter gets nothing but the milk of the sacred herd, which is kept for his use at the *Tiriari*; he holds office as long as he chooses, generally for three or four years. One is said to have been *Pâlâl* for fourteen years, but this is mentioned as something extraordinary.

---

* *Proceedings of the Board of Revenue*, No. 4,749, 29 July 1863, and *Mr. Grant's* Letter of the 17th idem. "Provision was always made in the leases for payment of *gūdu*, and for a few years it was enforced. But "the amount did not exceed a few annas, and the Todas did not care to ask for it."

† *Kraal*, a circular enclosure, in which cattle are penned at night, surrounded by a rough stone wall.

‡ *Tribes inhabiting the Neilghery Hills*, by Mr. Metz, p. 19.

They do not wear the ordinary *Pátkuli*, but a scanty black cloth called *Tunni*, made specially for them by the Badagas of Jakanēri.

"The preparations for this supposedly sacred office occupy a whole month, and the "exposure to which the aspirant to it is subjected is so great as to place his life in "some peril. For eight days and eight nights he must remain in the jungles without "a particle of clothing to protect him from the severity of the climate. His body is "at this time to be rubbed over with the juice of a certain tree called Fūr or Tūr, the "botanical name of which I do not know. After this the purifying juice is washed "off, and he is allowed to enter a small hut, which is the only shelter he is permitted "to have during the remainder of the period."*

II. *Varzhâls*, who undergo the same preparation as the *Pâlâls*, but for a shorter period. They are employed as village milkmen, and may be either Peikis or Pekkans. They hold office temporarily, and during their tenure must abstain from intercourse with women. Whilst employed in their official capacity they may only wear the langooty.

III. *Kokvali.* There is only one, who appears to be identical with the Varzhâl in all but the name; he lives at Tārnāt mand (*Plate* VIII.).

IV. *Kurpuli.* There is only one, who lives at the Kenna mand of Kândal, and must be a Kenna. In other respects he is the same as the *Varzhâl*.

V. *Pâlikārpâls* may be of any clan, but Peiki and Pekkan mands must have Peiki and Pekkan Pâlikārpâls. They are not obliged to abstain from intercourse with women, and can wear the *Putkuli* while performing their duties as village milkmen.

There are two kinds of temples:

I. *Boa*, a conical roofed temple surrounded with a low wall (*Plate* XIII.).

II. *Pâlthchi*, a temple resembling in outward appearance an ordinary house, but larger. Of *Pâlthchis* there are two varieties; the first the dairy-house, of which every *mand* possesses one at least; the second variety, though similar in appearance, is something more than a dairy-house, and wherever found, the mand is called by Todas *Etadmand* (*Great Mand*), and by Badagas *Mui mand*, in contradistinction to a *Buri* or common mand.

Both *Boas* and *Pâlthchis* are used as dairies, the only difference apparently being that the priests may live in the latter, and not in the former.

When a mand has two temples there are generally two priests, one a Varzhâl, and the other a *Pâlikārpâl*. Each has his own division of the village herd to milk, and his own temple in which to keep the milk and ghee. The *Boa*, if there is one, is appropriated to the *Varzhâl*.

There are four *Boas*:—

(1.) Called *Mânboa;* at Muttanâd *mand*, about four miles from Ootacamund on the left of the Segūr road.

* *Tribes inhabiting the Neilghery Hills*, by Mr. Metz, p. 19.

(2.) Called *Kiurzh*;* at the *Tiriari* mand near Sholūr.

(3.) Called *Tārzhva*; at the *Tiriari* mand on the Kūndahs.

(4.) Near Brikapatti; called *Mutterzhva.*

Formerly there was a fifth called *Katedva* near Mukkurti at Mudimand. It is now in ruins.

Every clan has its own *Muimands.* I give a list, with the name of the presiding God and Bell, where there is one.

Peiki Muimands (*Etadmands*).

Name of Mand.	Name of Temple and presiding God.	Name of Bell.
1. Karia	Marialph.	
2. Yemagal	Poltivasāri.	
3. Ebgôdu	Nalkanash.	
4. Kengôdu	Kyadf	Mírzhan. Ertâtu. Kírzhan.
5. Kundigôd	Térvalth.	
6. Melgod	Nirzâlva.	
7. Pilondugôd	Térvalth.	
8. Mardini	Nirzâlva.	
9. Denâdu	Apurshanash.	
10. Wongôd	Nirzâlva.	
11. Karimolu	Toriâldf.	

Pekkan Muimands.

Name of Mand.	Name of Temple and presiding God.	Name of Bell.
1. Manjakal	Môddva.	
2. Narigo	Tvarieldf.	

Kenna Muimands.

Name of Mand.	Name of Temple and presiding God.	Name of Bell.
1. Kandal	1. Torzhaldf	Narâl Kantshu.
	2. Karzhaldf	Ponâl Kantshu.
2. Kandiko	Térvalth.	
3. Ar	Tilthbóa	Karidzand (2 bells here so called).

* Measurements:—

From top of roof to ground	16′
Inside diameter, north to south	9′ 2″
Do. do. east to west	8′ 2″
Outer circumference two feet above ground	34′
Height of doorway, inner and outer	1′ 7″
Breadth do. do.	1′ 2″
From eaves to ground	3′ 5″

The door faces West. The interior is in two compartments, divided by seven thick beams standing on end. The centre beam, in which the inner doorway is cut, is about 1½ feet broad, and reaches from the ground to the conical top. The other six beams are of like thickness, but of less breadth and length.

Kuttan Muimands.

Name of Mand.	Name of Temple and presiding God.	Name of Bell.
1. Kodanâd	Músdshyáldf	Kérshandk.
2. Pangôd	Pêrgârsh.	
3. Âr	Tírzh pâlzh (in ruins).	
4. Nirzh	Ponarshaldf.	
5. Kanorzh	Muderzhva.	

Todi Muimands.

Name of Mand.	Name of Temple and presiding God.	Name of Bell.
1. Puirtāl	Térvalth.	
2. Kārzhtith	Kátŭtivâ.	
3. Âr	Kâjva	Kângŭar. Kânj.
4. Térshdêr	Korzhaldf.	
5. Kérkŏārzh	Musdshyáldf.	
6. Kúramârzh	Marzhaldf.	
7. Pun	Nirzālva	Ândk.
8. Tarār*	Terpivor; Tékva; Pēshhva	Ândk and Pândk (2 bells).
9. Nârsh	Mânboa. Ârialdf.	
10. Kúĕrsh	Kênaldf.	
11. Párzhtâr	Karzhaldf.	

The eleven *Muimands* of the Peikis belong to three families. Six belong to the present chief Muttivên.

Besides the above-mentioned deities, the Todas also recognise a Hunting God called Bētikhân, who lives at Nambilikote in Wainâd. They say he is a son of Dirkish (who was a son of Ēn, the first Toda) and "is now attended by Brahmans."

In spite of this formidable pantheon, the Toda religion is of the vaguest and smallest kind. Some old men of a devout turn of mind make salām to the rising sun (*Birsh*), and at some seasons to the moon (*Tiggal*),† and fast at eclipses, and occasionally they may prostrate themselves at the door of the *Pâlthchi*, but no one except the *pūjāri* attempts anything beyond this. "May all be well!" "May the buffaloes be well!" is the only form of prayer. What their idea of a God is, it is not easy to say. Except the Bells, to which the *pūjāris* occasionally offer libations of milk, they have no material object of worship; they do not appeal to their Mand God by name, nor do they seem to expect that he will show them special favour; in fact, the names of their Gods, like some of their funeral ceremonies, seem more like the fossil remains of an extinct religion, than parts of a living creed.

* Bad. Tārnāt. *Pl.* VIII.

† Sometimes they also salute a lamp when first lit. In all these cases the salutation consists in raising the right hand to the face, the first finger resting on the nose.

About Ootacamund a few Todas have latterly begun to imitate the religious practices of their native neighbours. In *Plate* xi. the right hand figure has his forehead smeared with ashes. Occasionally children's foreheads are marked with the Saiva spot, and my particular friend, Kinniaven, after an absence of some days, returned with a shaven head from a visit to the temple of Siva at Nanjanagudi. He assumed, however, the tone of an *esprit fort* on the subject, and said that his relatives believed in Nanjanda, and that he had gone to please them.

The only purely religious ceremony which the Todas have, is the *Kōna Shastra*, or annual sacrifice of a male buffalo calf. It may take place at any time of the year, apparently when it pleases the *pūjāri*. Any mand may celebrate the Kōna Shastra if the *pūjāri* is willing. The inhabitants of other mands of the same clan are duly invited. The calf, eight days old, is brought to a neighbouring *shola*. The Peikī *Varzhāl* comes with three holy branches of the *Tūr* tree, and repeats the names of all the gods of the four divisions; then the calf is killed with a branch of the *Tūr*. The flesh must not be boiled, but roasted on a fire,* made by rubbing together two sticks of the *neralu*, *muthu*, or *kem* trees, and eaten by the celebrants. Women cannot attend or partake of the feast.

The institution is *Māmūl*,† they say, and was ordained by Koten, their ancestor, by way of ensuring prosperity for themselves and their buffaloes.

Their domestic ceremonies are more elaborate and interesting.

I begin with those that are usual on the birth of a child.

As soon after birth as possible, a young buffalo calf is brought near the house; the father takes three small bamboo measures filled with water, and holding two of them close to the right side of the calf's hind quarters, pours the water from the third measure into the other two.

Two leaves of a tree are also brought; one is given to the woman, another held by the husband, who pours water from a measure into the leaf in his hand, and from it to that held by the woman.‡ The latter drinks and puts a drop into the child's mouth three times, after which the woman and child, accompanied by the husband, are removed to a separate hut (*Purzhārzh*) outside the mand, where they remain till the next new moon.

When she returns to her own house, a similar ceremony is repeated with milk, and a Pekkan man must be called to milk the buffalo.

In mands containing a conical temple (*boa*), the *Purzhārzh* is situated a long way off; in others it is close at hand.

When the child is a few months old, the father takes the child (if a boy) early in the morning to the door of the village *Pálthchi*, and prostrates himself there. The maternal grandfather then names the child. No particular custom seems to determine the child's name, except that they say that all their names of men, as well as of their kraals and

* Cf. *Exodus* xii. 9.

† *Māmūl* (custom) and *Shastra* (law or religion) are the invariable reply of a Toda when asked to give a a reason for his practices.

‡ A similar ceremony amongst the Brahmans is described by *Dubois* (*People of India*, *p.* 84). In this case the *Purohita* pours water into the hands of husband and wife, who drop part of it on their heads and drink the rest.

drinking springs, are names of gods. Female children are not taken to the *Pálthchi* and christened; there is no ceremony in their case. The mother calls her female child by any name she fancies. She will never give the child her own name.

Early betrothals are common amongst the Todas. The boy is taken to the girl's house and salutes his future father-in-law by lifting the feet of the latter to his forehead. An interchange of buffaloes completes the contract. When the time arrives for claiming his wife, the young man goes alone to the mand of his father-in-law, who gives him the girl, and a separate house to live in for a few days. There is another exchange of buffaloes, and the bride is taken home.

When two or more brothers* are the husbands of one wife, this ceremony is performed with the eldest alone.

---

* Names used to express relationships in TODA.

	English.	Toda.	Literal Meaning.
1.	Father	*Ēn, Eyan.*	
2.	Mother	*Aff.*	
3.	Son	*Măkh.*	
4.	Daughter	*Kukh.*	
5.	Father's elder brother	*Perudēn*	Great father.
6.	„ younger „	*Kirudēn*	Little do.
7.	„ elder sister	*Māmi.*	
8.	„ younger „	*Māmi.*	
9.	Mother's elder brother	*Māman.*	
10.	„ younger „	*Māman.*	
11.	„ elder sister	*Perudaff*	Great mother.
12.	„ younger „	*Kirudaff*	Little do.
13.	Father's brother's son	*An*	Brother.
14.	„ „ daughter	*Akkan*	Sister.
15.	„ sister's son	*Machen.*	
16.	„ „ daughter	*Tajmakh*	Female.
17.	Mother's sister's son	*An*	Brother.
18.	„ „ daughter	*Akkan*	Sister.
19.	„ brother's son	*Machen.*	
20.	„ „ daughter	*Tajmakh*	Female.

Nos. 5, 6, 13, and 14 at first sight would appear traceable to polyandry, but Nos. 11, 12, 17, and 18 create a difficulty.

Todas have no name for *husband* and *wife* beyond *Âlt* and *Tajmakh*, which simply mean *man* and *woman*.

In *Anthropological Journal* for *January and July* 1871, page 28, *ya* is said to be *father* in Toda. I do not find it so.

Male Names.

1. Kêvi, a sacred buffalo bell of a *Tiriari* is so called.
2. Pernâl, literally a great man.
3. Nárikút, (lit.) child of jackal.
4. Ponkút, (lit.) child of gold.
5. Tshinkút, (lit.) do.
6. Padrithzh, (lit.) name of a god who resides on a mountain.
7. Kêdâlvên, (lit.) the man of the funeral.
8. Âlvên, (lit.) a man.
9. Beltavên, (lit.) like silver.
10. Kirnâli. (lit.) little one.

Female Names.

1. Kâthaveli, (lit.) silver coin.
2. Darzthinir, (lit.) a jewel scale.
3. Tshinâb, (lit.) gold one.
4. Berzth, no meaning that I can find out.
5. Depbili, (lit.) silver ring.
6. Pondshulkammi, (lit.) gold ankle bells.
7. Kattshira, (lit.) Cutcherry, Sircar office.
8. Piltimurugu, (lit.) white ear ring in the top of the ear.
9. Piltzaras, (lit.) white ring.
10. Tâkém, (lit.) doctor. This child was so called because an European doctor cured it of an illness soon after its birth.

In the fifth month of a woman's first pregnancy, she marks her two thumbs in two places by a slight burn with a lighted rag.

In the seventh month, at the time of new moon, the woman's father visits the husband's hut. The husband asks "Shall I tie the *Tāli?*"* The father consents. The husband then asks "Shall I give a bow?" The father says "Yes." The husband makes a bow of the *Hubbe* shrub (*Sophora glauca*), the bark serving for the string. He takes this into a Shola in the afternoon, and gives it to his wife, who, sitting down before a jungle tree, in the stem of which a convenient hole can be found to place a small earthenware lamp, asks the name of the bow, holds it a little while, and then places it at the foot of the tree.

Each mand has a different name for the bow—

In Kāndal it is *Pirzhvâkham.*
,, Muttinâd ,, *Pirzhirzhk.*
,, Kodanâd ,, *Kurrkduvirzh.*
,, Manjakal ,, *Bellgârăff.*

They remain in the Shola all night, and eat their morning meal there, returning home in the evening. On this occasion the woman's father generally presents the couple with a *Nāga* (a buffalo heifer). I have tried to find out the origin and object of these customs, but can get no further than *Māmūl* and *Shāstra.* One man added "*By the Bow and Arrow*† *we have got a wife who is with child.*"‡

The most remarkable portions of the Toda ritual are those connected with the dead, in which there is much that is beautiful. A Toda always pays to the departed the respect of silence. A dead man's name is never heard again; his friends resort to any amount of periphrasis rather than profane by ordinary use "the household name of one whom God has taken."

They have two ceremonies; the "green funeral" (*Kordzai Kêdu*), which takes place soon after death, and the "dry funeral" (*Marvenâli Kêdu*), a sort of commemorative festival, sometimes performed by the relatives of a single person, but more frequently in honour of any number of one clan who may have died within a twelvemonth or so.

* The *Tâli* is the Hindu equivalent of wedding ring. It is either a gold ornament of a peculiar shape, or a necklace of beads, which is tied on the neck of the bride by the bridegroom at the time of marriage. Among the Todas a string of black beads represents the Tali.

† See *Coorg Memoirs*, by Rev. H. Moeqling, p. 40 :—

"As soon as a Coorg boy is born, a little bow of a castor-oil-plant stick (*Ricinus communis*), with an arrow "made of a leaf stalk of the same plant, is put into his little hands. He is thus, at taking his first breath, "introduced into the world as a future huntsman and warrior."

‡ A somewhat similar use of the bow is described in Dr. Leitner's account of Dardistan (*Ind. Antiquary,* No. 1, p. 12.) "When the bridegroom has to go for his bride to a distant village, he is furnished with a bow. "On arriving at his native place, he crosses the breast of his bride with an arrow, and then shoots it off. He "generally shoots three arrows in the direction of his home." Are these traces of "marriage by capture"?[1] That such marriages have been a recognised practice in India from ancient times is evident from Menu, iii. 33.

[1] See *Development of Relationships*, by Sir J. Lubbock · *Journal Anthropological Institute*, vol. for January, July 1871, page 8 :—

"Marriage in Rome was symbolised by capture or purchase, as among so many of the lower races at the present day. In fact the "idea of marriage among the lower races of men generally is essentially of a different character from ours; it is material, not "spiritual; it is founded on force, not on love, the wife is not united but enslaved to her husband."

Each clan has its own appropriate* days of the week for the green funeral, "according to the *Shastras.*"

The body is not removed from the place of death till it is carried to the burning place,† which the Todas call *Methgúdi* (*lit. Marriage temple*).

All green funerals are alike. I will describe one I saw near Kartêri, at the old burning ground of the neighbouring mands, an open space near a stream. The body was brought on a stretcher preceded by Kota musicians. It is not necessarily carried by the relatives, or even by men of the same clan. A rough hut (called *Nōlpali* for a man, and *Nirzhārzh* for a woman,) was built of boughs and grass, in which the body was placed. The women of the mand sat by it, and moaned in their peculiar manner, one of them meanwhile embroidering a strip of cloth for a purse. Four walking-sticks and several skeins of cotton-thread, each with a bunch of cowries at the end, were laid upon the body, which was wrapped in a new *pútkuli,*‡ the feet being tied together by the great toes with a piece of blue thread.

A rude circle§ about a yard in diameter was then made of single stones, leaving an entrance gap at one side. Outside this circle the body was laid, with the head opposite the entrance, and the nearest male relatives in turn, drawing their *pútkulis* over their heads,‖ took a wand (*Pett*), round which was tied a small rag, obtained from the *Pálál*, dug up the earth at the entrance of the circle, and muttering "*Purzhutukamā,*" "May I throw earth?" threw three handfuls into the centre of the circle, and three on the body. After this the body was carried back to the hut and placed on the ground outside, and the women sat round it as before. A large silver necklace (*Kévilth, Plate* XI., *Fig. b*), belonging to the widow, was laid on the breast of the corpse.

The funeral pile¶ was made of large logs on a space cleared for the purpose near the hut. The dead man's herd was driven up, and some fifteen or twenty Todas went to it, one of them carrying wreaths of leaves to throw at the doomed buffaloes. Two of the animals were seized by four or five men hanging to their necks, separated from the herd, and dragged to the hut, followed by the Kota musicians. A bell was then

---

* *For men.*

Peiki -	- Thursday, Saturday, Sunday.
Todi -	- Sunday, Tuesday.
Kuttan -	- Saturday, Sunday.
Kenna -	- Tuesday, Saturday, Sunday.
Pekkan -	- Tuesday, Thursday, Saturday.

For women.

All clans -	- Thursday and Saturday.

† Each clan has several *Methgúdis,* separate ones for men and for women. In this case, however, as the deceased was a poor man who had died while on a visit to relatives at a distance, his body was not carried back to the usual burning ground of his Mand.

‡ When death is imminent the patient is dressed in a new *Pútkuli* and other cloths.

§ The circle is called *Taal* (*Kraal*), and is made in imitation of a buffalo kraal. If there is a kraal near the *Methgúdi,* the body is taken there, and the stone circle is not made. It is never made for a woman.

‖ Compare 2 *Sam.* xv. 30; *Esther* vi. 12; and *Jer.* xiv. 3, 4.

¶ The wood of the *Eugenia Arnottiana* is always used at the green funeral, that of the *Olea robusta* at the dry.

tied round the first buffalo's neck, and the corpse was lifted and made to touch three times the side of the animal, which was killed by one blow from the back of an axe, and its body dragged up, so that its head lay close to that of the dead man, the hand of the latter being made to clasp the buffalo's horn (*Plate* XIV.) The bell was then transferred to the other buffalo, and the same process repeated. All the relatives seated themselves by the three bodies to mourn in couples, a man and woman putting their heads together and sobbing and moaning. After a little while each couple would separate, the woman saluting the man by raising his foot to her forehead (except in the case of the old women, when the process was reversed), and fresh pairs would be formed. As with other Eastern people, their sorrow is woeful to behold, the tears literally streaming down their faces and over their cloths. Their grief, however, is marvellously transient.

After this the widow sat alone mourning at the head of the deceased, and put three handfuls of grain into the pocket of his cloth. Then the body was placed on the bier, and laid on the ground beside the pile, which was lighted by the relatives, who, again covering their heads, made fire with two sticks.*

One side of the bier was cut into three and laid on the pile. *Sāmĕ* grain (*Panicum miliare*) and jaggery, the two great Toda luxuries, were then put into the pocket of the dead man's *pútkuli*, with two cheroots, some tobacco wrapped in red cloth, and the purse, embroidered by one of the mourners, containing five or six rupees in silver and a little gold coin.† A ring was put on the finger, and earrings in the ears. A bit of the skull with hair and one of the finger nails‡ were cut off by the relatives; these, I was told, would be kept till the dry funeral in a little hut built near the mand for that purpose, and a buffalo bell hung over them for the relatives to ring night and morning. The bell is not hung over the remains of a woman. After this, ghee was thrown on the pile; the body was swung three times over the flame and laid on the pile *face downwards*, a sort of imitation bier or hurdle, which had previously been placed under the body, being laid above it.

When the fire has burnt out, any coin or metal that may have been actually given to the flames, is recovered; usually they merely pass such articles through the flame by way of an offering.

No care is taken of the ashes, they "are left to the winds," as a Toda told me.

The dry funeral takes place within a twelvemonth or so after death, according to the pleasure of the relatives. Each clan has its own *kēdmanes*§ or funeral houses, different ones for men and women. They are sometimes near a mund, sometimes not, but always have a kraal at hand. They are like the ordinary Toda huts, but are sometimes decorated at the time of the funeral with silver coins. These are mostly rupees,

* A dry stick of the *Cœlcodaphne Wighiana*, about as thick as a man's thumb, is laid on the ground and held firm by the feet, a second stick is held upright between the two hands, the point resting on the horizontal stick: by twirling the upright with great rapidity between the palms of the hands fire is produced at the point of contact.

† Called by Todas *Bīrăn pănăm*. I think it is the same as the *Birianhana* given to a dying Badaga. This is a *Vir-raya* or Coorg-fanam.

‡ These appear to be specially sacred relics among the Buddhists also. Stupas covering a lock of hair, crown of skull, or finger-nail of Buddhist saints seem to have been common in the palmy days of Buddhism.

§ *Kēd* is the name given to the skull, hair, and finger-nail saved from the green funeral, which are tied between two pieces of bark.

but on one occasion I saw some old gold coins and a silver medal of the Nilagiri District Exhibition of 1869. The ceremonies occupy part of three days. The first is devoted to belling the buffaloes. The Kota musicians are in attendance; crowds of Badagas and other natives come to see the ceremony; shopkeepers bring biscuits and sweetmeats to sell, and the whole scene presents the aspect of a fair. Pending the arrival of the buffaloes, the Todas do a little dancing, escort monigars* or other guests of importance in procession to the spot, chanting "Hoh! Hoh!" in the deepest bass possible to the human chest, hold Panchayats† for settling disputes, and otherwise amuse themselves. Occasionally a man who is liable to inspiration, throws off his *pútkuli* and begins tramping up and down a line of Todas, shaking his head and trembling, while communicating the wishes of the god. On one occasion when I was there, no less than three went through this performance, professing to be possessed by Bēti Khân, the hunting god, who, however, seemed to have little to say beyond a lamentation, in the *laudator temporis acti* spirit, over the degeneracy of modern Todas as evinced by the decreasing number of buffaloes slaughtered. At last the herd of buffaloes, two or three for each of the dead commemorated, are driven up to the kraal, near which stands the funeral house. As the buffaloes approach the entrance, a crowd of young Todas, throwing off their *pútkulis*, rush into the kraal with them, seize them, and tie one or more bells to the neck of each, the women meanwhile weeping profusely. Ordinarily this finishes the ceremonial part of the proceeding, and the rest of the day is spent in eating and amusement; but on the occasion before alluded to, the buffaloes, distressed by their bells, made a rush at the wall of the kraal, and, in spite of the efforts of some Kotas, who fought valiantly for their next day's dinner, five of them escaped, and had to be followed a mile or two and brought back. This untoward event further induced a quarrel between the Peikis and Todis, one of the former having in his excitement struck a Todi, who left the place in dudgeon, and was not appeased till many influential processions and much Kota music had been lavished on him.

The second day's ceremonies are the most important. The young men spend the morning in dancing in the kraal, to the great annoyance of the buffaloes. Every now and then three or four single out a particular buffalo and seize it, hanging on by the neck and horns, hold it for a few moments, and release it. This requires some nerve in the leader of the party, as he makes the first rush alone, and may be thrown down and trampled on before the others come to his assistance. Even when three or four are hanging on together, a buffalo will sometimes lift them all off their feet.

This, however, is only by way of passing the time; the actual ceremonies are begun by placing the *kéd*, wrapped in a new *pútkuli*, on the ground within the stone wall surrounding the *kēdmane*. Fifteen or twenty men stand round it, shouting "*Hah! hoh! ēr kar ultamā*," ("May the buffaloes and calves be well,") or words of that kind; and one after the other lays his right hand on the *kéd*, covered by the *pútkuli*, and bows so as to touch it with the forehead. The *kéd* is then carried to the entrance of the cattle kraal, where a hole has been dug, and where the relatives and

* *Monigar*—properly *maniyakāran*, the head man of a village.

† *Panchāyat*, a native court of arbitration consisting of five or more members, usually chosen by the parties themselves for the settlement of petty disputes.

friends of the deceased in turn, covering their heads with their cloths, scratch up the earth with a stick (*Pett*), to which is tied a rag given by the *Pâlâl*, and throw three handfuls of earth into the kraal, and three on the *pútkuli*, as in the green funeral; each before throwing mutters "*Purzhutukamā*" ("May I throw earth") to a man of the Peiki class standing by the entrance, who replies "*Purzhut*" ("Throw earth.") At the funeral of a Peiki, one of the Tarserzhâl performs this office.

When each of the relatives has thrown his handfuls, the *pujāri* approaches with some garlands of creepers, which he throws at the buffaloes. At this signal, a crowd of young men leap into the kraal, the gate is opened, and, with a rush, men and buffaloes pour out in a cloud of dust, four or five men clinging to each animal's neck, while others urge it on with their clubs. The excitement and confusion are great, and the danger not small; as the buffaloes, blinded and terrified, tear wildly round the kraal and against its walls before they can be dragged out to the place of slaughter. This differs in different cases. At a Peiki funeral, where nine buffaloes were slaughtered, one was killed near a couple of posts about a hundred yards from the kraal, and the rest near the *kêdmane*, their bodies being laid in two rows with the heads together. At a Todi funeral near Tārnāt Mand, commemorative of a single death, one of the two buffaloes slaughtered was killed near the *kêdmane*, the other at the mand *Pālthohi*. Death is inflicted by one blow between the horns from the back of an axe. The *pútkuli* and *kêd* are then laid beside the carcases, and men and women sit down by them and mourn in couples, changing places from time to time as at the green funeral.

The next ceremony at a Todi funeral is most striking, and vividly recalls Mosaic sacrifices.

The Peiki *Varzhâl* carries a small urn-shaped vessel of leaves, stitched together, and filled with pieces of bark of the *Meliosma pungens*, to the mand herd, and sits a little way off, while the young men run in and seize a female buffalo and a calf. The latter is decorated with an iron bell, and held by two or three men, while the buffalo is dragged to a stone, to which the *pútkuli* and *kêd*, the deceased's stick, and a miniature bow and three arrows are brought. The *kêd* is untied, and the hair, &c. laid on a mimic stretcher (*Berrkvur*) about $1\frac{1}{2}$ foot long, roughly made of green sticks. The buffalo is half stunned by a blow between the horns from a big stone, and a clansman of the deceased, with an axe, makes a gash under its right foreleg. Into this wound the *Varzhâl* dips a few of the pieces of bark from the leaf vessel, and gives some of them to the kinsman, who smears the blood on the *kêd*, with some words which are differently reported by different Todas. The clearest sentence given is "*Karma odi ponā*," "May "the sin run away." Another man repeated an unintelligible sentence, which, however, contained the words *Karma*, sin, and *Amunâd*, heaven, so that the idea of a propitiatory sacrifice underlies the ceremony.

(They make rather a secret of this part of the proceedings, fearing, not unreasonably, that it may be objected to on the score of humanity, and I had to promise not to report the matter, or induce Government interference, before they would let me see what was done.) A Peiki man then puts on the *pútkuli*, in which the *kêd* had been wrapped, and a silver necklace, and taking the bow and arrows, the latter laid across the bow, as though in readiness for shooting, dips the points of the arrows into the blood on the *kêd*, saying "*Birzhutukamā*," "Shall I give the bow." After this they walk to another stone near the Kêdmane in procession, shouting "Hoh Hoh," the Peiki with the bow in the middle, and the *Varzhāl* in front, carrying the leaf vessel, out of which he takes two pieces of bark at intervals, throwing one behind him and another before him. The calf is dragged to this stone and let loose, when they all run after it, throwing themselves down at intervals so as to touch the ground with their foreheads, and shouting

Amunādga Sērumā
Karma dharma tilimā.

which may be rendered, "May he enter heaven, may it be well with his good deeds "and his sins."

The Peikis and Pekkaus do not sacrifice a buffalo, nor loose a calf at the dry funeral, but at the next new moon they slaughter a male buffalo, and bringing the blood in a leaf vessel to the *kêdmane*, sprinkle it on the kraal and the *Āzāram*.

The ceremonies are hardly concluded, before the Kotas descend upon the carcases of the buffaloes like so many vultures, and hack them to pieces, screaming and squabbling over the spoil, and carrying off the flesh in great lumps to their homes. It is curious that the Todas, to whose relatives the dead animals are consecrated, make no objection to this disgusting operation, though carried on at the very door of the *Kêdmane*. I asked a Toda once about it, and he replied, "*When the buffaloes are "alive they are ours; when dead they belong to the Kotas.*"

The *Kêd* is burnt about four o'clock on the following morning (they say the burning must be completed before dawn) at the *Āzāram*,* a single circle of large stones fixed in the ground not far from the Kêdmane. They first light a fire outside the *Āzāram*, and then spread the *pútkuli* with the *kêd* in the middle of the circle, and pile burning sticks on it until, with the help of ghee, they make a great blaze. They put on the inside fire the following articles:—

A *Kăf Kutli*, a sort of large knife or sickle wrapped round with cloth.
An axe.
Twenty-one bamboo measures ornamented with cowries, two anna bits, and coloured threads, and containing barley, kīre, and sāme grain.
Four or five cakes of jaggery.
A winnowing basket.
A basket for holding rice.
Three or four Toda walking sticks.
A straight pole (*Tarzh*) 20 feet long, ornamented with tassels and rosettes of cowries, and sometimes with a small silver umbrella. (*Plate* XI., *fig. b.*)
A palm-leaf umbrella.
A miniature bow and three arrows.† (*Plate* XI., *fig. a.*)
A purse.

* I could not ascertain with any certainty whether these stone circles, which are always to be found near the funeral mand, had been constructed in recent years or were of considerable antiquity. Their appearance, however, did not suggest any great age. From the Todas whom I questioned on the subject, it was very difficult to elicit any definite information; but the impression which their answers conveyed, was, that now and then they construct new circles, when they consider that the old ones have been used long enough.

† I am told that these are burned at the green funeral when the Kotas have time to make them, but they must not be made beforehand, or the man for whom they were intended would die; and as the Kotas will only work, and the Todas only burn on certain days, it must frequently happen that the two do not coincide.

The pouch of the *pútkuli* is filled with grain. Outside the *Āzāram* are burnt the miniature stretcher (*Berrkvur*), some half-dozen mimic buffalo horns of bamboo (*Kūter*), the dead man's bamboo milk vessel, and the *Pett*. All the silver ornaments are passed through the flame and removed, before the utensils, &c. are burnt. All the time the fire is burning, two Kotas are making night hideous with their discordant music, and all the Todas mourn and weep in couples, sobbing their rhythmical farewell to the dead:

* *Âmunâdga serumā,*
Karma dharma (pronounced *Karrm Dharrm*) *tihmā* *

Courtesy requires that all who attend the funeral should go through the form of mourning, but a brief display of mitigated grief contents mere acquaintances.

Just as dawn is breaking, the music is stopped, the mourning ceases, and in dead silence all cluster round the *Āzāram* for the impressive closing ceremony. Water is sprinkled on the embers, a large stone at the entrance of the circle † is taken up, and a pit dug under it, into which they scrape the ashes, and the stone is replaced.

At a Todi funeral a man goes three or four times round the circle ringing a bell,‡ followed by another with a chatty,§ but this is not done by all the clans.

Finally a dim figure enters the circle, and raising a chatty high over his head dashes it to pieces on the stone covering the ashes, ‖ bends down, touches the stone with his forehead, and hastens away. All the others perform in turn the same prostration, and flitting silently down the hill—a procession of hurrying shadows—fade into the mist through which twinkles the distant fire at the *kēdmane*. Imagination might easily transform them into the departing spirits of the propitiated dead.

They tell me that they have a tradition that after putting their foreheads to the stone, they must get away as quickly as possible, and without looking back. The natives of the plains have, I believe, a similar superstition.¶

At a woman's dry funeral, instead of the bows and arrows, a rice-beater is burnt, and last of all the *kēdmane* itself, a remarkable symbolical acknowledgment of the exceptionally important position which the Toda women occupy.

Thus the Toda funeral, like the Badaga song which describes a future state,** ends in note of despair, a mournful suggestion that, after all, their cares for the dead may be in vain. Surely those who instituted these remarkable ceremonies must have recognised the significance of that time-honoured symbol the "broken pitcher;" a type of irremediable

---

* This is the only thing in the shape of verse I know among the Todas.

† At a Todi funeral near Tānāt Mand the entrance was N.N.E., but this does not seem to be always the case. Some more modern *Āzārams* might be examined to ascertain this, which is important in connexion with the orientation of the cairns.

‡ Not a sacred bell, but one that the Kotas keep and bring with them to the funeral.

§ An earthen pot.

‖ Dubois, People of India, p. 290. At a Brahman funeral "the chief of the funeral taking on his shoulder a pitcher of water goes three times round the pile, letting water run over it through a hole in the vessel, which he afterwards breaks near the head of the corpse."

¶ Among the Todas, according to Dr. Pope, the same word, Bhūt, stands for ghost and demon. Possibly the interment of the last relics of the dead is felt as breaking his last link with the living, and giving him over to the disembodied army of Bhūts. The dread of ghosts, or belief in the evil power of the spirits of bad or unmarried men is very common in India.

** Dravidian Folk songs, by Mr. Gover.

destruction, and of usefulness gone by for ever, contrasting pathetically with the hopes of immortality implied by the previous elaborate provisions for the future welfare of the dead. Such a recognition, however, implies a widely different religious life from that of the modern Toda. It is startling to contrast the respect for the dead to which this ritual testifies, with the utter indifference shown by the present race, not only to the disposal of the buffaloes, but even to the fate of old *Āzārams*. Numbers of these are to be found in different parts of the hills, but the Todas do not even always claim them as theirs; and in no case object to their being examined and destroyed. The sacrifice of the buffalo, the sprinkling of blood, the loosing of the calf,* and all the striking symbolism of their funeral rites, have no meaning for the present generation. Like the numerous gods who are never worshipped, and the preparatory penances of the priests who perform no priestly offices, these are but the strangely suggestive relics of a bygone faith.

The burning at funerals of a mimic bow and arrow together with the daily-used implements of the deceased, and the importance assigned to the bow in the marriage ceremony, seem to me inexplicable, except on the theory that the bow was once the chief weapon of the Todas, although they are ignorant of its use now.† This view is in a measure confirmed by the Todas' admission that their ancestors ate samber flesh, and that they would gladly do so now if they could obtain it; and by the fact that they still recognise, and make offerings to, a hunting God under the name of Bêtikhân, who, though he now resides in a temple at Nambilicotē beyond Gudalūr, is, they say, the son of their ancestor Dirkish.

The question then arises: how and when did the bow fall into disuse with the Todas? a disuse the more strange, because some of the jungle tribes near the base of the Nīlagiris are still expert archers.

The answer would seem to be found in the tradition mentioned by Colonel Ouchterlony, viz.—that before the Badagas and Kotas came to the Hills, the Todas lived only by their herds, and wore leaves. As far as the leaf dresses go, the story seems apocryphal. If the Todas had only adopted clothes after the arrival of the Badagas and Kotas, their garments would probably have Badaga or Kota names, whereas *pútkuli, tharp, kônu, &c.*, are among the few Toda words which Mr. Metz can trace to no Dravidian roots. Besides, a hunting race would certainly wear skins: however, the story probably contains some truth. Before the cultivating tribes settled in the Hills, the Todas, unless they killed their cattle, would have no means of obtaining solid food except by hunting, for their traffic with the Western Coast must have been too inter-

* The idea of the Scapegoat, Egyptian I believe, as well as Jewish, has more than one Indian illustration. The Baigas, who exercise priestly offices among the Gonds, loose fowls occasionally on this principle, while among some of the tribes of the N.W. Provinces, an inanimate representative is chosen in the shape of a sieve or winnow which is beaten in every corner of the house and then thrown outside the village, to carry away the poverty of the people. (*Tribes of the N.W. Provinces, Sir H. Elliot.*)

† I do not overlook the fact that both Badagas and Kotas burn the bow at their funerals; but this I think is borrowed. That the Badagas do copy the Todas, is evident; for although they do not kill a cow, they go through the form of dragging one up to the funeral pile, seizing a diminutive country cow by the neck and horns, and pulling it along with a ludicrous imitation of the Todas' struggles with their powerful buffaloes.

The Badagas have also adopted the *Têr* or funeral car of the Kotas, an innovation which astonishes the Gurus from Mysore who occasionally visit the Hills.

The Todas and Kotas have a good deal in common, of which I shall speak afterwards.

mittent and insignificant to be depended on for subsistence. Probably they were then expert in the use of the bow, but when they found that they could obtain from the cultivators a share of their produce, such an idle race as the Todas would naturally abandon the toilsome and precarious occupation of hunting.

The disuse of the bow is thus, to a certain extent evidence of an improvement in the material condition of the Todas, though unaccompanied by any advance in civilization: still, as they themselves admit that it would be convenient to supplement their food by samber* flesh, their present inability to procure it, shows how easily a semi-savage race may lay aside and forget† arts of obvious utility as soon as the pressure of absolute necessity is withdrawn.

It is noteworthy that this indication of a still wilder life than that of the modern Toda, should occur side by side with traces of so much higher a religious condition.

The disposal of the body is suggestive. Col. Dalton, in an account‡ of somewhat similar funeral rites among the Kols, observes that some of the accessories of their ceremonial suggest the idea that their dead were originally buried, not burnt. The Toda ceremonies convey this impression with still greater clearness. The *Berrkvur* probably represents an actual bier, and the sprinkling of earth on the body and in the circle, as before described, leads almost inevitably to the conclusion that the body was formerly buried, *and that the stone circle was the original burying place.*

The minor observances present coincidences interesting, but of little ethnological importance, such as the dread of looking back, as old as Orpheus and Eurydice; and the three handfuls of earth which recall our own funeral rites.

It would be desirable to obtain detailed accounts from eye-witnesses of the ceremonies of other Indian Hill tribes, and of the Low Castes of the plains. It seems to me that it is in such observances, rather than in the every-day life of these tribes, that the most valuable indications of their previous condition are to be found; because, while circumstances necessarily affect their ordinary life, customs of this kind may remain unchanged for centuries.

---

* Sāmber, commonly known as the Indian Elk, a large kind of deer.

† Vide—Sir J. Lubbock *On the origin of civilization and primitive condition of Man*, page 331 :—

"The art of spinning and the use of the bow are quite unknown to many races of savages, and yet "would hardly be likely to have been abandoned when once known"!

Sir J. Lubbock, *Prehistoric Times*, page 451 :—

"Many again, of the ruder arts, as for instance the manufacture of pottery, and of bows, are so useful, "and at the same time, however ingenious in idea, so simple in execution, as to render it highly "improbable that they would ever be lost, when they had once been acquired"!

‡ Col. Dalton's *Kols of Chota Nagpore. Transactions Ethnological Society, Vol. VI., New Series, page* 37. He says that among the *Hos* and *Moondahs* a corpse is burnt in a very stout coffin furnished with projections as if to facilitate transport. With the body are burnt all the clothes and ornaments of the deceased, and what money he had with him at his death. The larger fragments of bone are afterwards selected (the rest being buried at once) and hung up for some time in a place where they may be constantly viewed by the mother or widow. After some time a large monumental stone is brought to the family burying ground. The bones are carried in procession to the houses of relatives, who mourn over them, and to the favourite haunts of the deceased, preceded by men with drums, and girls carrying empty and half broken pitchers, which from time to time they reverse. Ultimately the procession circles round and round a large hole at the burying place, the bones are placed in a new earthen vessel, and deposited with a quantity of food in the grave, which is covered by the monumental stone.—Compare the reversed pitchers and interment in an earthen vessel with the account of cairns at the end of this volume.

The Todas, as we have said, believe in a Heaven and Hell, the latter represented by a river or swamp full of leeches. The road to *Âmunâd* (Heaven) lies across this stream, and those who have already reached their Paradise, make for new-comers a bridge formed of a single thread, which will bear a good man, but breaks under the weight of a sinner, and precipitates him into *Pûfĕrigĕn** (Hell) (from *pûf*, leech; *ĕri*, place; *gĕn*, water), where he remains until he has expiated his offences. I asked particularly what became of the slaughtered buffaloes meanwhile, but my informant had evidently taken this economical question into consideration, and replied that they crossed higher up, and were utilized by the dead man's family until his penance was over.

Âmunâd is presided over by Ēn, a deified Toda, on whose authority the Todas believe it to be "a good place." Their description of it however does not seem attractive. They say that here men's arms and legs are poisonous, so that by culture they wear out the earth, but that in *Âmunâd* the tables are turned, and the arms and legs of the cultivators are gradually worn down to the elbows and knees. When they have arrived at this stage, they return to earth. This seems a strange form of the common tradition of antagonism† between the earth and its inhabitants. As Todas cannot be accused of wearing out the earth by culture, this peculiarity of *Âmunād* probably only affects strangers. It is curious to find this prejudice against agriculture expressed in almost the same terms as far back as the time of Menu. *Cf. Institutes, X.* 84. "Agriculture is a mode of subsistence which the benevolent greatly blame: for the iron-mouthed pieces of wood not only wound the earth, but the creatures dwelling in it."

The bridge of thread recalls the Mahomedan Al Sirât, and the Badagas have a similar tradition, which receives a curious illustration from the actual practice of the Khāsias, when carrying home the remains of any of their number who may have died at a distance. "The dead, they say, have not the strength or ability to wade through water, and if they trust themselves to it, would be carried down the stream, never to be recovered. They, therefore, stretch a thread of cotton from one bank to the other, and, if the breadth is great, this is kept clear of the water by sticks planted in the bed of the river, and notched at the top to receive it. If the running water should be very narrow, merely a stick is laid, or even a stalk of grass is considered sufficient to form a bridge for the dead man's soul. The line of thread is called the 'string bridge'"‡

Our own old superstition about the inability of witches to cross running water seems a reproduction of the same idea.

Language. The Todas have no written language. Captain Harkness§ speaking of their dialect says, "It appears to be quite distinct from the languages of the surrounding countries. With the Sanscrit it has not the least affinity in roots, construction, or sound, and if I may venture to say so, as little with any Asiatic language of the present day."

Major Ross King gives a similar account in the *Journal of Anthropology* for July 1870.

---

* Dr. Pope (*Outlines, &c.*) says "pûf, an insect, is probably old Kanarese-purlu. It must, however, be stated that the words in which *f* is found are precisely those which it is most difficult to trace."

† Compare *Genesis* i. 28, and iv. 12; also *Moor's Hindu Pantheon*, page 248, story of Prithu and Prithivi.

‡ *On the Stone Monuments of the Khāsi Hill Tribes*, by Major H. H. Godwin-Austen. *Journal of Anthropological Institute*, October 1871, Vol. I., No. II.

§ *Neilgherry Hills*, p. 25.

Little was known of the Toda language in Captain Harkness' time. Since then it has been studied and analysed, and both in grammatical structure and inflexional forms, it is found to resemble closely the other Dravidian* languages of Southern India.

Tamil and Canarese derivatives form the bulk of the language. Out of a hundred words commonly made use of by a Toda, Mr. Metz finds at least eighty to be identically the same with, or derived from, words used by his Dravidian neighbours: other philologists might find more.†

Mr. Metz has kindly furnished me with a vocabulary (Appendix A.) giving the correct rendering in Toda, Kota, Kurumba, Irula, and Badaga, of all the words contained in Dr. Hunter's *Comparative Dictionary of non-Aryan languages of India and High Asia.*

To this vocabulary Mr. Metz and I have prefixed a table of letters with the corresponding sound of each in some European language. We have followed, as far as possible, Dr. Pope's *South Indian Alphabet,* to which however a few additions have been found necessary, in order not to sacrifice the sound or the derivation of words; ‡ for instance, Todas for the most part pronounce the long *a* like *a* in *all.* To have rendered the *a* by ŏ or *au* would have obscured the derivation in many cases: ex. gr., Tamil pāl milk = Toda pâḷ (paul).

Dr. Pope's object was the simple transliteration of South Indian written characters, not the representation of the sounds contained in all the dialects written and unwritten. For philological and ethnological objects, which presumably the Government have in view in ordering inquiries such as I am conducting, simplicity is less important than the accurate rendering of every sound by a distinct character, so as to facilitate comparison and analysis by philologists personally unacquainted with the dialects. Moreover at present none of the systems of transliteration proposed by Sir W. Jones, Drs. Wilson, Caldwell, Pope, and others, have commanded universal acceptance; and the result is that even the various written characters are not always uniformly rendered, while the unwritten dialects depend for their orthography on the taste and fancy of the speller. The consequences of this are well illustrated in Dr. Hunter's work. He has necessarily compiled his Dictionary from various vocabularies, spelt upon no uniform system, and has wisely refrained, as he says, "from corrections in languages of which he was ignorant."

---

* With regard to the theory propounded by Mr. Gover in *The Folk-songs of Southern India,* of the Aryan origin of Dravidian languages, an extract from a letter of Dr. Gundert's, with which Mr. Metz has favoured me, may be interesting:—

"Thus much I think I myself know, that no one acquainted with both families of speech will ever make "Dravidians into Aryans. How much the former have borrowed from the latter is well known. That the "latter in turn have borrowed words from the Dravidian, I have, I think, proved in greater detail than is to "be found in Caldwell."

† Dr. Caldwell (*Comp. Gram.* p. 16) says, "Of all the Dravidian idioms the Tamil is that to which the "Tuda language is most nearly allied."

Mr. Metz thinks that it is more nearly connected with old Kanarese, but that it is as distinct a dialect as Tulu.

Dr. Pope ("*Outlines of Tuda Grammar,* § 44") says, "The language seems to have been originally old "Kanarese, and not a distinct dialect."

Mr. Burnell has noted the large proportion of Sanscrit words in the Toda vocabulary.

‡ Since the above was written, Dr. Pope's "Outlines of the Tuda grammar," written for Colonel Marshall's book, has been printed. The vocabulary, however, contains different words; the spelling also is rather different, as is inevitable, when no recognised system exists.—*Ed.*

For the Toda language he has consulted two vocabularies under the respective names of Toduva and Toda,* which he thinks may possibly refer to different dialects; not unnaturally, since the former systematically follows the phonetic, and the latter what may be called the derivative system of spelling. Thus he gives, for *Four*—

Toduva = *Nonk.*
Toda = *Nánk.*

In this case the compiler of the former simply regarded the sound of the word, whereas the author of the latter was mindful of the derivation from the same root as the Tamil *Nālu,* Canarese *Nālku.*

The same difference occurs in the next page, where Six is rendered—

Toduva = *Or.*
Toda = *A'r.*

Again Dr. Hunter has apparently been compelled to depend for some dialects on writers who were very sparing of diacritical marks, and did not always distinguish even between long and short vowels. Thus *Three* is written—

Badaga = *Muru* instead of *Mūru.*
Kurumba = *Mudu* „ *Mūdu.*

And Thirty in both languages is *Muvattu* instead of *Mūvattu.* Four, *Nālku,* is given correctly, but Forty is written *Nalvattu,* instead of *Nālvattu,* and One hundred is *Nuru* instead of *Nūru.*

Every page almost of the Comparative Dictionary would supply similar instances.

Dr. Hunter himself is aware of, and regrets, the imperfection of his materials. He says (p. 18), "The attempt to represent tones was, after mature consideration, given up. "Of the consonants little need be said, except that I have not ventured to improve "the apparent accuracy of the book by a manufactured uniformity. The temptation "to do so has presented itself on every page. The letters d, ḍ, r, for example, and "particularly ḍ and ṛ, are very often used indiscriminately, some of the compilers of "the lists writing ḍ generally as *r*, others putting *d* instead of ḍ. * I thought it better, "even where it might be clear which was the correct form, to print the words as they "stood in my MS. lists, than, for the sake of appearances to venture on corrections "from analogy." After giving one or two instances in which such corrections would have led to error, Dr. Hunter says, "This confusion I chiefly regret, because it has "rendered it unsafe to complete what I had hoped would form the most important "feature of the book, to wit, a table of non-Aryan phonetic changes. * * * "Until a table of phonetic changes is constructed, and its laws ascertained, researches "into non-Aryan speech will remain destitute of the exactitude of Indo-Germanic "philology."

As the Government have interested themselves in the history of the lower Indian races, it seems to me desirable that they should do, what no one else in India can, viz., stamp with authority some one well-considered Indian alphabet for scientific purposes, on

* *Vide* page 17 of Dr. Hunter's *Comparative Dictionary of the non-Aryan languages, &c.* Referring to Toduva, and Toda, he speaks of them as "representing the same language, or varieties so close as to seem "scarcely deserving of separate places."

the principle of the "Universal Alphabet" proposed by Dr. Lepsius.* The actual adoption of Lepsius's system seems to me undesirable, because the great number of sounds it comprises, and the consequent complexity of diacritical signs used, are not requisite for Indian vocabularies, and would be unnecessarily bewildering to amateur compilers.

I would suggest that the Government of Madras, for instance, should endeavour to obtain the services of such men as Dr. Caldwell, Dr. Pope, and Mr. Metz, to draw up a table of signs which should represent all the sounds to be found in the different dialects of the Presidency. This list might be then forwarded to the other Provinces, in order that philologists there might add letters expressive of any sounds in Northern languages which are not found in the Dravidian dialects. When a general alphabet had been agreed upon, it should be sent to every district as the basis for vocabularies of the ruder and less known dialects. If the vocabularies thus formed, were again submitted to competent philologists for correction of the orthographical errors, into which ignorance of derivation might lead compilers, they would afford a reliable basis for the comparative philology of India.

The vocabulary in the Appendix is simply an attempt to render correctly, with due regard to derivations, the sounds of certain words in the Hill dialects; it has no pretensions to anything more.†

History and Tradition.

The Todas have hardly a tradition or legend of any sort from which information as to their former condition can be obtained. They believe that their ancestors always inhabited these hills, that is (for their ideas on the subject seem chiefly negative) they have no knowledge or belief of their having migrated from elsewhere. Mr. Metz thinks the Todas came from the neighbourhood of Kāligāl (Collegāl), because he has often been asked for news of the relatives, who, they believe, still reside there. I cannot find, however, that any Todas are now known in that neighbourhood. Mr. Minchin informs me that there are three colonies of Todas in Wainād, one at Dēvāla, and two on the eastern slopes of the Neliyālam Peak range. Those at Dēvāla, he says, reside in houses of bamboo, built with gable ends, like the huts of the Paniers, and occasionally work as house-builders for the bazaar people, but live chiefly by the sale of ghee and milk. They are Peikis, and say that they left the Nīlagiris sixty years ago to find a better sale for their produce. This account of themselves is confirmed by the fact, that within my own knowledge the dry funeral of two of them has been celebrated at the funeral mand of the Peikis near Ootacamund.

Little more information is to be derived from foreign sources. The Badagas are said to have come to the hills in consequence of the troubles that followed the fall of Vijayanagar, *i.e.*, about three centuries ago; but their songs and stories depict the Todas much as we see them now. I think, however, we may infer that the latter were more numerous, from the fact of their having been able to exact the *gūdu* in the first instance, whereas now, with all the help afforded by long custom, they have at times difficulty in collecting it. Moreover, there are still traces to be found of old mands

* Such an alphabet is not open to the objections which historians and geographers urge with much reason against every method of transcribing names of places and other well-known oriental words which will render them unintelligible to the ordinary reader, because it is simply wanted for philological purposes.

† I believe that since the above was written the Government of India have authoritatively prescribed a system of transliteration, how obtained I do not know.—*Editor.*

long ago deserted, some of which by the girth of the trees which have since grown up in them, have evidently been abandoned for centuries.

It would appear that the Todas have always maintained some intercourse with the western coast, as the cowrie necklaces of the women imply. The earliest notice of them I know of, is to be found in the Journal of the Archbishop of Goa, Aleixo de Menezes; Coimbra, 1606, the following extract from which has been kindly furnished me by Dr. Gundert:—

" From Malabar the Vicars' regular report, from their hitherto neglected and paganised churches, came in to Goa (in 1599). At this time two Cattanars had been to Todamala in the country of the Zamorin, 50 leagues distant from the furthest churches. There (in Todamala) there are still Christians, who speak a language different from the Malabar language. They call their god 'Bidi'* (=fado, fatum). They have a Trinity of persons, viz., an old man, a youth, and a small bird. They say Thomas taught them, but because the king of Mylapūr killed all Christians, they took refuge on these mountains, that there their Cattanars have died, their books have been lost, and all idea of God has disappeared, but still they have a picture very much injured of that Trinity. The objects of that picture they try to keep in mind. They knew that in Cochin there were people of their own caste, on which account they called the two Cattanars brothers, and summoned men and women together to hear them, when the Cattanars explained from the picture the Trinity to the people. The Jesuit Roy was very glad of this report, and spoke of it as not a singular instance. In other places also (near the hills) remains of former Christian congregations were discovered. He (Roy) became Bishop of Angimale in 1601, and Archbishop of Cranganore in 1605."

This report seems to have led to further investigations, as we find by the following abstract of a manuscript in the British Museum kindly furnished me by the Reverend Mr. Whitehouse:—

At the synod of Udiamparūr in the state of Cochin,† held under Archbishop Menezes in 1599, information having been received that there were certain villages of Christians in a country called Todamala, who anciently belonged to the Syrian church of Malabar, but then had nothing of Christianity except the bare name, it was ordered that priests and preachers should be sent thither immediately to redeem them to the Catholic faith, baptize them, &c. Francisco Roy, the first Roman Catholic Bishop of the Syrian Christians, in 1602 sent a priest and deacon of the Christians of St. Thomas with a good guide to find out the place and collect information. They reached the Todamala; but, as the account brought back by them, was not so sure and complete as was desirable, Bishop Roy requested the Vice-Principal of the Jesuits to depute a priest of his own order to make further inquiries. The Rev. Jacome Ferreiri was selected for this mission. He started from Calicut, the place of his residence, and was permitted to return safely, after undergoing great exposure and fatigue, with a good deal of information about the hill tribes, their manners and customs, but with no tidings of any Christian colony, which had either become extinct or removed elsewhere, if it had ever been there at all.

---

* Dr. Gundert says, "Bidi or Vidhi is a well-known name of Brahma."

† Todamala is included in a list of Christian churches given in Assemani Bibl. Orient., but this only refers to the date of this same synod.

At Calicut he wrote a formal report, dated April 1st, 1603, from which the following particulars are gleaned :—

He proceeded viâ Manarecate 13 leagues inland from Tanūr. A native convert, a nephew of the Samuri Rajah, accompanied him, and some others. Their route led them over steep and rugged mountains, infested with elephants and tigers. At Manarecate they were told that the Todamala was 6 Canarese or 12 Malabar leagues distant, and that it would take them two days and a half to reach their destination. Here they provided themselves with extra clothing as a protection against the cold of the mountains, and also provision for their journey. The Nairs who accompanied them wisely left their weapons behind them, lest the hill people should take alarm. The evening of the second day from Manarecate* found them at the foot of a steep hill up which their route lay. On the third day they reach a Badaga village called Meleuntao (? Mēlūr or Mēlkūndah), containing between one and two hundred inhabitants. The priest and deacon previously sent are said to have arrived thus far. Here they met also with the chief of the Todas, who agreed to call his people together so that they might have an opportunity of conversing with them. On the following day the Jesuit father tried to converse with the Badagas on the subject of Christianity. He also had an interview with the Toda priest called Pallem (Pâlâl) outside the Badaga village, which he would not enter for fear of pollution. They saw some Toda women, and gave them looking glasses and hanks of thread, with which they were much pleased. The third day of their sojourn on the hills was spent in a visitation of some of the Toda settlements, which are very correctly described, as also their dress, diet, manners, and customs. They could not give much account of their own origin, and gave no information leading to the supposition that either they or their ancestors ever had anything to do with any form or profession of Christianity. They simply said that they had heard that their ancestors came from the East, that one party settled on these mountains, and another party descended into the plains. Their number was supposed to be about 1,000, scattered pretty equally over four mountain districts. Feeling the cold, and the Samorin's nephew beginning to be indisposed, they now began to arrange for their descent into the low country. Ere they left, they promised to return within a year, and make a longer stay. Circumstances however prevented them from so doing. The friendly Badagas showed them a better road than that by which they made the journey there.

Very probably the records of the Portuguese missionaries on the Western Coast would furnish us with further information regarding the Todas.

The only other notice (also furnished by Dr. Gundert) I possess, is the following:

Il Viaggio all' Indie Orientale del padre F. Vincenzo Maria di S. Caterina da Siena, Procurator Generale dei Carmelitani scalzi. Roma 1672, Venetia 1683.

" The Todri, a small tribe of rather fair people on the mountains behind Ponāne in " the kingdom of the Zamorin, pray to the buffaloes by which they live. They choose the

* Mr. Whitehouse says, "I think the Manarecate must be the place called Manaur in Ward's Government " Survey Map, about Lat. 11°, Long. 76° 30″, because it was 13 leagues inland from Tanor, and from thence " 12 leagues to the Todamala. There is a Manaar at the foot of the Sundapatti Ghât, but this is too near. " This idea receives support from Buchanan's Journey through Mysore and Canara, Vol. ii. p. 484, where he " speaks of a tract of land occupying part of the mountains between Malabar and Coimbatore, divided into two " districts, Attapadi and Agrata-Cadava, and says that the pass leading to Attapadi is called Manarghât."

" oldest buffalo cows, hang a miserable little bell on their necks, this is enough to ensure " the buffaloes adoration. The buffaloes are permitted to go about free everywhere, also " into the fields to graze, and everyone considers himself fortunate if they eat something " of his property. Though the buffaloes are very often killed by tigers, the Todas do " not slacken in their worship."

The Carmelite made his journey in 1657, and only heard these reports on the Coast.

The Todas themselves have a few stories, which, however, it is very difficult to extract from them. The elder men, who are the chief depositaries of the mythological learning of the tribe, are, native-like, very averse to questions (which always seem to bring before them visions of taxation), and apt to profess entire ignorance. Such traditions as I have obtained, are of no historical importance, but may have some ethnological value, in common with the legends of most rude tribes. I give them, therefore, much in the form in which I received them.

A Pekkan man, Kiniaven, one of my intimate acquaintances, when asked whether his people had any songs like the Badagas, said yes, they had songs, and after entreaties for a specimen, began a queer monotonous sort of drone through his nose. He said there were no words to the song, but when pressed as to the meaning, and what they thought about when singing, he replied they thought about the names of their gods, which he enumerated. After racking his brains a little more, he discovered that they also thought about Dirkish the son of Ēn. What about Dirkish? Of what Dirkish said in lamenting his father Ēn. What did Dirkish say? "Where have you gone, why have you left us, " have you gone to Heaven, what shall I do," &c., &c. Did they sing anything else about Dirkish? Yes, they sang that Dirkish made everything, the kraals, the buffaloes, the Todas, the *pâltchis*, &c., &c., with childishly minute emuneration. Whether these lugubrious "songs without words" really are supposed to convey an idea of Dirkish's labours or lamentations, I cannot say; but the most discriminating ear could not discover any appropriate variations in tune. By further inquiries, I discovered that Ēn was "the first Toda who came" (he had previously said that they were created on the hills), he went to heaven by way of the Avalanche, and was no more seen; that his son was Dirkish, who built the munds and temples *and the Cairns on Seven Cairn hill*,* *and Nātanēri hill*,† no others; that all the other cairns were built before the Todas came up; that Dirkish also divided the Todas into five tribes; that he did not die, nor go to heaven, but resided as a god on Seven Cairn hill. On being asked who told them all this, they said Kotēn told them, Kotēn was one of their ancestors, and brought up the Kotas. On another occasion they said the Kotas were also born on the hills, and explained the discrepancy, by saying that Kotēn had first bargained with the Kotas saying "You shall be my people, and make pots for us." Possibly the claim of the Kotas to dead buffaloes, mentioned before, formed part of this agreement.

Up to this point I had to extract Kiniaven's information piecemeal, but afterwards, finding, I suppose, that no fatal consequences followed his indiscretion, he became communicative, and volunteered the following stories, which he related with, for a Toda, great fluency.

I subsequently verified the stories in all essential points, by inquiries from other Todas.

---

* Close to Mūttināḍ mand, near the top of the Segūr Ghât. † To the right of the Croormand road.

First Story.

A Pekkan* Ēn, and his wife who was with child, went from Kūltul mand to Okadnâdmand. The husband brought fibres of a thorn tree, and in due course the wife brought forth a pumpkin!!† The Pekkan said, "What! this child is dead, we must make a *Kêd.*" They made a *Kêd,* and when the fire touched the pumpkin it split in two, and one half contained a male child; they brought it to Ootacamund, and it lived there, until one day the father found it playing in the kraal, and blew some dust on it, when it became a kite, and flew away. In those days the gods used to assemble on Doddabett, and the kite used to sit with them. One day the gods took counsel, saying "Why does the kite come here, let us drive him out;" so one of them, named Kodātha, took the kite home to Kodātha-betta (Hulikaldūrga), and pushed him over; the kite, in falling, caught hold of a bamboo, with which he returned, and struck Kodātha's head, so that it split into three pieces. Again the kite joined the assembly of the gods, who said, "The kite does everything; will he turn backwards the stream of Piowakmund? will he catch hold of the sun?" The kite turned back the stream, and tried to catch the sun, first with iron, then with bell-metal chains, both of which melted; at last he made the hook and part of the chain with stone, and caught the sun, and brought it down to Nérvēnmand. Then the world was dark: then the gods went to the kite and said, "You are very great, let the sun go;" so he let the sun go, and the river return to its course.

Before death began, one Ēn, a Todi of Muttanâd Mand,‡ used to go to the other world and return, accompanied by Ponetwan of Okadnâdmand. One day when they were in the other world, the kite came and said to the people of Okadnâdmand, "Ēn and Ponetwan will not return, therefore tie bells to thirty buffaloes and make the *Kêd* ceremony on their account;" and they did so. As Ēn and Ponetwan returned, they met buffaloes with bells coming; so Ponetwan cried, "The kite has done this;" and he touched the buffaloes with his forehead and wept, and his tears became a spring of water; and he blew his nose and there sprang up a tree. Then both said, "They have killed buffaloes for us, we must go back to the other world;" so they went, and took the buffaloes with them. Afterwards a man died in a circle of stones on the right hand side of the road to Kalhatti.§ People tried to lift the body, but could not, so they burnt him there. As there were no posts to the circle, they made women with rice-pounders stand at the entrance all night, and next day the buffaloes were killed.

---

* A Pekkan of Manjakal Mand.

† Comp. *Ramayana, book* 1, *chap.* xl. Soumati, the wife of king Sagara of Ayodhya, gave birth to a pumpkin, which broke, and from it issued the 60,000 sons she had been promised. Afterwards the 60,000 were reduced to ashes in an encounter with Vishnu, but obtained Swarga on being sprinkled by the Ganges, by the advice of Garuda, whose appearance seems to make it possible that the Toda story may really be a corruption of this very old legend.

‡ To the left hand of the Segūr road, near the top of the Ghât close to Seven Cairn hill. The "Boa" (*Plate* XIII.) is at this mand, which from the position it holds in all these stories, I imagine to be one of the oldest.

§ Nearly opposite Muttanâd Mand. There are several circles here, some apparently kraals. I dug out the circle built on rock and found that it had nowhere more than a foot of soil above the rock, so that the posts could not have been fixed. There are many *Ázārams* on a neighbouring hill, and the place seems to have been an old funeral mand. This story looks like an invention to account for this abortive kraal, when the real story was forgotten.

As the Paikāra *Tiriari* buffaloes had gone with Ēn and Ponetwan, Pūrsh, Ēn's daughter, went to the other world and brought them back. But when they returned, they said, "We will not give you our milk, Pūrsh; let our calves have it." Pūrsh went and told this to Ēn, who said, "Give the *Tēd* tree bark to the buffaloes, and they will cease to speak, and you can take their milk." Again, Pūrsh went to ask for the golden milk-vessels and churn, which she had left in the other world; but Ēn said, "You left them here, and I will not give them back: use bamboos for milk vessels, and make a churn with five branches like the kafle flower,* and do not come here any more."

When Ēn was gone, there was no head of the Todas, so Pūrsh was made head; and she lived at Muttanâd temple (*Plate* XIII.), and established the *Pâlâls*, *Tiriaris*, *Mands*, and *Boas*. One day an army of horsemen from Mysore came near; when Pūrsh heard of it she said, "Let them all become stones;" so they were turned into stones;† but a few escaped. After this another troop came, and halted at Segūr. Four of them came up the hill, captured a Todi, and asked him, "Who turned the first army into stones?" and they bribed him to tell them of Pūrsh's curse. Then the Mysoreans returned and told their chief; and he said, "Take mutton, and throw it at Pūrsh's door, and the flesh will expel the god." They did so, and Pūrsh came out like a fire, and was transformed into the hill behind Muttanâd Mand.‡ Then the Mysoreans came up and plundered the Todas. Before this time the Todas used to see and speak to their gods, but from the time Pūrsh disappeared, and from the day that a Toda betrayed his people, the gods are seen no more of men.

Second Story.

Kotēn, Tekudi, and Elna were three brothers, who lived respectively at Hona Mand, Tārnāt Mand (*Plate* VIII.), and Muttanâd Mand.§ The wife of the former cursed her husband, saying, "You possess no *Kotagiri*, no *Tiriari*." Kotēn went to his brother and said, "I am cursed, I can't eat or go to the house; give me a *Tiriari* and some Kotas." Then Tekudi gave him a *Tiriari* bell and buffaloes from the Muttanâd *Tiriari*, and Elna gave him a Kota man and woman.

Kotēn went off with these to the Kundahs, and established a *Tiriari* and *Pâlâls*, and placed the Kotas at the Kundah *Kotagiri*, called by Todas Mērkōkâl.‖

When the Paikara Pâlâl drove Elna's buffaloes to the Sholūr Tiriari, where the god Ênta presides, the buffaloes refused to go, and said they could not go without the bell which Tekudi had taken. The Pâlâl told Elna, who told Ênta. He said he would give a stick, which was to be given to a Pekkan of Manjâkal Mund, who was to take a horn to be cut from the head of a living buffalo, and blow it in front, when the buffaloes would follow. Even now when the Paikara buffaloes go to the Sholūr Tiriari, a Pekkan must go in front with a horn, and the horn is blown every evening when the Pâlâl has finished his meal. Enta added that he would kill Tekudi by a bow and arrow within eight days.

* Such as the Todas still use. Two are seen in *Plate* IX. leaning against the hut.

† A variety of this story is connected with some upright stones, apparently slabs from a half-destroyed cairn, near Mr. Findlay's plantation at Kodanâd. Mr. Findlay tells me that he was told by a Toda, that these were once soldiers who insulted the Pâlâl of a neighbouring Tiriari, whereupon he threw some milk over them and turned them into stones.

‡ The hill nearest Muttanâd Mand is Seven Cairn Hill, connected with the story of Dirkish.

§ All these mands belong to the Todi clan, which is the largest, and possibly the oldest from its position in these stories.

‖ Mērkōkâl means the Kota village of the Kūndahs. Mēr is the Toda for Kūndahs, and Kōkâl for Kota village.

As Tekudi came from Tarnât Mand one day, an arrow appeared in the shape of a bird screaming. Tekudi looked up and the arrow dropped into his eye. The arrow was one that a lame Toda, lying down and by means of his legs,* shot by command of Ênta into the air.

Tekudi fell on his back and died, and a Toda man with him put a stone on his head and on each of his hands and his legs. The stones are still to be seen on the road to Paikāra. The man accompanying Tekudi, reported what had happened to the people at Tārnāt Mand, and they all went out to see, and found some hair on the stone which had been placed over the head, and some blood, but no corpse.

After this, Kotēn went to a Kurumba village in Bāni Shīma,† and on his return, when bathing in a stream, a hair of a golden colour came to his hand; he followed it up stream to find the owner of the hair, and saw a Swāmi ‡ woman, by name Têrkosh, whom he married. After this, Kotēn returned home to his mand near the Avalanche. Kotēn slept on a deer skin, wore a silver ring, and carried a spear, bow, and arrow. On the night of his return he went to sleep, and in the morning nothing was found of him but his spear and ring § and some blood on the deer-skin. He and Têrkosh were transformed into two hills, which are now known by the names of Kotēn and Têrkosh, on the Sisapāra side of the hills, to which both Kurumbas and Todas pay occasional ceremonial visits.‖ The Kurumbas light a lamp on the hill Têrkosh. When the Todas see these two hills, they sing the song about Kotēn.

Elna had five or six hundred cattle at Muttanâd. When milking them in front of the mand, samber used to come out of the *shola* and bell and make a noise, which made all the buffaloes run away. So Elna built the wall which now appears at Muttanâd Mand.¶

Third Story.

Ēn's father was called Pith, and he and his father made the Mands. Ênta, Pith, and Dewak were born at the same time, all Swâmis in the form of men, and are recognised by all Todas as gods. There were no Todas when they were born. Ēn one day said, " What's the use of being quiet?" and took a stick and thrust it in the earth, from whence came eighteen hundred common buffaloes, followed by a Toda holding a buffalo's tail. Ēn's wife did the same a little way off, and out came two thousand

---

* Compare *Elphinstone's History of India,* Appendix iii., page 268.—" The peculiar Indian bow, now only " used in mountainous countries, which is drawn with the assistance of the feet, and shoots an arrow more than " six feet long, is particularly described by Arrian, &c." This incident confirms in a measure the testimony as to the use of the bow afforded by the marriage and funeral rites.

† Bāni Shīma, the country of the Bhawāni (Bhowāny) river.

‡ Swāmi, God or Lord; used here as an adjective.

§ Nīrvēn, the present head of the Todi clan, possesses a ring, an ordinary silver ring of large size, which is said to be Kotēn's ring. Nīrvēn claims to be a direct descendant of Kotēn. He professes to have lost the spear.

‖ Thus five gods are connected in these traditions with different hills, viz.:—Dirkish, Kodātha, Pūrsh, Kotēn, and Tērkosh. If the Todas originally deified every hill, not an unnatural worship for mountaineers, the number of their gods, otherwise astonishing, is accounted for. The Todas, in common with the other hill tribes, still offer ghee to be burnt at Maleswaramalē.

¶ This seems to have been concocted to account for the existence of the wall which runs round the crest of the hill and forms a peculiar feature at Muttanâd Mand.

white buffaloes, also a big bull and cow buffalo which disappeared again. Ēn took a rib from the side of the Toda man holding the buffalo's tail, and made a woman, and from these two came all the Todas. Ēn had a son Pauv. Pith, Ēn, and Pauv made all the mands and *tiriaris.* They themselves became *Pâlâls*, and built temples. When a white buffalo died they buried it within a circle of stones now called *Āzāram.*

Pith and Ēn lived in Ēnnâd Mand. A quarrel took place between them, and Ēn set fire to the temple wherein Pith slept. Pith flew out and went to *Âmunâd.* Ēn and Pauv remained making *pūjā** and building mands. Pauv milked the buffaloes morning and evening, and churned. He used to wear a ring, and one day seeing the reflection of the ring in water, and thinking the ring had fallen in, he went down into the water and never returned.

Ēn had "something like a feather." One day looking "into it" he saw Pauv grazing the buffaloes (that had been buried) in *Âmunâd.* Ēn then told the Todas he must go to *Âmunâd.* They said they would go also. Ēn said, "No, you must remain "here, I will go," and he took the white buffaloes and went away, leaving a tiger which he kept for a dog to look after the common buffaloes. The tiger did so for two or three years, till one day, when coming home with the buffaloes, he saw a cat catch a rat, and asked the cat for some of the flesh. The cat gave him some. He wanted more; when the cat said, "Can't you catch a buffalo and eat;" and showed him how. After this, the tiger daily eat a buffalo, and the Todas asking him where the missing buffaloes were, he said he did not know. Afterwards the Todas found him out and drove him away.

These stories may serve, I think, to explain the report of the Cattanars quoted above. When I asked Kiniaven about Bidi or Vidhi, he at once said Pith, and told me that Pith had formerly a temple, at which the Todas used to prostrate themselves, but which had now fallen into disuse; an example of that decay of the Toda religion, of which we find many traces.

If, as one of my informants stated, Pith's son Ēn was the father of the kite, the story of the Trinity is explained.

As for the accounts of the flight from Mailapur, (St. Thomé), that, reading Buddhist or Jain for Christian, is the story of the Kurumbas. Very likely the Cattanars encountered both races. The Kurumbas do not now own to any traditions; but two centuries and a half ago, when the power of their kinsfolk of the plains had not long been destroyed, they may have retained some reminiscences of their former state.

The singularity of the Toda religion, and especially the absence of idols, has induced all sorts of theories as to their origin. Another tradition, mentioned by Mr. Whitehouse, is that they were Manichæans, an idea probably gathered from their reverence for sun and fire, and indifference to material objects and tokens of worship, and from their ascetic system, corresponding in many particulars with the ideal "elect" life of the Manichæans.

That the Todas ever were really either orthodox Christians or Manichæans, seems improbable. Considering the anxiety always shown by Roman Catholic missionaries to

---

* *Pūjā*, worship.

discover and turn to account any resemblances, real or apparent, between the heathen religions in possession, and that which they sought to introduce, the Cattanars may be forgiven for their mistake; especially as in a different form, it has been repeated by the modern writers who have enlarged on the simple virtues of the Todas, on their desire for instruction, their freedom from idolatry, and consequent readiness to accept Christianity, under the common delusion that the soil which has proved too sterile to nurture a false religion, is the fittest for the reception of the true. Mr. Whitehouse's manuscript shows that further inquiry did not confirm the tale of the Cattanars. I know of no Christian remains of any sort on the Nīlagiris, nor can I find, in the customs of the Hill tribes, anything that can reasonably be referred to a reminiscence of Christianity. Mr. Metz derives Peranganād (Toda *Pirgâr*) from Feringhi; but we have no evidence, as to the origin or antiquity of the name, that can warrant us in attributing it to the existence of ancient Christian settlements.*

If not Christian, however, the Toda religion is singular enough. Its trace of element worship, trace of ancestor worship, and strong pastoral colouring are almost Vedic; while the omission from their Pantheon of the regular gods of the plains, in any of their innumerable forms, indicates long isolation.

Some few of their customs resemble those of the various Kol tribes. The similarity in the funeral rites of the Ho and Mūndah Kols of Nagpore has already been noticed; the Larkā Kols have the same singular law of inheritance, by which the house becomes the property of the youngest son; they also offer a young buffalo once a year (like the Peikis); but it is to the well-known goddess Bhawāni; and they break a pot at funerals, their dead being sometimes burnt, sometimes buried.†

* While these pages have been passing through the press, Mr. Whitehouse's interesting narrative of the Syrian Church of Malabar (Lingerings of Light in a Dark Land, being Researches into the past History and present Constitution of the Syrian Church of Malabar, by the Revd. Thomas Whitehouse, M.A.) has been published. In this work, page 133, the author expresses his decided opinion that "there is no reason whatever "to believe that the Todas of the Nilagiris were ever in any way associated with either the Christian or "Manichean settlers of the Low Country or of the Coast of Malabar, or had ever known anything of "Christianity, even so much as its external forms."—*Editor.*

† The following description of some of the Papuans applies word for word to the Todas:—

"Sie haben religiöse Gebräuche und Uebungen welche, mit einigen anderen Erscheinungen in ihrem Leben, "mit ihrem jetzigen Culturzustande ganz unvereinbar erscheinen, wenn man darin nicht die Spuren einer früher "hohern Bildung erkennen will."

"They have religious customs and practices, which, as well as some other circumstances in their life, seem "quite irreconcileable with their present state of civilization, unless we recognise in them the traces of a formerly "higher culture."—*Trench's Study of Words, page 22, note.*

It need hardly be said that it was not intended in this work to enter on the vexed question of the origin of civilization. The cases of the Todas and Kurumbas were considered on their own merits without bias in favour of any theories about Primeval man, and the evidence of their degradation is given for what it is worth. That such instances of decay exist can hardly be questioned; whether they are the rule or the exception will probably not be soon, if ever, determined. Meanwhile, to ascertain facts about the tribes in question seemed more germane to the matter than to discuss theories of civilization.—*Editor.*

CHAPTER III.

THE KOTAS.

NAME—CENSUS—PHYSICAL APPEARANCE—MODE OF LIFE—EMPLOYED AS ARTIZANS BY OTHER TRIBES—RELIGION, RITES, AND CEREMONIES—LANGUAGE—HISTORY.

The name is found variously spelt. Kota, Kotar, Kotĕr, Kohatūr. The derivation is uncertain. Kohata or Gohata, cow-killer, has been suggested, but this seems doubtful. The Todas call them Kuof, or cow-people. They recognise no caste among themselves, but are divided into *Keris*,* and a man of one *Keri* must seek a wife in another. In one *Kotagiri* † inhabitants belonging to all three *Keris* are found.

They numbered at the last census 1,112, inhabiting the four divisions of the district, as follows :

—	Todanâd.	Mekanâd.	Peranganâd.	Kūndanâd.	Total.	Male.	Female.
Villages -	2	1	2	1	6		
Inhabitants -	420	243	331	118	1,112	534	578

A seventh *Kotagiri* near Gudalūr is not included in this district.

Physical appearance.

Dr. Shortt thus describes‡ the Kotas :—

" *Physical appearance.*—They are well made and of tolerable height, rather good " featured and light-skinned, having a copper colour, and some of them are the fairest " skinned among the Hill tribes. They have well-formed heads, covered with long " black hair, grown long and let loose, or tied up carelessly at the back of the head. " An average of 25 men gives the following measurements, &c. :—Age, 27·68 years; " height, 62·61 inches; circumference of head, 20·95; neck, 11·95; chest, 30·68; arms, " 8·76; thighs, 15·52; length of arms, 30; hands, 7; breadth of hands, 3·25; length " of feet, 10; breadth of feet, 3·50 inches; weight (avoirdupois,) 105·20 lbs. They " have a slightly elongated face with sharply defined features; the forehead narrow " but prominent, and occasionally protuberant; ears, flat and lying close to the skull. " The growth of hair from the verge of scalp to eyebrows, 2½ inches distant; eyes, " dark brown, of moderate size and deep set, varying in colour from Nos. 1 to 5, in " Paul Brocas' Tables; eyebrows, dark and bushy, with a tendency to approach, " frequently united to each other; nose, as a rule, smaller and more sharply defined

---

* *Keri*, street.

† Kurumbas and Irulas call their villages - Motta.
Todas " " " - Mand.
Badagas " " " - Hatti.
Kotas " " " - Kōkal.
Kotagiri is the Badaga name for the Kota villages, lit. Kota hill.

‡ *Hill Ranges of Southern India*, Part I., page 54.

" than in the Todas, ridged and slightly rounded, and pointed at the extremity, 2 inches " in length; alæ of nostrils expanded, measuring $1\frac{1}{4}$ inches in breadth; mouth, of " moderate size and well formed; teeth, well grown and regular; lips, of fair size " and well compressed; chin, well set and small. Altogether they may be pronounced " tolerably good-looking, and the general aspect of the countenance indicating energy " and decision.

" The women are of moderate height, of fair build of body, and not nearly so " good-looking as the men. An average of 25 women gives the following results:— " Age, 32·44 years; circumference of head, 20·36; height, 57·98; circumference of " neck, 10·70; chest, 29·30; arms, 8·20; thighs, 14·63; length of arms, 26·52; length " of hands, 6·50; breadth of hands, 3; length of legs, 35; length of feet, 9·25; breadth " of feet, 2·25 inches; weight (avoirdupois) 96·24 lbs. Most of them have prominent " foreheads, with more of a snub nose and a somewhat vacant expression." (*Plates* xv. *to* xx.)

There are, as already observed, but seven Kota villages, of which six are on the Nīlagiri plateau, and the seventh near Gudalūr in Wainâd at the foot of the Nīlagiris. *Mode of life.*

Badaga name.		*Toda name.*
(1.) Menāda	in Kundanâd	Mērkōkāl.
(2.) Tirichigidi	in Todanâd	Tirichigād.
(3.) Padugula* or Kuruvōje	in Todanâd	Kuruguli.
(4.) Kolamalē	in Mekanâd	Kolimal.
(5.) Mēlkotagiri or Perangāda†	in Peranganâd	Mēlkōkāl.
(6.) Kīlkotagiri or Kinnāda	in Peranganâd	Klikōkāl.
(7.) Kalagāsa near Gudalūr		Kallgōdi.

The following description of their villages I quote from Dr. Shortt:—‡

" They form large communities, each village containing from thirty to sixty or " more huts, of tolerable size, built of mud walls, and covered with the usual thatch " grass, somewhat after the style of native huts in the plains; but the arrangement " of the dwellings is far from being neat or prepossessing in some villages. The " floors are well raised from two to three feet above the soil, with eaves or a short " verandah in front, and a pial or seat on either side of the door, under the eaves, " on which the people squat themselves when idle. The size of the doors giving " entrance to their huts measures 46 × 26 inches."

The pillars of some of their verandahs are of stone, neatly sculptured by low-country stone cutters. Each village has one or two houses set apart for women for purification purposes. On several of the stones, forming the wall in front of the rows of houses in Kuruvōje (Padugula), I found that lines had been chiselled for the games of *Hulikotē* and *Kotē*.§ The former is played with pieces, two of which represent tigers, and the remainder sheep; the latter is a kind of labyrinth, the problem being to get into the centre.

* See *Plate* xxi.

† The European settlement commonly known as Kotagherry, is close to this *Kotagiri*, whence it derives its name.

‡ The *Hill Ranges of Southern India*, Part I., page 55.

§ See App. B.

In agriculture they are quite on a par with the Badagas, and raise the same crops. They seem, however, not to care to extend their cultivation, as they are the only handicraftsmen on the hills, and their services in that capacity are in great demand.

They keep herds of cattle, but do not milk them either for sale or consumption.

"The Kotas are the only one of all the hill tribes who practise the industrial " arts, and they are therefore essential almost to the very existence of the other classes. " The work in gold and silver, are carpenters and blacksmiths, tanners and rope- " makers, umbrella-makers, potters, and musicians, and are at the same time cultivators " of the soil. They are, however, a squalid race, living chiefly on carrion, and are on " this account a bye-word among the other castes, who, while they feel that they cannot " do without them, nevertheless abhor them for their filthy habits." *

When a Badaga and Toda meet, the former lays his hand on the head of the latter by way of salutation, but no such familiarity is permitted to the Kota by either race; a Kota, meeting a Toda or Badaga, raises both his hands to his face, and salāms to them from a distance. Kotas are not allowed to approach a Badaga temple.

It is odd that their disgusting food seems to agree with them: they are active muscular fellows, with twice the strength of a Badaga.

Every village has three or four forges, where they work with the usual native bellows, pincers, and hammers. In one village I saw a European anvil. There is iron ore in small quantity on the plateau, but no attempt is made to smelt it. The metal used by the Kotas is brought up from Coimbatore in a semi-fused mass, full of impurities. The Kotas display much more energy and muscle than the other tribes. If you watch a Badaga and Kota at work together, removing a huge slab, you will see the latter straining every nerve till he freely perspires, while the former remains as dry as dust.

The women make clay pots on a wheel, work in the field, cook, and fetch water and firewood. The potter's wheel is a disc of wood, with a blunt iron point, on which it revolves:† the socket is a hole in a stone, fixed permanently in the ground, in front of their houses.

Each Badaga village has its Muṭṭu Kotas‡ in the neighbouring Kotagiri, and each Muṭṭu Kota does artizan work for certain individual Badagas of the village, and receives in payment at harvest time a *Kanduga* (forty Madras measures) or half a *Kanduga* of each sort of grain harvested. The Todas also have their Muṭṭu Kotas, who are paid with the hides of dead buffaloes, and sometimes with ghee. The Kurumbas pay their Muṭṭu Kotas in grain, the Irulas in plantains and grain. On the whole they make a good livelihood, especially as their music and dancing are indispensable at feasts,§ and are necessarily well rewarded, performers often receiving ¼ rupee each.

For a list of Kota garments, ornaments, and household utensils, see Appendix B.

Laws of inheritance.

As with the Todas, to the youngest son is left the house and the charge of the mother. The rest of the property, real and personal, is divided equally among the sons, the youngest taking his share.

---

* *Tribes inhabiting the Neilgherries*, by the Rev. F. Metz.

† v. *Plate* XVII.

‡ From *Muttuva*, Kanarese, to touch.

§ v. *Plate* XVIII.

They hold the land around their villages at easy rates from Government, under Ryotwāri tenure.

The substantial cultivators of each village pay *gudu* to the Todas, who in return are expected to honour Kota feasts and ceremonies by their presence.*

Dr. Shortt says,† "In confirmation of their having followed the Todas as settlers "on these Hills, they hold the best lands, and have the privilege of selecting the "best whenever they wish to extend their holdings."

They hold the lands immediately surrounding their villages. I do not know that it is better land than what surrounds Badaga villages. They have not now the privilege of selecting the best land, nor, as far back as the office records go, can I find that they ever had.

Religion, Rites, and Ceremonies.

Each *Kotagiri* has at least two temples. Kolamalē has three, two dedicated to Kāmatarāya, and one to his wife Kahasamma or Kalikai. They are all of the shape of the one in *Plate* XXII., with the exception of one of the two at Padugula, which is in the form of a Toda *Pâlthchi*.‡

From traditions of the Todas and Kotas, Padugula appears to be the oldest and the original settlement of the latter. This may be thought to receive some confirmation from the fact, that Padugula is the only *Kotagiri* in the Malād,§ a district inhabited solely by Todas, and the only village in which one of the temples is in the form of a Pâlthchi. When I asked the Padugula Kotas how the Toda *Pâlthchi* came there, they said, "Are we not *Annatāmalu*" (brothers)? Mr. Metz tells me that he has heard the Badagas say, "Did not the Todas make the people of Padugula, Kotas?"

Their priests are of their own tribe. There are two to a village, one called Devādi, whose office is hereditary. If the family fails entirely, recourse is had to inspiration for the choice of another. The second is appointed by the Devādi. Neither lives in the temple; they cook food before it at the feast of Kāmatarāya, and distribute it to the householders, sow and reap the first handfuls of grain at the proper seasons, and make the first obeisance to the corpse at a funeral. The Devādi is liable to be possessed by the Deity.

Generally they recognize but one god, under the name of Kāmatarāya, and his wife, each represented by a thin silver plate.

Tradition says of Kāmatarāya, that, perspiring profusely, he wiped from his forehead three drops of perspiration, and out of them formed the three most ancient of the Hill tribes, the Todas, Kurumbas, and Kotas.‖ The Todas were told to live principally

---

* By some accounts the Kotas contribute some of the articles burnt at a Toda dry funeral, receiving the dead buffaloes in return.

† *Tribes inhabiting the Neilgherries*, p. 54.

‡ This *Pâlthchi* is shown in *Plate* XXI. It is dedicated to Urupâl, who, however, they say is the same as Kāmatarāya. The *Pujāri* boils rice in this temple at the sowing and reaping seasons, and distributes it to all the heads of families in the village; and when the crops come to ear, he makes ghee and lights a lamp there. There is no temple to Kahasamma in this village.

§ The Malād, called by the Todas Mârzhâr (mountains), is the western part of Todanâd, inhabited almost exclusively by Todas.

‖ Compare Scandinavian legend quoted by Mr. Walhouse (Mad. Jour., Vol. iv., New Series) of the giant Ymir. "Whilst he slept, a man and woman sprang from an extraordinary sweat under his left arm." The story closely resembles a Chinese one quoted by Mr. Walhouse, also the Vedic legend of Purusha.

The Bhats of the North-West Provinces sometimes claim to be produced from three drops of sweat on Siva's brow.

upon milk, the Kurumbas were permitted to eat the flesh of buffalo calves, and the Kotas were allowed perfect liberty in the choice of food, being informed that they might eat carrion if they could get nothing better, a permission of which they have freely availed themselves.

Of late years the Perangāda and Tirichigidi people have set up a new deity, under the name of Māgāli, represented by an upright stone. The origin of this worship is accounted for as follows :—

A virulent disease carried off a number of Kotas of Perangāda, and the village was abandoned by the survivors. A Badaga named Munda Jogi, who was bringing his tools to the *Kotagiri* to be sharpened, saw near a tree something in the form of a tiger, which spoke to him, and told him to summon the runaway Kotas. He obeyed, whereupon the tiger form addressed the Kotas in an unknown tongue, and vanished. For some time the purport of this communication remained a mystery; at last, however, a Kota came forward to interpret, and declared that the god ordered the Kotas to return to the deserted village, on pain of a recurrence of the pestilence. The command was obeyed; a *swāmi* house was built on the spot where the form appeared to the Badaga, (who doubtless felt keenly the inconvenience of having no Kotas at hand to sharpen his tools); and goats and fowls are still sacrificed to Māgāli every year, the astute interpreter and his descendants holding the office of priest.

The Badagas have an annual festival in honour of Hetti, a village heroine who, on the death of her husband, voluntarily killed herself to accompany him to Swarga.* The Todas are invited to the feast, but the Kotas are not allowed to join, so they have a Hetti of their own.

The chief Kota festival, however, is the annual feast of Kāmatarāya, called *Kambata* or *Kamata*.† This lasts for about a fortnight. On the first evening the priest lights a fire in the *swāmi* house, and then brings it to the principal street of the village, where it is kept up during the whole of the feast. On the second day no work may be done, except digging clay and making pots, but no particular ceremonies take place on this or the three following days.

On the sixth day men are sent to fetch bamboos and rattan, and on the seventh the two temples are newly thatched and decorated; it is essential that this should be accomplished before nightfall.

The eighth and ninth days are spent in feasting. Contributions of grain and ghee are demanded from all the neighbouring Badaga villages, and cooked in the enclosure of the temples. Only boiled grain, ghee, and a sort of pea soup are eaten on this occasion. A portion is laid before the temple, then the priests eat, and afterwards the rest of the villagers, all sitting in a row before the temple.

The tenth day is passed in dancing; the Kotas dress up for the occasion, wearing the long robes shown in *Plate* XVIII., and borrowing jewels of all sorts from the Badagas, who are obliged to propitiate their artizans by attending and contributing on this occasion.

On the eleventh day they decorate themselves with leaves, tie buffalo horns to their heads, and go through various appropriate pantomimes. The women also dance at this

---

* Swarga, the Hindu Paradise.

† Most of this information has been kindly furnished by Mr. David Cockburn of Kotagherry.

feast only; they sing at the same time, which is an improvement on the drum and horn accompaniment of the men's dancing.

On the twelfth day they make a fire inside their temple, by drilling a pointed stick round and round in a hole in a piece of dry wood, bring a bit of iron, and go through the form of heating and working it up by way of "making *shāstras*," and say to the god, "Let all be well and prosper."

During a woman's pregnancy the husband leaves his hair and nails uncut. Three *Birth.* houses are built for women to occupy after the birth of children, or at other times when they are considered unclean. Immediately after birth the mother and child are removed to the first hut, a temporary erection of boughs called *Vollugūdu*, from *vollu* inside and *gūdu* nest, where they remain for thirty days. The second and third months are spent in two permanent huts called *Tēlulu*. A woman with her first child, on leaving the *Vollugūdu* for the first *Tēlulu*, must make seven steps backwards among seven kinds of thorns strewed on the ground. Some *Kotagiris*, however, have only the *Vollugūdu*, in which the woman remains for a month, and the treading on thorns takes place when she leaves the *Vollugūdu* to return home. This is *Māmūl*, no other reason is of course discoverable. On leaving the second *Tēlulu*, the mother generally goes to a relative's house for three days; if this is not convenient, she returns home. Her husband purifies the house on her return by sprinkling it with cow-dung and water. On the seventh day after this a feast is given to the relatives, the child is fed with "congee," and the paternal grandfather (or, if he is dead, the father) names it.*

Ten Male Names.

	Name	Meaning
1.	Kurumbane.	
2.	Kambata.	Name of God.
3.	Kose,	
4.	Chinapa.	Father of people.
5.	Mosale.	Crocodile.
6.	Angāra.	
7.	Paria.	
8.	Kounda.	
9.	Jogi.	Devotee.
10.	Mala.	Mountain.

Female Names.

	Name	Meaning
1.	Mādi.	Goddess.
2.	Nīji.	
3.	Puyı.	
4.	Teinti.	
5.	Mēngi.	
6.	Tēgi.	
7.	Tausi.	
8.	Kempi.	Red one.
9.	Dōni.	
10.	Vērkārji.	

Names of Relations in Kota.

Father's elder brother	*Aıan or Talālaian.*
Do. younger do.	*Karālaian.*
Mother's elder brother	*Māmne.*
Do. younger do.	*Do.*
Father's elder sister	*Māmi.*
Do. younger do.	*Do.*
Mother's elder sister	*Tolājav.*
Do. younger do.	*Kunnājav.*
Son	*Main.*
Daughter	*Magu.*
Father's brother's son	*Karāl.*
Do. do. daughter	*Aktan or Katāj.*
Father's sister's son	*Mago.*
Do. do. daughter	*Māmi or Mago.*
Mother's brother's son	*Ēil.*
Do. do. daughter	*Ēil or Tammachinichi.*
Do. sister's son	*Ānna.*
Do. do. daughter	*Ākne.*
Elder brother	*Anne.*
Younger do.	*Kerāl.*
Elder sister	*Ak.*
Younger do.	*Katāj.*

Marriage. When a boy is from fifteen to twenty years old, his parents ask in marriage for him some girl of six or eight. If her parents consent to the betrothal, the boy with his parents goes to their house, salutes them by bowing his head and clasping their feet, and presents them with a *Bīrianhana* of gold and ten or twenty rupees. Amongst well-to-do Kotas some jewels are presented to the girl at this time. This ceremony is called *Bali med-deni*, from *bali*, bracelet, and *med-deni*, I have made, and can only be performed on Tuesdays and Fridays; some say only on Tuesdays. When the girl becomes of age, she is sent at the request of the boy's relations to his father's house, a feast is given with music, and the bridegroom's mother ties on the *Tāli*, in this case a silver necklace made by the Kotas.

In some places the bridegroom goes to the bride's house and presents her with the *tāli*, two *madige* or brass armlets, and a *bali* or bracelet.

The Kotas marry only one wife, unless she should be barren, when they may take another. In this case the two wives live in the same house.

Widows may re-marry.

Funeral. A *Tēru** or scaffolding hung with cloths is erected before the dead man's house. The corpse is laid on a cot and placed under the *Tēru*. All the relations assemble and salute the body, the elder putting their foreheads to the dead man's forehead, the younger to his feet. After dancing round the corpse for some hours they remove the *Tēru* and carry the corpse to the burning place.†

The Toda and Badaga masters of the deceased attend the funeral, bringing two or three male buffalo calves for slaughter, or a cloth or two. If more calves are brought than can be eaten by the assembled Kotas, the remainder are kept or sold by the relations. Before the body is burnt a blessing is invoked on the village, the spirit of the dead being implored to allow no more deaths there. A cow is then driven once or twice round the corpse and killed, and the dead man's hand clasped round the horn, as among the Todas. When all is ready for the burning, the widow lays her *Tāli* and other ornaments on the body and retires. These are, however, removed before the pile is lighted. The body is burnt face upwards, as with the Badagas and Kurumbas.

With the body of a man are burnt, an axe, a handkerchief, a chopper, a small knife, a *buguri*, one or two walking sticks, an umbrella, and some cheroots.

With a woman a rice measure, rice beater, sickle, winnowing basket, and umbrella, her cloth and jewels in every-day wear.

The next day the bones are collected, placed in a pot, and buried near the burning place, a stone being placed over them. The skull, however, is kept till the dry funeral. This must take place on a Monday or Thursday. Eight days notice is given to the relatives of all the dead to be commemorated, who assemble at the dry funeral

---

* This custom has been borrowed by the Badagas. I do not known whether it exists elsewhere, but have never heard of it. I find however in the legend of Bhutala pandya (Mad. Jour. July 1864), who is described as instituting the law of inheritance peculiar to the west coast, that he ordered that "Nale Upparige" (a litter with upper story), and in case of a chief Púmáda Kaimáda Upparige (litter with stories adorned with flowers, &c.) should be used at funerals. Tēru literally means a car.

† In Kota language *Duē*.

"Due," which is not the same as the green funeral one. The former is always, the latter only sometimes, surrounded by a circle of stones.

Each skull is wrapped in a new cloth and placed on a cot, and first the men and then the women assembled bow to each in turn. The Todas and Badagas again supply a number of buffaloes or common cows, varying according to the estimation in which the dead men are held. A bell is hung round the neck of each buffalo to be killed; these are not sacred bells, but belong to private houses. The animals are made to touch the cots on which the skulls are laid, and are then killed. Some, however, I am afraid, are only disabled and left to die, as their flesh is not at once required.

With each male skull is burnt an axe, stick, and umbrella, a knife, a bow and three arrows, a basket, and a long pole.

With female skulls the rice beater, &c.

The sickle, jewels, &c., are taken out of the fire, and water is sprinkled on the ashes from a chatty, which is then broken. The ashes are not buried, but left where they lie.

The Kotas appear to have borrowed their funeral rites to a great extent from the Todas. The *Tēru* is however original (and is imitated by the Badagas); and the exact reversal of the Toda practice with regard to the disposal of the ashes is curious, and strengthens the presumption that in both cases the body was originally buried, since it seems necessary that there should be one burial and only one.

Language.

See Appendix A.

History.

The Kotas profess to have no traditions of any kind. They even pretend ignorance of the story of Kotēn, though it is pretty evident from their manner that they do know it. Some declare that they were born on these hills, others that the inhabitants of each *Kotagiri* came from a different part of the neighbouring plains. On the whole, I am inclined to believe that the Toda story is true, and that the Kotas were a caste of artizans, brought from the plains to work for the Todas on certain conditions; the right to dead buffaloes being probably one.

M. R. R. Rāmiah, a Deputy Superintendent of Mysore, who was kind enough to make some inquiries for me, reports that "Lingayet Panchālas (workers in metals) and Huttagars are called Kotars in this part of the country (Harihar), and they worship Kāma (god) and Kurymena (goddess)." Also that a caste of the same name exists in Mārwār and Guzerat.

Buchanan says that Kamachuma or Kalima, the wife of Siva, is worshipped by the Panchāla.*

* Anglice, the five castes of artizans who eat together and intermarry.

CHAPTER IV.

THE KURUMBAS.

CENSUS—DIVISIONS—MODE OF LIFE—EMPLOYED AS PRIESTS BY BADAGAS—RELIGION, RITES, AND CEREMONIES—HISTORY—SETTLERS IN TONDA MANDALAM—TRACES OF, AT SEVEN PAGODAS—NOTICES OF DRAVIDA AND OF PALLAVA PRINCES—CONQUEST BY CHOLAS—SUBSEQUENT HISTORY—HATRED AND FEAR THEY EXCITE.

The Kurumbas of the Nīlagiri district, according to the last Census, numbered 613. There are, however, many more in the forest tracts of Malabar, just outside the limits of this district.

In the Tabulated Census Returns they are entered under the following castes or divisions :—

—	Arakādu.	Budunatham.	Mēkanād.	Mulaicheppi.	Peranganād	Semhanarē.	Sembanatham	Todanād	Aranjur.	Koondahs.	Vagapanē	Velleri Kambē	Total.
Ela Kurumban - -	—	29	—	—	—	—	—	—	—	—	—	—	29
Karmadiya Kurumban -	—	—	—	—	7	—	—	—	—	—	—	—	7
Kurumban - - -	41	11	60	23	201	2	1	6	36	15	2	55	453
Kurumban Okkiliyan -	—	4	—	—	—	—	—	—	—	—	—	—	4
Male Kurumban - -	—	109	—	—	—	—	—	—	—	—	—	—	109
Pāl. Kurumban - -	—	11	—	—	—	—	—	—	—	—	—	—	11
				Male 330	Female. 283				Total	-	-	-	613

They generally, however, say they have no caste, but are divided into *bīgas** or families, which do not intermarry. It is difficult to get a complete account of the tribal divisions recognised by them.

One man will name you one (his own); another two divisions; another three, and so on. The head man of the village in *Plate* XXVI. enumerated four :—

1. *Botta Kurumbas*, who live on the northern slopes, and near the Mysore Ditch.
2. *Kambale* do., who make blankets (cambly), and live in the low country, in the Konguru (Coimbatore).
3. *Mullu* do. (he did not know where they lived).
4. *Anda* do., who, like himself, live on the eastern slopes. Pāl Kurumbas are also vaguely mentioned sometimes.

---

* Bīga means literally a lock.

He said he knew nothing of the *Naya, Malsar*, or *Pania Kurumbas*, and that none of the four classes would intermarry or eat with each other. On my expressing surprise at this, he sniffed angrily, and said, "What! are we Moplahs?"—a view of the relative position of the races which would probably take the Moplahs by surprise. There are also some in the Bhawāni Valley who call themselves "Jain Kurumbas," a name which is said to be derived from honey, the collection and sale of which forms the main part of their occupation. The Malsar (lit., I believe, Male Arasu, king of the hills) occupy the western slopes.

The following description of the physical characteristics of the Kurumbas is taken from Dr. Shortt, *Tribes of the Neilgherries, p.* 46:— ***Physical character.***

"The Kurumba tribe are small in stature, and have a squalid and somewhat "uncouth appearance from their peculiar physiognomy, wild matted hair, and almost "nude bodies. An average of 25 Kurumbas gives the following measurements, &c.:—

"Age, 30·20 years; height, 60·64 inches; circumference of head, 20·24—short "from end to end with a lofty crown or dome, and a prominent forehead; neck, 11·04 "inches; chest, 30·15; arms, 8·77; thighs, 15·27; length of arms, 29·50; length of "hand, 6·75; breadth of hands, 3·18; length of legs, 35; length of feet, 9·75; breadth "of feet, 3·25 inches; and in weight (avoirdupois) 100·44 pounds. They have a "shortish and spare form of body, with a peculiar wedge-shaped face and obtuse facial "angle; cheeks hollow, with prominent malars or cheek bones; slightly pointed chin; "eyes moderately large, and frequently bloodshot; colour of irides dark brown (No. 1 "of Paul Brocas' Tables); the nose has a deep indentation at the root about 1¼ inches "in depth, which is general, and when contrasted with the profile, or line with the "ridge of the nose and *os frontis*, it gives them a very peculiar expression of feature. "Distance of growth of hair from root of nose to scalp, 2¼ inches; length of nose, 1¾; "alæ, widened; nostrils, exposed; breadth of nostrils, 1 inch and 5 lines, ridge slightly "depressed. The hair is long and black, and is grown matted and straggling, somewhat "wavy, and is sometimes tied into a knot, with a piece of cord on the crown or back of "the head, while the ends are allowed to be free and floating. They have scarcely "any moustache or whiskers, and a straggling scanty beard; occasionally one is met "with who has a full moustache, whiskers and beard. They are as a body sickly-"looking, pot-bellied, large-mouthed, prognathous, with prominent out-standing teeth "and thick lips—frequently saliva dribbles away from their mouths.

* * * * *

"The women have much the same features as the men, only somewhat softened in "expression, and slightly modified in feature, with a small pug nose, and surly aspect. "Their general appearance is anything but prepossessing. Hair tied at the back, "carelessly divided in the centre, and the sides scraggy. Some of them are of small "stature and coarse build; others smaller and of delicate make. An average of 12 "gives the following measurements. I regret that I was unable to complete the usual "number of 25:—

"Age, 17 years; height, 54·25 inches; circumference of head, 19; neck, 9·75; chest, "26·25; arms, 7·75; thighs, 11·50; length of arms, 24·50; length of hands, 6·75;

" breadth of hand, 2·38; length of legs, 33·10; length of feet, 8·25; breadth of feet, " 3·15; weight (avoirdupois) 68 pounds." (*Plates* I., XXIII. *to* XXV.)

Mode of Life. They live on the slopes in villages called *Mottas*, four or five houses generally form a village (*Plate* XXVI.). The walls are made of wattle and mud, and the better sort have the fronts white-washed and covered with rude drawings of animals and men in charcoal and red earth. They store their grain in large oval baskets (*Plate* XXIII.), and for bottles they use gourds. They clear a patch round about the village, and sow the ground with *Rāgi* (*Cynosurus corocana*), *Tennē* (*Panicum Italicum*), or *Kīrē* (*Amaranthus tristis*). They dig up roots (called *Gāsu**) for food, and collect jungle produce, honey, resin, gallnuts, &c. which they barter with low country traders, and they are clever in catching game in nets, and dispose of the flesh in a surprisingly short time. They pay no *gudu* to the Todas.

Of late years many of them have taken work on adjoining coffee plantations. One I know, was even a maistry for many months, having been advanced to this position mainly because the Badaga coolies on the estate, afraid of his powers of sorcery, refused to work with him unless he was propitiated with the pay of a maistry. The youngest son inherits the house, other property is equally divided.†

The women cook and fetch water, and are fond of ornaments, wearing many bead necklaces, nose and ear rings, and glass and iron bracelets (*Plate* XXIII., LXXVIII.) when circumstances call for an elaborate toilet. This is not a tedious operation, as their only garment is the *Tundu* (lit. a piece) reaching from under their arms to the knee. When I suddenly came upon two women at a *Motta* the other day, one ran in, and bringing out a new *Tundu* threw it over the back of the younger, who adjusted it in its place, and dropped what looked like an old pocket handkerchief. She was now in her best attire, and the old *Tundu* was taken inside.

The men make baskets of ratan, nets of *oilhatti* thread, and milk vessels out of bamboo stems. They play on the clarionet, the drum, and the tambourine, the same as Kotas, and also on the *Buguri*, in use with Todas and Badagas. They usually attend all Toda funerals, and add their quota to the instrumental part of the performance. Ordinarily they have no turban; they wear the *chila*, a large cloth like that worn by Badagas, the waistcloth, and the *languti*. They profess to abstain from beef, but they will eat the flesh of young male buffaloes when offered by the Badagas for slaughter on certain ceremonial occasions.

They have no monigar, but generally some one of them is recognised as the head man of the *mottas* of the neighbourhood. Their villages, however, are so dispersed over the slopes and base of the hills, that the inhabitants of one locality know nothing of those at a distance. They can hardly be said to have any tribal existence as it were, but are isolated scattered families.

---

* There are two kinds of *Gāsu*, one wild (*Dioscorea alata*), and one cultivated (*D. globosa*). The latter is grown as follows:—A lump of the root is planted in a wide pit about a foot deep, so as to leave a couple of inches above ground and four or five times as much below. In nine months it fills the whole pit, and is then dug up.

† Another Kurumba said that the eldest son got the house and hatchet.

The foregoing description applies to the Kurumba villages specifically called *Kambês*, the inhabitants of which have intercourse with the Badagas, Todas, and Kotas on the plateau, and even labour on coffee estates. There are Kurumbas who live further down in the denser jungle at the base of the hills, whose houses and lives are of a ruder and wilder fashion.*

---

* In the plains the Kurumbas or Kurubas are found, both as a partially civilized low caste living in or near villages, and as a wild jungle tribe.

It will be seen by the following extracts from Buchanan's Journey, that some of the tribal divisions they recognise, correspond with those vaguely enumerated by the hill Kurumbas.

" The Curubaru are of two kinds, those properly so called, and those named Handi or Cumly Curubaru. " The Curubaru proper are sometimes cultivators and possess the largest flocks, but they never make blankets. " The Handi Curubaru abstain entirely from cultivation, and employ themselves in tending their flocks and " manufacturing the wool. The Handi Curubaru, or in the singular number Curuba, are a caste living in the " Harupunya-halli and Chatrâkal districts, and are of Karnâta descent, but many of them have now settled on " the banks of the upper part of the Krishna river in the Maratta dominions. All those who have settled in " that part of the country being horsemen, they are called Handi Ravalar. In this country they confine " themselves entirely to the proper duties of their caste, which are to rear sheep, and to work up wool into " blankets. They can eat with the other tribes of Curubaru, but do not intermarry with them. They are " allowed a plurality of wives, and their women continue to be marriageable after the age of puberty. Widows " may live with a second husband as left-hand wives (Cutigas). The Handi Curubas eat sheep, fish, venison, " and fowls. They hold pork to be an abomination, and look upon the eating of the flesh of oxen or of buffaloes " as a dreadful sin.

" When a Curuba dies, his property is divided equally among all his sons. The deities whom this caste " consider as their peculiar objects of worship are Bira Deva, and his sister Mayava. Bira is, they say, the " same as Isvara, and resides in Cailâsa, where he receives the spirits of good men. Bad men are punished in " Naraca, or by suffering various low transmigrations. There is only one temple of Bira, which is situated on " Curi-betta, or the sheep-hill, on the banks of the Krishna near the Poonah. There is also one temple " dedicated to Mayava at a place called Chinsuli, near the Krishna.

" These deities do not receive bloody sacrifices, but are worshipped by offerings of fruits and flowers. " The Pujâris at both these temples are Curubaru, and, as the office is hereditary, they of course marry. Once " in four or five years they go round distributing consecrated powder of turmerics and receiving charity. " Besides the worship of the deities proper to the caste, the Curubas offer sacrifices to some of the destructive " spirits, such as Durgava, Jacani, and Barama Deva. The Guru of the caste attends at feasts and sacrifices, " and punishes transgression against the rules of the caste by fine and excommunication. At marriages, " building a new house, &c., the astrologer of the village, who is a Brahman, attends."

" The Curubaru are an original caste of Karnâta, and, wherever they are settled, retain its language. " They are divided into two tribes, which have no communication, and which are called Handi Curubaru and " Curubaru proper. These last, again, are divided into a number of families, such as the Ani or elephant " Curubas, the Hâl or milk Curubas, the Colli or fire Curubas, the Nelli Curubas, the Coti Curubas, &c.

" These families are like the Gótrams of the Brahman, it being considered as incestuous for two persons " of the same family to intermarry. The proper duty of the caste is that of shepherds and blanket weavers. " The Curubaru are, besides, Candachaca or militia, cultivators, Attavana or armed men, who serve the Amildar, " post-messengers, and porters. They are allowed animal food, but in most places are not permitted to drink " spirituous liquors. In other places this strictness is not required, and almost everywhere they intoxicate " themselves with palm wine.

" The Curubas believe that men who die unmarried become Virikas, to whose images, at a great annual " ceremony, offerings of red cloth, jaggery, &c. are made. If this feast be omitted, Virikas become enraged, " occasion sickness, &c.

" The peculiar god of the caste is Bir-uppa, one of the names of Siva. The priests are Curubas. In some " districts they offer animal sacrifices to a destructive spirit called Batte Devaru."

" The Curubas here (between Sira and Seringapatam) have a book called Tiraga Cha-pagodu, which gives " an account of the tribe. They say that at a temple near Mercasua, where one of their tribe acts as Pujari, " the image represents a man on horseback with the *Linga* round his neck and a drawn sword in his " hand."

It is these that Dr. Shortt,* alludes to in the following words :—

"The various dry grains, chillies, Indian corn, yams, and some of the commonest " vegetables are grown by them in extremely small quantities, but, as a rule, they do " not cultivate. Frequently, a piece of jungle is rudely cleared, the soil roughly broken " up, and such seeds as they can obtain from the villages in the vicinity (plains) are " scattered on it; sometimes patches of land at a distance from their abodes are culti- " vated in like manner. They also have the plantain, mango, jack, and other fruit " trees, which in a manner grow wild in the vicinity. When their cultivation is at some " distance, the family remove thither during harvest time, inviting their friends to join, " and reaping only so much as is requisite for their immediate wants. The grain so " reaped is broken between stones into rough meal, and boiled into porridge or baked " into cakes. They never store the produce of their harvest, or preserve any for future " occasions, but eat while they can procure it, living in idleness and making merry while " the supply lasts. Sometimes the community unites, and live on the produce of a " single family, moving in succession from one patch of cultivation to another; and " when the whole of the cultivated plots are exhausted, there is no other resource left " them but to fall back on the produce of their fruit trees in the neighbourhood, such " as the Jack and Plantain, with other wild fruits; or the community scatters, each " family taking a different direction towards the jungles, in search of honey, edible roots,

---

In the Coimbatore district the Curubaru are also employed in making blankets, and keep for that purpose the woolly sheep called Curumbar.

South of the Kaveri, Buchanan mentions more Curubaru, as follows: "The Cad Curubaru are a rude tribe " of Karnata, exceedingly poor and wretched. They build miserable low huts, have a few rags only for " covering, and the hair of both sexes stands out matted like a mop. Their persons and features are weak " and unseemly, and their complexion is very dark.

" In the intervals between crops they work as day labourers, or go into the woods and collect the roots of " wild yams (*Dioscoreas*), part of which they eat, and part exchange with the farmers for grain. They also " hunt small game.

" They confine their marriages to their own tribe. The Gauda or chief man of the village is present at " the ceremony, which consists of a feast. During this the bridegroom espouses his mistress by tying a " string of beads round her neck. They can eat everything except beef. Some of them burn, and some bury " their dead.

" They make offerings of fruits to a female deity called Bettadu Chicama. There is a temple dedicated " to her near Nunjanagudi. There is also in this neighbourhood another rude tribe of Curubaru called Betta " or Malayu, both words signifying mountain.

" They are not so wretched as the Cad Curubaru, but are of diminutive stature. They live in poor huts " near the villages, and the chief employment of the men is cutting timber and making baskets. With a " sharp stick they dig up spots of ground in the skirts of the forest, and sow them with ragy. They never " intoxicate themselves, but may eat any kind of animal food except beef. Some burn, others bury their dead.

" The god of their caste is Ejuruppa, who seems to be the same as Hanuman, but they sometimes address " Siva. To the god of their caste they offer fruit and a little money."

A slave caste of Malabar is called Curumbal or Catāl (sing.) Curumbalun or Catālun (plu.): "The deity " is worshipped by this caste under the name of Malaya-devam, or the god of the hill, and is represented " by a stone placed on a heap of pebbles. Their place of worship is on a hill called Turuta Male in " Curumbaca Nādu. To this place they annually go and offer prayers, coco-nuts, spirituous liquors, and such " like.

" The dead bodies of good men are burned, but those of bad men, in order to confine their spirits, are " buried."

A letter from the Sub-Magistrate at Gudatur enumerates three divisions among the Kurumbas of Wainâd Mulla, Kurali, and Jain or Chēn. The first-named worship "Durga Bhagavati," and "Thalacholan dēvam," whom they propitiate with offerings of cooked rice at a temple called Puthadi. The priests at this temple are Brahmans. The Kurali and Chēn Kurumbas offer fruit and uncooked rice to Bhadra Kali and "Toriville." They have no priests.

* *Tribes inhabiting the Neilgherries*, page 49.

" and fruits. They are fond of the chase, and are expert in waylaying and destroying " animals, either by nooses, nets, or rude constructions of stone gins. Thus they fre- " quently live on the flesh of the Sambre, spotted deer, squirrel, wild cats, rats, snakes, " &c. Sometimes they engage themselves as labourers, and are very expert in felling " jungles and forests, cutting wood, squaring timber, &c., but don't take kindly to other " kinds of manual labour. Frequently, they are so hardly pressed from want, that the " men take to the jungles, and the women to the villages in the vicinity, where they " crave for and receive the refuse rice, rice-water, &c., and will sometimes do a little " work in cleaning, winnowing, or grinding grain, for which they receive wages from " the women of the different villages, in the shape of small quantities of cooked food " or grain."

Religion, Rites, and Ceremonies.

Some Kurumbas whom I have met with, profess, in answer to inquiries, to worship Siva, and occasionally women mark their forehead with the Saiva spot.

Others, living near Barliār, worship Kuribattrāya* (lord of many sheep), and the wife of Siva under the name of Musni.

They worship also a rough round stone under the name of Hiriadēva, setting it up either in a cave or in a circle of stones like the so-called "Kurumba Kovil" of the Badagas (*Plate* XXVII.), which the latter would seem to have borrowed from the Kurumbas; to this they make *pūjā*, and offer cooked rice at the sowing time. They also profess to sacrifice to Hiriadēva a goat, which they kill at their own houses, after sprinkling water, and eat, giving a portion of the flesh to the *pūjāri*. Others say they have no *pūjāri;* among such a scattered tribe customs probably vary in each *motta*. They do not consider the stone as a *lingam*, although they profess to be Saivites. They make no *pūjā* at home. They profess some small caste scruples, and will not eat with any tribe but the Badagas; but they will accept uncooked food from Todas, though not from Kotas.

Each Badaga *Grāma*, with its group of villages, keeps a Kurumba priest called Kāni Kurumba (*Kanike*=offering), who performs annual ceremonies for the Badagas at seed and harvest time, and is called in on all occasions of blight and murrain to propitiate or scare the demon of disease. The office is hereditary. In April and May, before sowing time, a goat or young male buffalo is supplied by the cultivators, and the Kāni Kurumba is summoned to make the sacrifice. Surrounded by the villagers, the officiating priest cuts off the head of the animal, and sprinkles the blood in three directions, East, West, and South, and also on a water-worn stone, which is considered as a "*hutu* (natural) *lingam*." No words are spoken, but, after the sprinkling, the Kurumba clasps his hands behind his head, shouting *Do Do Do* three times, and bows his head to "Mother Earth." The priest gets the head, and the Badagas the body, of the goat, which is taken home and eaten. In the Jakanêri Grāma this ceremony is performed at the cromlech (*Plate* LXII.); in Tenād, at a rude circle of stones (*Plate* XXVII.) surrounding a water-worn stone for a *lingam*. They call the place the "*Kurumba Kovil*" (Kurumba Church).† At harvest time the Kāni Kurumba gathers the first fruits, and makes a garland to tie

* More probably I think Kuri-betta-rāya (lord of the sheep-hill). *See* note *ante*.—*Ed.*

† Cf. Colonel Meadows Taylor's article in Eth. Jour. vol. I. No. 2, in which he says that a natural rock surrounded by a circle of stones is still used as a *place of sacrifice by shepherds.*

on the *B(l)aka;* four posts of wood which usually stand in front of Badaga temples. This office is a profitable one, if we may trust a Badaga song, which relates how Unigamāda, a Kurumba lad, was engaged to be Kāni Kurumba for the whole of Todanād, with the promise of a measure of grain and ¼ rupee from every house, which yielded him three pits-full of grain and 750 rupees. He also got 2½ rupees from every rich Toda of Mallādu, so that he became possessed of three stables full of cattle, fifty young buffaloes and thirteen pair of oxen.

There seems to be no marriage ceremony amongst the Kurumbas; no early betrothals. The son chooses for himself, and, if he is well-to-do, will aid his father in giving a feast to the neighbours to celebrate his wife's advent to her new home. Widows may re-marry.

They have no birth ceremony. When the child is three months old there is sometimes a christening feast, when the father names the child.*

Funeral Ceremonies.

Their funeral ceremonies resemble those of the Badagas, but are not so elaborate. They call the relatives together at the last, and those who can afford it administer a small gold coin (the *Bīrianhana*) to the dying man. After death they erect a small *Tēru* (car) hung with cloth, and place the corpse under it. Round the car they dance with music, and afterwards making a pyre of faggots they give the corpse and the car to the flames. Nothing is burnt with the body but the car and the cloth. After cremation it was not usual to take further trouble; the ashes and remains are left to the jackals and the winds.

They have no dry funeral like the Todas and the Kotas, but on occasions at long intervals, when a Kurumba has become rich enough to feast his neighbours, he will give a *Manemele* in honour of the dead for years previous. At these times a loftier car is built, and the tools of the dead commemorated, are put in a cot underneath. Goats and fowls are killed, and the blood is sprinkled, to gain the favour of the gods. The Kurumbas and Irulas round about are all invited, the Todas and Badagas too, and the music, dancing and feasting are kept up for a week.

The Kurumbas near Rangaswāmi's Peak told me that some Kurumbas buried their dead, but that they themselves burned theirs, and that the nearest relatives next day took some boiled rice in a cloth and a small round stone, and perhaps a bone from the funeral pile, and deposited them for the dead in the *Sāvumane* (death-house) belonging to the *Motta*. At Barliār they do the same. These *Sāvumanes* are small cromlechs of three upright stones and a covering slab; they said they did not now make them, but that they used those made by their forefathers.

---

* *Male Names.*

1. Chitta
2. Masana
3. Komara
4. Andi
5. Bella - - white.
6. Sevana - - like *Siva.*
7. Nanja - - a name of *Siva.*
8. Modea
9. Kenjala
10. Kutti

Female Names.

1. Hāla - - milky.
2. Tippi - - dungheap.
3. Timi
4. Dundi
5. Biri - - heroine.
6. Masani
7. Belli - - white.
8. Bendi
9. Yerangi - - name of *Rama.*
10. Bidigi.

Two Kurumbas who came to the Kūndah *Kotagiri* (bringing their hoes to be sharpened by the Kotas) from a *Motta* in Malabar in the Adipati *Grāma*, about two days journey S.W. from Kīlkūndah, told me that they buried their dead, and made a circle of small stones round the grave.

They knew of no god peculiar to the Kurumbas, nor had they any temple, but at a certain season they took offerings of plantains to the *Pujāri* (a Tamil man) who attended on Maleswara (lord of the mountain), the god who lived on a hill known by that name.*

They further told me that they had no marriage or birth ceremonies, nor any funeral rites except dancing and music; that they lived on grain, jungle roots, and the flesh of animals, which they shot with matchlocks, and that they had no domestic animals of any kind.

Insignificant as the Kurumbas now are, they seem to have played no unimportant part in Indian history. *History.*

They are chiefly known to us as the former possessors of Tondamandalam, a province whose boundaries are differently described in different stanzas quoted by Professor Wilson,† but which undoubtedly comprised the sea-coast from Pulicat to Cuddalore, and extended West at least as far as the foot of the Eastern Ghauts, possibly over a considerable part of Mysore, where to this day the Kurumbas or Kurubas are numerous.

The following succinct account of this kingdom is given in Mr. Taylor's Abstract of the Mackenzie MSS.‡ The manuscript treats of various matters connected with the districts of N. and S. Arcot, Chingleput, &c.

" Sec. 7. Ancient history of Tondamandalam, and its earlier inhabitants called " Vedars and Curumbars. After the deluge the country was a vast forest inhabited " by wild beasts. A race of men arose, who, destroying the wild beasts, dwelt in certain " districts. There were then, according to tradition, no forts, only huts; no kings, no " religion, no civilization, no books; men were naked savages; no marriage institutions. " Many years after the Curumbars arose in the Carnatic country; they had a certain " kind of religion; they were murderers; they derived the name of Curumbars from " their cruelty. Some of them spread into the Drāvida-dēsam as far as the Tonda-" mandalam country. They are now found near Uttramelūr, but more civilized. They " ruled the country some time, but falling into strife among themselves they at length " agreed to select a chief who should unite them all together. They chose a man, who " had some knowledge of books, who was chief of the Dravida country, and was called " Comanda Curumba Prabhu and *Palal* raja. He built a fort in Puralūr. He divided " the Curumbar land into twenty-four parts, and constructed a fort in each district.§ " Of these the names of ten are Puralūr, the royal fort, Callatūr, Amūr, Puliyūr,

---

* A very high cliff overlooking the Bhawāni Valley and held sacred by the surrounding tribes, Irulas, Kurumbas, Goundas, &c. See account of the Curumbalun of Malabar, p. 52, note.

The Todas and Badagas also contribute some of the ghee which is annually burnt on the top of the peak. Cf. Buchanan's account of the Curumbalen. See note ante.

† *Des. Cat. Vol.* I. *p.* 191.

‡ *Catalogue Raisonné, III.* 430; *Mad. Jour. VII.* 310.

§ These are the kottams, still recognised divisions (from kôte, fort). Mr. Ellis says that the divisions, kottam and nādu, were introduced by the Kurumbas.

" Chembūr, Uttri kādu, Kaliyam, Venguna, Icattukottar, Paduvūr. While they were " ruling, there was a commerce carried on by ships. As the merchants of Caveripum " patnam, (the Χαβῆρος of Ptolemy) sought trading intercourse with them, the " Curumbars built the following forts for trade: Pattipulam, Salacupam, Salapākam " Meyūr, Cudalūr, Alampari, Maracānam, whence, by means of merchants from " Cāveripumpatnam and the Curumbars, a commercial intercourse by vessels was " carried on. They flourished in consequence, and while they were still without any " religion, a Jaina ascetic came and turned them to the Jaina credence. The Basti " which the Pural king built after the name of that ascetic is still remaining. (Puralūr " is at the Red Hills near Madras.)

" They were shepherds, weavers, limesellers, traders. While living thus, various " kings of civilized countries made war upon them, as the Chola and Pāndya kings " and others.

" Being a wild people who cared not for their lives, they successfully resisted their " invaders, and had some of the invading chiefs imprisoned in fetters in front of the " Pūral fort.

" Besides they constrained all young people to enter the Jaina religion, in con- " sequence of which vexation a cry arose in the neighbouring countries. At length " Adondai of Tanjore formed the design of subduing them; a fierce battle was fought " in front of the Pural fort, the Curumbars fought with great bravery, and two thirds " of Adondai's army was cut up. He retreated, overwhelmed with grief, to a place " still called Cholanpédu. While meditating retreat, Siva appeared to him in a dream, " and promised him victory, guaranteed by a sign. The sign occurred, and the Curumbar " troops were the same day routed with great slaughter; the king was taken; the Pural " fort thrown down; and its brazen gates fixed in front of the shrine at Tanjore. A " temple was built where the sign occurred; and a remarkable pillar of the fort was " fixed there: the place is called Tirumulivásal. A sort of annual ceremony is " practised there.* After some more fighting the other forts were taken and the " Curumbars destroyed.

" Adondai brought the Vellazhar and settled them in the country. The name of " Curumba-bhumi was discontinued, and the country was called Tonda-mandalam."

Mr. Ellis † gives a list of the twenty-four kottams of Tonda-mandalam, amongst which are the ten above named; and the Mackenzie MSS. contain many notices of Curumba forts in that part of the country.

The following confused traditions seem to refer to the Kurumba dynasty.‡ " Account of Puthupatnam near Sadras. In the 2301st year of the Caliguga (B.C. 800) " there were two Rakshasas named Chaturangan and Balarangan, who were very " powerful and lived in Chaturanga patnam (Sadras). These cleared the forest from " Mailapūr (St. Thomé) as far as to Cudalur (Cuddalore), and destroyed the wild beasts. " Mavali Chairavarti is traditionally said to have been their descendant."

---

* This place (says Mr. Taylor) attracted my attention some years since, but I could not get any satisfactory explanation of the annual commemoration. It is about 12 miles W.N.W. of Madras, and one mile N. of the railroad.

† *Mirasi Right*, p. 286.

‡ *Cat. Rai. III.* 398.

A legend follows, designed to fix the locality of the account of Mahābali to this neighbourhood; but the incidents differ from the usual narrative.

" The Jainas afterwards had an ascendancy in this neighbourhood, and seventy-" two families built the town called Puthupatnam (or new town). Seventy-two head " men amongst them rode in palanquins. A chief to the north of them fought with " them. He was named Purushottama Prabhu. After much loss on both sides he " was taken and killed, by being fed with rice without salt. In consequence of the " cruelties of the war, a town received the name of Kodavu patnam. It is then stated " that they fought against " Sanatcumara," and, being denounced by him, a mud-" shower descended and destroyed their towns, and the sea overflowed them. Thus " from Mailapūr to Cudalur not one stone upon another now remains of their " habitations."

Another legend of the Jains of Mailapūr states that they were twice warned by a vision to move further inland, their former town being in each case destroyed by the sea.*

" Account of the Mauradya of Immudipatnam.† Formerly the Curumbars kept " herds and flocks in this neighbourhood, whence their town was called Pattipulam. " Certain old coins have been found there. Remains of their fort appear. Roman coins " have been found there. The people had a town on the sea shore for the purpose of " trading. There is a large stone inscription, said to have been engraved by the " Curumbas, but now illegible. There were certain large jars containing bones, which " some years ago, after being examined, were cast into the sea." (Compare account of kistvaens at Panduvaram Deval, given later.)

The last quoted tradition indicating the practice of urn-burial is noteworthy in connection with other MSS., which describe *pandu kulis* ‡ as abounding in that part of the country, and, amongst other more or less fabulous accounts of their origin, ascribes them to the Kurumbas. Many *pandu kulis* are said to exist near Puralūr. Sir Walter Elliot § possesses a copper spear-head, ornamented with a lotus, which was found in this neighbourhood. The greatest interest, however, attaches to the seaports in possession of the Kurumbas. Sala cupam is Saluvan kuppam near the Seven Pagodas, Alamparva and Cudalur are well known.

Sir Walter Elliot ‖ describes various coins found on the sea coast, from Cuddalore to Pulicat (the exact N. and S. limits of Tonda-mandalam), some very primitive, and considered by Sir Walter to belong to the oldest extant description of Hindu money. Others " belong to a remarkable series of thin and frequently broken coins, found along " the shore to the South of Madras (after the sand has been disturbed by storms); in " company with Roman, Byzantine, and a few Chinese coins. The figures are often " struck with considerable elegance, the obverse being always a bull, sometimes with a " short legend, and various reverses * *. There can be little difficulty in attributing " this series to the aboriginal people of Dravida-desam, the Curumbas and their princes " of the Pallava race. These coins may be assumed to have been struck in the 7th or " 8th century; the representation of a ship indicates the existence of commercial " pursuits; and the fact that all the specimens in our possession have been picked

* *Cat. Rai. III.* 372.
† *Cat. Rai. III.* 399.
‡ Cromlechs or Kistvaens.
§ *Madras Jour.* IV. N.S., 157.
‖ *Madras Jour.* vol. III. N.S.

" up on the sea-shore between Madras and Cuddalore, and that they are found with " copper coins of the Lower Roman Empire and with Chinese money, shows that the " commerce must have been extensive."

The seafaring Kurumbas of Tondamandalam would seem to have a claim to some of the remains at the Seven Pagodas. Dr. Babington,* mentions that four Sanscrit inscriptions had been sent him from the neighbourhood of Mamallapūram, all of which proved to be identical in substance, though written in three different characters; his translation is as follows.

"1 and 2. Siva, the beautiful, sits in the broad lake Siras, which teems with lotuses, " resembling variegated gems, and is full of water for sprinkling the much-loved Kāma- " rāja, who puts down the pride of his enemies, who is the receptacle of glory, and is " earnest in worshipping Siva.

"3. He (Kāma-raja) who dwells on the heads of his enemies, caused this temple " of Siva, which resembles the temple of Kailasa, to be erected for the happiness of " the world."

"4. May he who bears Siva in his mind, engrossed by devotion, and the earth on his " shoulders, with as much ease as if it were an ornament, long prevail."

"5. Atiranachanda, lord of kings, built this place. May Siva the beloved, accom- " panied by the daughter of the snowy mountain, be present in it for ever."

Unfortunately the locality of only two of these inscriptions (identical in character) is mentioned. These are both on the walls of a temple containing a *lingam*, near Saluvan Kuppam, on the frieze of which Sir W. Elliot deciphered the name Atiranachanda-pallava in two different characters. This inscription therefore, wherever found, belongs to the Kurumba dynasty.

The same slokas, transposed, and with some additions, form the inscription on the Ganesa temple at the Seven Pagodas. (This is written in a fourth character; a fifth is found in the inscriptions on the Rathas,† also Sanscrit). The sloka with the name of Atiranachanda, however, is replaced by one which ascribes this building to "Ranajaya Stambha." Two out of the four characters exhibited by the first five inscriptions are, according to Dr. Babington, varieties of Grantham, and two of Deva-nagiri, but unfortunately he does not say which is which.‡

---

* *The Seven Pagodas, by Capt. Carr.*

† This would seem to be the oldest character, as Prinsep says that it corresponds closely with that found on the oldest pure Hindu coins.

‡ The fact of their being in Sanscrit is suggestive, taken in connexion with the following statement of Dr. Caldwell's (Dravidian Comparative Grammar, p. 58).

"The higher antiquity of the literary cultivation of the Tamil may be inferred from Tamil inscriptions. In " Carnataka and Telingana every inscription of an early date, and the majority even of modern inscriptions, are " written in Sanscrit. Even when the characters employed are the ancient Canarese or the Telugu, it is " invariably found that Sanscrit is the language in which the inscription is written if it is one of any antiquity. " In the Tamil country, on the contrary, all inscriptions belonging to an early period are written in Tamil, and " I have not met with or heard of a single Sanscrit inscription in the Tamil country, which appears to be older " than the fourteenth century."

If this is the case, then the Sanscrit inscriptions at the Seven Pagodas probably belong to the Kurumbas, a people who came from the north, and whose descendants (in this district at all events) speak Canarese, and the Tamil ones to their Chola conquerors, and this is confirmed by the fact, that a Tamil inscription, which by Sir W. Elliot is considered the earliest, is dated in the reign of "Sri Koppari Kesari Varma, also called Sri Rajendra Deva of the prosperous Chola-mandalam."

[" That

The traditions preserved in the Mackenzie MSS repeatedly suggest the occurrence of some great catastrophe, or series of catastrophes, along the S.E. coast line. Wariūr or Uriyūr, once the capital of the Cholas, is said to have been destroyed by a shower of mud. A large trading town at the mouth of the Kāverl (probably the Χαβηρος of Ptolemy) is credited with the same fate.* Some connexion between the Kurumbas and these cataclysms is suggested by the stories of the Jains of Mailapūr and the south coast, quoted above. Such a cyclone as, in our days, desolated Masulipatam, would quite warrant these stories, and might have permanently altered the coast line to the extent indicated by the isolated pillar in the sea at Mamallapūram.

The downfall of the Kurumbas may have been assisted by some such natural catastrophe, and there may be after all a residuum of truth in the often repeated and often contradicted story of the—

"Works of wonder the devouring wave
Had swallowed there."

Tondamandalam appears to have been the more modern name of the Kurumba kingdom. In older traditions it is generally called Drāvida. Whether the Drāviras mentioned in Menu† are the Kurumbas or their savage predecessors, I do not know; nor is it clear whether Drāvida then meant Tondamandalam, or was used generally for the south of India. In the Ramayana, we find Cholas, Drāviras, and Pāndyas mentioned separately; in the Mahabhárata, although the Drāviras are again mentioned, the *kings* of Chola and Pāndya only came to Yudhishthira's sacrifice, which would seem as though Drāvira as a kingdom was not known.

In the Kongu-desa-rajakal‡ we find that Druhva-niti raya, whose father began to reign in S.S. 288§ = A.D. 366 (the date of his own accession is not given), conquered the Kerala, Pāndya, Drāvida, Andhra, and Calinga countries. This is the first mention of Drāvida; Chola, Pāndya, Kerala, and Malayāla occur much earlier in the record. All traditions make the Kurumbas the first *settlers* in Tonda-mandalam, occupied before their advent only by the Vedars or wild jungle tribes. The positive statements, however, as to their migration from the north, and the fact that one account assigns a date so reasonable as the time of Salivahana for their arrival, compared with the thousands of years with which Pāndyas and other dynasties are credited, suggest that they were comparatively modern colonists.

Pliny mentions the Darangæ, possibly the Drāvidian Kurumbas, next to the Pandæ.

"That these Tamil inscriptions," says Sir Walter (Seven Pagodas), "were posterior to the formation of "the Atiranachandesvara Mandapam, the Rathas, and the temple cut out of a single mass of rock, is established "by the invocation of Adisandesvara (Atiranachandesvara, the lingam set up by Atiranachanda) in the "inscription on the rock" (dated in the reign of Vira Chola). It is strange that all these inscriptions are Saiva, whereas all tradition makes the Kurumbas Buddhists or Jains. A grant of Prithuvi Kongani of Kongu mentions a Jain temple built by the grand-daughter of Pallavâdhiraja. (*Indian Antiquary,* vol. ii., p. 161.)

* *Cat. Rai.* III., p. 387.

† "The following races of Kshatriyas by their omission of holy rites, and by seeing no Brahmans, have gradually sunk among men, to the lowest of the four classes :—Paund'rakas, Odras, and *Draviras;* Kambojas, Yavanas, and Sakas; Paradas, Pahlavas, Chinas, Kiratas, Deradas, and C'hasas." *Menu,* X., 43, 44.

‡ *Mad. Jour.,* vol. xiv.

§ By an inscription translated by Mr. Price of Mysore (*Ind. Antiquary,* i. 363) it appears that this date is just a century too early.

Ptolemy does not give this name,* but his map of India shows many towns on the sea-coast between the Krishna and the Kāveri, amongst others, Alasinga emporium and Codduva, which one is tempted to identify with Alamparva and Cuddalore. On the whole the scanty notices of Drāvida we possess, agree with the first-quoted tradition, which indicate that the Kurumbas colonized the country under chiefs, and had been settled there for some time before they took, or were taken by, a king.

Of the Pallava princes little is known. Sir W. Elliot says,† "Previous to the arrival "of the first Chalukya in the Dekhan, the Pallavas were the dominant race. In the "reign of Trilochana Pallava, an invading army, headed by Jaya Sinha, surnamed "Vijayaditya of the Chalukya Kula crossed the Nerbudda, but failed to secure a "permanent footing. Vijayaditya lost his life in the attempt, but his posthumous son, "Raja Sinha, also known as Rana-raga and Vishnu Varddhana, renewed the contest "with the Pallavas, in which he was finally successful, cementing his power by marriage "with a princess of that race. The son of this marriage was Pulakesi, and a *sāsanam* "of his bears date S.S. 441=A.D. 489." The struggle between the various branches of Chalukyas and Pallavas was, however, renewed and carried on for centuries. The great-grandson of the Pallava princess claims, in an inscription of A.D. 584, to have defeated the Latas, Malavas, Gurjaras, and Pallavas.‡ "In a copy of a grant at Pithapur in "my possession," says Sir W. Elliot,§ "Vijayaditya, founder of the Chalukya dynasty "of Kalinga, about the middle of the sixth century, is described as destroying the "southern king Trilochana Pallava, and, by the decree of fate, losing his life in that "country. From the title Pallava, it may be inferred that this chief was of the same "race, and probably of the same family as Kāma Raja, surnamed Jayarana Stambha "and Atiranachanda Pallava.

"Another inscription of Vicramadityā, sixty or seventy years later, says, 'Moreover "'Pallava Mardu was overcome by this lord, Sri Vallabha, &c. &c. He has justly "'assumed the title of Sri Vallabha, being in the unprecedented possession of Kanchi "'(Conjeveram). He is also rightly entitled to the name of Rājamalla, having con-"'quered the chief (Pâlaka) of the Mahā-malla race.'"

Mr. Price of Mysore,‖ in commenting on a copper-plate inscription found at Nāga-mangala, says: "I have a Chalukya inscription, in which the first Vikramaditya is "stated to have 'become the possessor of Kanchipura by the conquest of Pallava Pati, "'whose insults threatened destruction to the dynasty resembling in purity the rays "'of the moon,' i.e., the Chalukyas who were of the lunar line. The next king, "Vinayaditya Satyasraya, who began to reign A.D. 680, is described as having destroyed "the power of the Trairājya Pallava.¶ Previously to this, however, we find from the "present inscription that Pallavendra Narapati had suffered defeat from Raja Sri

---

* Ptolemy's Sora regia Arcati has been identified with Arcot, and the Soræ Nomades with the Kurumbas, but not, I think, on valid grounds. General Cunningham has shown that the position of Sora must be far to the north of Tondamandalam (*Ancient Geography of India: cf. Caldwell's Dravidian Comparative Grammar, Introduction*), and Arcot is never mentioned among the towns of the Kurumbas. Moreover Hiouen Thsang describes Joriya or Choliya, a land scantily inhabited by heretics and infested with wandering robbers, in about the locality of Ptolemy's Soræ Nomades, at a time when the Kurumbas were flourishing in Drāvida.

† *Mad. Jour.*, vol. iv., N.S.

‡ *Ind. Antiquary*, I., 158.

§ *Seven Pagodas*, 126.

‖ *Ind. Antiquary*, II. 155.

¶ Another inscription of Vinayaditya boasts that he "churned the lords of Kānchi and Siugala Dwipa" (Ceylon).

"Vallabhākya of the Kongu line" (or Kongani Mahadhi III., the 20th of Mr. Dawson's list, who seems to have reigned towards the end of the sixth century). In spite of the boasted victories of the Chalukyas, it is clear that Drāvida was powerful and prosperous in the seventh century, since the Pallava prince could "threaten destruction" to the Chalukyas; and this is confirmed by Hionen Thsang's* narrative. He describes Drāvida as having a circuit of 1,000 miles. "Its northern boundary may therefore be approximately defined," says General Cunningham,† "as running from Kundapur, on the western coast, viâ Kadur and Tripati, to the Pulicat Lake, and its southern boundary from Calicut to the mouth of the Kāveri." Kanchi is said to have been at that time five miles in circumference. The people are described as devoted Buddhists (in great contrast to those of Malakuta or Madura, where heretics abounded, and convents were in ruins), and 100 convents gave shelter to 10,000 monks. Kanchi seems to have belonged to the Drāvidas only in these high and palmy days, when their territory had been enlarged at the expense of their Chola neighbours. A Chola king claims to have founded the city, and heretical Cholas from Kanchi are mentioned in the early traditions of Madura. An inscription of the Chalukya king, Pulakēsi who was reigning in A.D. 489, asserts that he "burned Kanchi, the capital of Chol."

Hionen Thsang's omission of Chola from the list of South Indian kingdoms‡ has been often remarked on. It agrees, however, with the inscriptions above quoted, none of which notice Chola, and suggests that the power of the Cholas stood very low at this time, which would account for the extensive dominion assigned to Drāvida.

The date of Adondai's conquest cannot be fixed with certainty: all accounts make him the natural son of a Kulottunga Chola, but unfortunately the dates assigned to the latter vary by some centuries. Wilson says that, "on the whole the weight of testimony places that prince, who is best known as Kulottunga Chola, about the end of the 9th or beginning of the 10th century." A village tradition preserved in the Mackenzie MSS. makes "Tondaman Chakravarti" (Adondai) reign in the 7th century.

Mr. Ellis§ adopts the latter date; and Mr. Prinsep‖ places the defeat of the Kurumbas in the 15th century.

The various lists of Chola princes, given in Mr. Prinsep's Useful Tables, make confusion worse confounded by their variations. The only authentic records of the Cholas, according to Sir Walter Elliot, are those which concern the four princes of that family who ruled over the Eastern Chalukya kingdom of Vengi. Sir Walter has kindly furnished me with the following corrected dates of these kings:

Rajendra Chola - - - -	A.D. 1063	reigned 49 years.
Vikrama Deva Kulôtunga Chola -	1112	15
Raja Raja Chola - - - -	1127	1
Vira Deva Kulôtunga Chola -	1128	56

* Hionen Thsang, a Buddhist pilgrim, travelled in India in the middle of the seventh century.

† *Ancient Geography of India*, vol. I.

‡ General Cunningham is doubtful whether to identify the Choliya of Hionen Thsang with Zora or Jora, near Kurnool, which he considers to be Ptolemy's Sora, or to accept M. Julien's suggestion that the names of Choliya and Drāvida have been transposed in Hionen Thsang's narrative, and that Chola is intended. The description of Choliya, however, as a country of desert plains, and wild marshy lands scantily peopled, could hardly have ever been applicable to the fertile district of Tanjore; and if the limits assigned to Drāvida and Malakuta are at all nearly accurate, little room is left for Chola, which must have been tributary, or very much weakened and reduced.

§ *Mirasi Right.* ‖ *Useful Tables.*

Vikrama Dēva, son of Vīra, was expelled from the Chalukya dominions, and Sir Walter thinks it doubtful whether Vīra really maintained his authority there during his whole life.

Happily for our present object, this minute fragment of genuine history gives us the date of Rajēndra, whose name appears in an inscription (dated in his ninth year) near the Varaha Swāmi temple at the Seven Pagodas. The conquest of Tondamandalam therefore probably took place before his time.

The Kongu-dēsa rājakal throws some light on the subject. It states that Gandadēva, king of Kongu, went into the Drāvida-dēsam, and conquered the king of Drāvida who ruled in Kanchi-patnam, and imposed tribute on the country. No date is given, but by a calculation from preceding dates, Mr. Taylor makes out, that Ganda began to reign in about A.D. 800.* The king of Chola is mentioned separately.

Somewhere about the end of the ninth century† Kongu-desa was annexed to the Chola dominions, and from this time the succession of Chola kings is given as follows:—

1. Adityavarma raya (son of Vijayadi Raya).	Conquered Kongu desam.
2. Vira Chola - -	In alliance with the Pāndyan king, conquered many countries. At his death he gave Chola-dēsam to a younger son, Desotya-rāya, and Drāvida-dēsam to his eldest son, Harinjaya-rāja.
3. Desotya-raya.	
4. Parantaca, son of Harinjaya, called also Hari mali.	Conquered the Pāndiya king and took tribute.
5. Divi or Hari-tittu - -	His country was invaded by Vīra Pāndyan, who is said to have been defeated, but apparently close to the Chola capital, Tanjore. He afterwards went to conquer Uttra-dēsa, but returned apparently unsuccessful.
6. Hari-Vari Deva, brother of Divi.	Was crowned, apparently during his brother's lifetime, to govern during an expedition undertaken by the latter against the Pandyan king, whom he defeated. "Therefore, as he had conquered a king of kings, "he acquired the title of Raja Raja," "*he*" being apparently Hari-Vari.

The Pandyan's mother being a relative, peace was soon made, and the story proceeds as follows:—

"Amarbhujangan, this general (of the Chola Raja) set out with the four kinds of "forces towards the west to the mountain named *Saiza*, and thence proceeding to fight "against the Kerala-dēsa (Malabar), he heard that its king was performing the "*Chaturbalayanam* and other ceremonies, in consequence of which he became greatly "incensed and conquered (took) Kotur, Indragiri, Nīlagiri-dūrga,‡ and other places;

* Mr. Taylor's translation, Mad. Jour., XIV.

† The last king of the older dynasty was reigning in A.D. 877.

‡ It does not appear whence the general started, but one would imagine that one of the "girs" (hills) must have been Hūlikal Dūrga, overhanging the Coimbatore country. The inhabitants are not mentioned. Nīla vali durga is mentioned later on in the MS. among the conquests of Peddata Raya Bellala.

"and as the entire strength of that king failed him, he embarked on board ship, and fled "into an island in the midst of the sea.

"Subsequently this general of the Chola Raja, according to the permission of his "master, collected and deposited all the plunder of riches, acquired in this invasion, "in the Saiva temple on the top of the ghaut; and in the extreme west he fixed a con-"quest pillar (*jaya-stamba*) with a flag to denote his victory to that point, and he thus "acquired great fame in the world."

"* * * He went to fight against the Calinga desam, and taking "thence tribute he went to the Nirmata (Nerbudda) country, and there also conquered "many kings, and in the south he erected a pillar of victory on Mahendra mountain. "Then he conquered Vaidumba-rāya, Kama-rāya, Dhana pallia,* Bhima rāya, Amma-"rāya, and other kings.

"* * * Then the Congu-dēsa and Carnataca-dēsa being subject "to him, he, the Maharāja Chola-raja, gave the name of Raja-Rajapuram to the "town of Keriur, &c. At the same time he performed many other charities, S.S. 926 = "1004 A.D."

With Hari-vari the history of the Chola kings ends, and the MS. goes on to the Bellāla or Oyisala family, who seem to have been chiefs of Talkād, and to have gradually extended their power in consequence of the "Carnataca Congu desa, which had been "accustomed to pay tribute to the Chola kings, being in the hands of *palliya carar* "(chiefs)." The first date given is A.D. 1069, but the Bellālas do not seem to have been important till the time of Peddata raya, circ. 1092 to 1140. He claims to have defeated the Chola-raja and established his independence, and his son is said to have ruled Kongu as well as Karnataca, and received tribute from Drāvida.

It appears from this extract that Drāvida was among the Chola dominions soon after the conquest of Kongu. As, however, a Kāma-raya (the title given to the Pallava princes by the inscriptions near the Seven Pagodas) was afterwards conquered by Hari Vari's general, and as, according to tradition, Puralur, not Kanchi, was the capital of Tondamandalam at the time of its conquest, it seems probable that the Pallavas retained possession of the sea-coast strip for some time after a great part of their territory had been lost to invaders from Kongu and Chola. If, as Mr. Dawson suggests,† Hari Vari is the Pandi Chol who was defeated and slain by the Chalukya king of the Western line Ahava Malla, he must have preceded Rajēndra, who very early in his reign defeated Ahava Malla, and survived him many years.‡ In that case Amarbhūjangam may be the Adondai of tradition, but this can only be supposition in the present state of our knowledge. All that seems clear is that Drāvida was an independent kingdom, with Kanchi as its capital, as late as the ninth century, and that it was subject to Rajēndra in 1072.

The Kurumbas do not seem to have confined themselves to Drāvida. A Kurumba Nâd in Malabar is said to take its name from a Kurumba chieftain, to whom it was

* The old Buddhist kingdom of Dhanakakata would lie on Bhujanga's route to Vengi. Mr. Hunter mentions Pahlava (? Pallava) princes of Dhanakakata, but I do not know on what authority.

† *Journal R. A. S.*, vol. viii., *History of the Kongu or Chera kingdom.*

‡ An inscription of Rajēndra's which states that he recovered Vengi, and fulfilled the vows of his elder brothers, tempts one, in spite of the date given in the Kongu-desa-rājakal, to guess that he was a younger brother of Hari-tittu and Hari-Vari. The Cholan occupation of Ceylon begins in 1059, just at the time of Ahava Malla's victory.

granted by the last Cheraman Perumal. (Dr. Day thinks in the fourth century, but if, as some tradition says, this Perumal became a Mussulman and went to Mecca, it must have been much later) The Kurumba family soon became extinct, and the later rajas of KurumbanÂd claimed to be Kshattriyas.

The following notices of later Kurumba history are gathered from vague traditions, chiefly in the Mackenzie MSS., and are given for what they are worth.

The final subjugation of the maritime portion of Drāvida seems to have reduced Kurumba society to its primitive elements. Individual chiefs retained possession of their forts,* and they seem to have profited by the subsequent troubles of the Cholas to recover partial possession of Tondamandalam, but they enjoyed little power or importance until the confusion that followed the destruction of Wārangal by the Mahomedans in 1323. Shortly after this Hari-hari and Bukka Rāyar, Kurumba† chieftains and fugitives from Wārangal, founded the last great Hindu dynasty at Vijayanagar, and its rapid rise to power brought a sort of Indian summer upon the Kurumbas throughout the South of India.

"In the time of the Rāyars‡ the Kurumbas ruled in many places. They constructed "forts and tried to make the Muthaliars and Vellarzhars render them homage."

In "Narvapālliyam they built forts, causeways, &c." At Gingi§ another shepherd dynasty gave place, in Fusli 710, to a Kurumba tribe called Vadaga Yediar, North country shepherds, the first king being called Kobilingan. (The name suggests that the Kurumbas had now become converts to the god of the strongest battalions, to whom they have adhered steadily ever since.)

An independent chief at Gingi, however, could hardly be tolerated even by a kinsman, and Kobilingan or his successor was dispossessed in Fusly 800 by orders of "the "mahā-rāja of Anaconda, Vijayanagar, and Pennaconda."

To this period belongs the "Kurumba prince of Alakapuri" mentioned in the chronicle of the Sēthupathis of RamnÂd.‖ This document asserts that the Sethupathis held suzerainty over Madura for eleven generations, and actual possession of it for three, after which they were driven to the South of the Kaveri by the "Kurumba prince of Alakapuri," and finally Madura and Tanjore were taken from them by the officers of the Vijayanagar kings. This story agrees with another tradition quoted by Mr. Taylor,¶ which states that the Maravas reigned over Madura for 608 years, after which the Northern Nayaks drove them away.

As the Nayaks certainly had considerable trouble in reducing the Maravas to order, there is probably some truth in the story; though it is hard to believe that the latter could have extended their conquests North of the Kāveri. Where Alakapuri is, I do not know. An Alaga exists near Madura, but this is too far South.

---

* Sir W. Elliot (*Numismatic Gleanings, Mad. Jour.*, vol. IV., N.S.) gives an inscription from Narayanavaram in S. Arcot, which records the gift of a village to the temple of Parasara by one Pallava Rāya, who had received it from Nāgadēva the lord of Potappinādu in the 13th year of Uttama Chola! or S.S. 1027 = A.D. 1105. Perhaps this may have been one of the fallen royal family, but the dates cannot be right, as Rājēndra was reigning in 1105.

† Hari-hari and Bukka Rayer are only once called Kurumbas, I think by Professor Wilson in the preface to his Descriptive Catalogue. The Kongu-desa-Rajakal only says that both the Vijeyanagar dynasties were Yadava. The evidence of other MSS., however, as to the improved fortunes of the Kurumbas under the first dynasty corroborates the statement of Wilson.

‡ *Cat. Rai.*, III., 420.

§ *Cat. Rai.*, III., 38.

‖ *Des. Cat.*, I., 196.

¶ *O. H. MSS.*, II., 181.

The Kurumbas paid dear for their temporary elevation; amid the troubles of a minority the Kurumba line of Vijayanagar came to an end (circ. 1508 A.D.), and Narasimha Rayar founded a new dynasty. His son Krishna Rāyar, who raised Vijayanagar to the highest pitch of power, seems to have devoted his energies, as much to consolidating and settling his vast dominions, as to defending them against foreign enemies. Warlike families, chiefly Telugu, received grants of districts in various parts of the county, and specially in Madura, where a long period of anarchy had favoured the wilder tribes, on condition of extirpating the Kallars, Vedars, and Kurumbas, who appear to have been included in a common proscription. The Kurumbas probably, however, enjoyed a pre-eminence in persecution. Krishna Rāyar was not likely, under any circumstances, to have overlooked the tribe of his predecessors, but unluckily the Kurumbas seem to have made themselves specially obnoxious to their neighbours.

We find that the Muthaliars and Vellārzhars, from whom the Kurumbas had tried to extort homage,* "at length went to a barber's, and, promising a gift of land, asked of him " counsel how to destroy the Kurumbas. It was the custom of the Kurumbas that, if one " of their people died, the whole family should have the head shaved; one of the seniors " of the tribe of Kurumbas died, and by custom the whole tribe at one time sat down to " have their heads shaved.† The aforesaid barber, on this occasion, charged all his " assistants each one to kill his man, which they did, by each one cutting the throat " of the person shaved. The women thus suddenly widowed, had a great fire kindled, " into which they leaped and died." No local habitation is assigned to this story, but an allusion to Sadras suggests that the massacre took place in that neighbourhood.

At Narvapālyam, the Wiyalvars, a tribe said to have come from Ayodhya during the time of the Kurumba ascendancy, were bribed by the Rāyars to destroy the Kurumbas, which they did with the help of the Rāyars' troops.

At "Marutam near Kanchi in the Utramēlūr district," the Kurumbas had a mud fort "covering more than forty acres of ground." In the time of Krishna rāyar, his dependant, the raja of Chingleput, fought with them, and after some time the Kurumba chief was unjustly put to death, and the Kurumbas were destroyed. These are probably specimens of many an unrecorded tragedy. As far as the Kurumbas were concerned, the persecution was effectual. They "fell like Lucifer," leaving no trace of their former greatness, except the strange tradition of hatred which makes the "shepherds an abomination" in modern India, as in ancient Egypt. On the Nīlagiris their reputation for witchcraft procures them such fear and detestation from the other tribes, that Mr. Metz tells me he has repeatedly been implored to show his friendship for the Badagas by helping them to rid the district of the Kurumbas. A large proportion of Badaga songs record the villanies of the unfortunate wizards, who have not unfrequently forfeited their lives to their bad name.

On one occasion, about thirty years ago, a wholesale massacre by the Todas brought the perpetrators within the grasp of the English law; but the Badaga songs suggest that a good many imaginary injuries have been avenged more quietly. It is curious that all tradition, ancient and modern, taxes the Kurumbas specially with cruelty.

---

* *Mad. Jour.*, VII., p. 321; *Cat. Rai.*, III., p. 422.

† I cannot find that any such custom now exists among the Kurumbas of the Nīlagiris.

In the plains, if less detested, they are held in no high estimation.*

Dubois† says, "There are still a great many detached castes in the southern parts of "India, besides those we have mentioned; all living in a state of degradation and "contempt. Amongst others there is that of the Kurumbars or Kurubaru. The "baseness of their nature and their total want of instruction seem to justify the detesta-"tion in which they are held by the superior castes of Sudras * * * * "The meanness of their employment (care of sheep) seems to spread its influence over "their manners. Being confined to the society of their woolly charge, they seem to have "contracted the stupid nature of the animal, and from the rudeness of their nature they "are as much below the other castes of Hindus, as the sheep are beneath the other "quadrupeds." "As stupid as a Kuruba" is, according to Dubois, a common proverb; and the one redeeming point in our eyes, conveyed in the saying, "A Kurumba always speaks the truth,"‡ apparently does not go for much among their native neighbours.

Since they settled on the Nilagiris the Kurumbas' history is a blank. They own to no traditions, and we have no means of judging even how long they may have inhabited these mountains, except that they and the Todas are generally said to have been the earliest settlers. Their religion and customs, however, are so much less singular than those of the Todas, that one infers, either that they are later comers, or have had more communication with the plains.

---

* I have been told that in Ceylon Kurumba is used for rogue.

† *People of India*, p. 472.

‡ *Eth. Jour.*, Vol. I., No. 2 (Sir W. Elliot).

CHAPTER V.

THE IRULAS.

CENSUS—PHYSICAL CHARACTERISTICS—MODE OF LIFE—RELIGION—LANGUAGE—HISTORY.

The following return shows the number of Irulas by the last census.

Arakadu	Arnvadi	Budnatham.	Kodadu.	Mêkanâd.	Malachepp.	Peranganâd.	Sembanarê.	Sembanatham	Segûr.	Todanâd	Kunjapanê	Siralcambê	Vagapanê	Vellerycumbê	Ootacumund	Total.
160	105	250	30	5	52	6	45	72	24	334	139	99	50	98	1	1470 { The numbers of Males and Females are equal.

They have no castes or divisions.

Physical characteristics.

Dr. Shortt says*:—

"The following is the result of the weight and measurements of an average of "25 men:—Age 26·68 years; height, 61·78 inches; circumference of head, 19·83; "neck, 11·39; chest, 29·91; arms, 8·42; thighs, 15·17; length of arms, 30; "hands, 6·50; breadth of hands, 3·25; length of legs, 34·50; feet, 9; breadth of "feet, 3·25; weight (avoirdupois) 96·20 pounds."

(*V. plates* I., XXVIII. to XXXI.)

Those I have seen, struck me as having a more marked Mongolian type of feature than the Kurumbas. Their cheek-bones were more prominent, the nose shorter and flatter. At the same time the difference is inconsiderable; for, when once I saw on a coffee estate several Kurumbas and Irulas together, with turbans on, I was unable, after a fair trial, to class them correctly.

The agent of the estate, however, after several years acquaintance with them, said he could always, without fail, distinguish a Kurumba from an Irula, although unable to explain exactly how he did so. He thought the difference mainly lay in the points I have alluded to.

Mode of life.

They live, like the Kurumbas, in *mottas* (*Plate* XXXII.) on the slopes and at the base of the hills.

Round about their houses they cultivate a patch of land, scratching the soil with a hoe, and sowing *Tennē* (*Panicum italicum*), *Ragi*, or *Kirē*, holding in some cases pattās from Government. They pay no *gūdu* to the Todas. Quantities of plantain

---

* *Tribes inhabiting the Neilgherries*, page 62.

trees seem to be their delight, and form quite a forest round the villages under Rangaswami's Peak. In some instances Irulas and Kurumbas live together in one motta, and their habits of life are identical.* They frequently attend the Metapoliam market, and barter jungle produce for salt, tobacco, and cloths, &c. The walls of their houses are made of split bamboos (*Plate* XXVIII.); I have not seen any ornamented with drawings, as is common with the Kurumbas. They will eat any kind of flesh but that of buffaloes or cows, from which they profess to abstain. Women do not eat with the men. The men shave their heads and wear the *Kudumi*.† They possess all the musical instruments known on the hills, except the Kota horn, and amongst themselves they dance to the sound of the clarionet and drum as vigorously as any of the other tribes; but, unlike the Kurumbas, they do not attend and play at the Toda or Badaga ceremonies.

Their property, real and personal, is divided among the sons, with the exception of the dwelling house, which, with the responsibility of the charge of the females and minors, goes to the eldest son in addition to his share

Buchanan‡ when staying at Danayakankotē paid a visit to the hill slopes to westward, under Rangaswāmi's Peak, and thus describes the Irulas :—

" The love of the marvellous, so prevalent in India, has made it commonly reported, " that these poor people go absolutely naked, sleep under trees without any covering, " and possess the power of charming tigers, so as to prevent those ferocious animals " from doing them any injury. My interpreter, although a very shrewd man, gravely " related that the Eriligaru women, when they go into the woods to collect roots, " entrust their children to the care of a tiger.

" On the hills the Eriligaru have small villages. That which I visited, contained " seven or eight huts, with some pens for their goats; the whole built round a square, " in which they burn a fire all night to keep away the tigers. The huts were very " small, but tolerably neat, and constructed with bamboos interwoven like basket-work, " and plastered on the inside with clay. These people have abundance of poultry, a " few goats, and in some villages a few cows, which are only used for giving milk, as " the Eriligaru never use the plough. They possess the art of taking wild fowl in nets, " which adds to their stock of animal food; and sometimes they kill the tigers in spring " traps, loaded with stones, and baited with a kid. Near their villages they have large " gardens of plantain and lime trees, and they cultivate the neighbouring ground after " the Cotucadu fashion, changing the fields every year. One of the articles raised by " this means is a new species of Amaranthus, the seed of which they grind to flour, and " use as a farinaceous substance. I have sent it to Dr. Roxburgh, under the name of " *Amaranthus fariniferus*. Besides cultivating their gardens and fields, the Eriligaru " gather wild yams (*Dioscoreæ*), and cut timber and bamboos for the people of the low " country. Both men and women take an equal share of the labour in cultivating their " fields. They have the advantage of a tolerably good soil, and a part of two rainy

* Some ethnologists hold that there is an unmistakeable difference between savages pure and simple, and the degraded descendants of a civilized race. I doubt if the most careful study of the Kurumbas and Irulas would enable any one to decide which were the Vedars or jungle tribes of all past traditions, and which the offspring of the people who sculptured the Rathas at Mamallapuram and traded with Byzantium and China.

† *Kudumi*, a species of scalp lock.

‡ *Journey, &c.*, vol. I. page 460.

" monsoons; yet, although they have fixed abodes, and of course gardens, they are " greatly inferior to the subjects of the Pomang-gri, and other rude tribes who inhabit " the hilly parts of Chittagong. Their huts are much poorer, and their persons are " miserable. Both men and women are clothed with dirty cotton stuffs, but in much " smaller pieces than those used by the other inhabitants. They speak a bad or old " dialect of the Karnáta language,* and must be therefore of a different race from the " Eriligaru that I saw at Rama-giri, who spoke a dialect of the Tamul."

Rangaswāmi's peak may be called the headquarters of the Nīlagiri Irulas. In the vicinity of the peak there is a considerable village of them. To the inhabitants of this and the surrounding *mottas* Buchanan's description fairly applies.

But, as with the Kurumbas, so with the Irulas, sportsmen may here and there find families of them squatted in the denser part of the jungles at the foot of the hills, north, east, and south. The struggle for existence is much more severe to the inhabitants of these isolated settlements, and Captain Harkness' account † may be taken as a fair sample of their mode of life:—

" The generality of this tribe are poor, indolent, and miserable.

" By the sale of the produce of the forests, such as wood, honey, and bees' wax, or " of the fruits of their gardens by those who take a little pains to cultivate them, they " are enabled to buy grain for their immediate sustenance, and for seed; but as they " never pay any attention to the land after it is sown, or indeed to its preparation, " further than partially clearing it of the jungle, and turning it up with the hoe, or, " what is more common, scratching it into furrows with a stick, and scattering the " grain indiscriminately, their crops are of course stinted and meagre. When the corn " is ripe, if at any distance from the village, the family to whom the patch or field " belongs, will remove to it, and constructing temporary dwellings, remain there so long " as the grain lasts. Each morning they pluck as much as they think they may require " for the use of that day, kindle a fire upon the nearest large stone or fragment of rock, " and when it is well heated brush away the embers and scatter the grain upon it, which " soon becoming parched and dry, is thence readily reduced to meal. This part of the " process over, or as soon as the rock has cooled, the parched grain, which in the mean- " time has been partially cleansed of the husk, is, with the assistance of a smaller stone, " rubbed into meal, mixed up with water, and made into cakes. The stone is now " heated a second time, and the cakes are put on it to bake, or when they meet with " a stone which has a little concavity, they will, after heating it the second time, fill the " hollow with water, with which, when warmed, they mix up the meal and form a sort " of porridge. In this way the whole of the family, their friends, and neighbours will " live, till all the grain has been consumed; and it seems to be considered among " them as superlative meanness to reserve any, either for seed or future nourishment. " The whole of this period is a merrymaking time, they invite all who may be passing " by to partake of the produce of the field, and to join in their festivities. These " families will now be invited in return to live on the fields of their neighbours; and " when the whole of the grain of the village has thus been consumed; and this, at best, " is generally but a very small quantity, they have again to trust to the precarious

* This is a mistake; according to Mr. Metz, Irula is a dialect of Tamil.

† *Neilgherry Hills*, page 98.

" subsistence which the produce of the forests or their gardens yield. Many of them " live, for the remainder of the year, on a sort of yam, which here grows wild, and " which, after the name of these people, is called the Erular root. To the use of this " root they accustom their children from infancy, and when it fails them, which is " sometimes the case, they have then hardly any resource from starvation. As it " becomes scarce in the vicinity of their village, they wander through the forests in " search of it. If they find it, or if they are successful in the chase, or in the " ensnaring of wild animals, they are enabled to support themselves till the change of " season again brings forth those natural productions, by the sale of which they are able " to purchase a little grain; or as labourers are now required by the cultivators of the " plain, they readily engage themselves at a reduced rate of wages. It is during the " winter of their year, or while they are wandering about the forests in search of food, " that, driven by hunger, the families or parties separate one from another, each eager " only to satisfy his own craving. On these occasions the women and young children " are often left alone, and the mother, having no longer any nourishment for her infant, " anticipates its final misery by burying it alive."

Religion. Rites and ceremonies.

They are followers of Vishnu under the name of Rangaswāmi. On the top of Rangaswāmi's peak they have two temples, consisting of circles of rough stones, each enclosing an upright stone, the larger called Dodda (great) and the smaller Chikka (little) Rangaswāmi. The latter has not been long set up; they say he was but lately born. An Irula *Pūjāri* lives near the temples, and rings a bell when he performs *pūjā* to the gods. He wears the Vishnu mark on his forehead. His office is hereditary, and he is remunerated by offerings of fruit and milk from Irula worshippers. Every year about sowing time there is a large feast at the temples, which is attended by the Badagas of the surrounding district, who bring offerings of plantains and milk to propitiate the Irula god. No animal sacrifices are performed there.

Each Irula village pays about two annas to the *Pūjāri* in May or June.

They say that there is also a temple at Kallampalla in the Sattya Mangalam Tāluq, north of Rangaswāmi's peak. This is a Siva temple, at which sheep are sacrificed: the *Pūjāri* wears the Siva mark. They don't know the difference between Siva and Vishnu. At Kallampalla temple is a thatched building, containing a stone called Mariamma, a form of Durga, the well known goddess of small pox, worshipped in this capacity by the Irulas. A sheep is led also to this temple, and those who offer the sacrifice sprinkle water over it and cut its throat; the *Pūjāri* sits by, but takes no part in the ceremony. The body is cut up and distributed among the Irulas present, including the *Pūjāri*.

In their own houses they make no prayer or *pūjā* of any kind. Like the Badagas, they will not work at cultivation of any sort on Mondays or Saturdays, though they will dig for roots.

They will not eat with any hill tribe except the Badagas.

As far as I can ascertain, they have no marriage or birth ceremony. There are no early betrothals; but when a boy is of age, he chooses a wife for himself, and gives five or ten rupees to the girl's father, and perhaps a glass bead necklace to the bride, but there is no tying of the *Tāli*. Brothers and sisters and cousins do not intermarry; widows may re-marry.

About a week after birth the child is named by the father or by a rich relative.*

They bury their dead, placing the body in a sitting posture in the grave, dance and play round the corpse, light a lamp which they put inside, and block up the grave with wood and earth. They do not build a *tēru* like the Kotas, nor give the *Birianhana* to the dying man.

Each corpse is laid in a separate grave, over which the relations place a small upright stone about a foot high.

Each *motta* has its own burial ground. They bury with the body the cloth commonly worn by the deceased, and some rice, and with a rich man, sometimes an axe.

They have no commemorative ceremony.

Language. The Irula language is a dialect of Tamil. (*See* Appendix A.)

History. The Irulas belong to the Vedars, or hunting people, whose expulsion from, or extermination in, the settled parts of India is constantly recorded by traditions.

Buchanan identifies the Eriligaru of Mysore with the Chensu, Chenju, or Chenji existing in Kurnool and other districts, who seem to have been the most important of the wild tribes. They and their chiefs find frequent mention in the Mackenzie MSS. In Madura, according to the traditions of a Poligar family, they were able to ravage this country to the gates of the capital in the course of the last century. One of the Mackenzie MSS., however, describes the Irulas as a distinct and more peaceable tribe. At all events, there is no reason to suppose that they were ever anything but a jungle race, and it is needless to say that they have no traditions of their own.

---

* It was with the greatest difficulty I could get male and female names out of the Irulas whom I brought to my tent, as the most intelligent that could be found. It was not that they had any objection to give the information, but simply that their limited range of experience had not acquainted them with names enough. After at least an hour's reflection, during which they were evidently taxing their memories to the utmost, they could only enumerate eight women's names :—

Male Names.

1. Masana.
2. Virasa.
3. Ranga.
4. Rāma.
5. Kēla.
6. Linga - Name of Siva.
7. Kāla.
8. Dāsa - Slave, servant.
9. Sevana - Name of Siva.
10. Kangāla.

Female Names.

1. Pāli.
2. Masani.
3. Sevani.
4. Panichi.
5. Keppi.
6. Rāmi.
7. Resi.
8. Manithi.

CHAPTER VI.

CAIRNS AND CROMLECHS.

DEFINITION OF NAMES.—SITUATION OF CAIRNS AND BARROWS—EXTRACTS FROM DIARY—RESEMBLANCE TO EUROPEAN SEPULCHRAL TUMULI—CLAIM OF THE TODAS TO THE CAIRNS AND BARROWS DISCUSSED—STONE CIRCLES—SITUATION OF CROMLECHS—MODE OF PHOTOGRAPHING—INSCRIPTION IN MĒLŪR CROMLECH—KISTVAENS—ACCOUNTS OF SIMILAR REMAINS IN OTHER PARTS OF INDIA—FURTHER INVESTIGATIONS REQUIRED.

The terms Cairn, Cromlech, Kistvaen, &c. have been used so vaguely and received such different meanings from different authors that it seems better to begin by defining clearly the meaning attached to each in this report.* No special correctness is claimed for the definition, but it seems as plain and consonant to common usage as any other.

By cairn, then, is meant a circular enclosure formed either by a rough stone wall, or heap, or by single stones. Toda, *Phin;* Badaga, *Hok-kallu,* navel stone. (*Plates* XXXIII., XXXIV.)

By barrow, a mound of earth encircled by a ditch, and sometimes also by one or more circles of stones. Badaga, *Pongui,* gold-pit. (*Plate* XXXV.)

By kist-vaen, a vault of large stone slabs, closed on every side, but sometimes with a round hole in one of the walls, with or without a surrounding stone circle or tumulus. Badaga, *Mōriaru mane,* Morier's houses. (*Plate* LXIV.)

By cromlech, a similar enclosure open on one side. When these contain sculptured slabs, they are called by the Badagas, *Sela kallu,* by the Kurumbas and Irulas, *Bīra kallu,* stones of a hero, and by Todas and Kotas *Pāndavaru mane,* Pandava's houses. (*Plates* XLV., &c.) Those without sculptures are called by the Badagas, *Gattige kallu,* throne or seat stones, and the modern ones used by the Kurumbas are called *Bīra kallu,* hero stones, or *Sāvumane.* The Āzāram is a circle of stones, in which the relics preserved from a Toda green funeral are burnt, the ashes being buried under one of the stones.

To begin with the cairns and barrows, which are by far the most numerous of the monuments on the Nīlagiris. They invariably occupy commanding situations on the tops of hills and ridges; often several cairns and barrows lie together, but some are single.

They abound in most of the inhabited parts of the hills, but only a few small ones are at present known on the Kūndahs, and these are on the eastern side of that range, not far from the villages and mands near the Avalanche bungalow.

This is what one might expect, since the rain and cold of the Kūndahs must always have made them almost uninhabitable except during the dry months, when they are resorted to for pasturage.

---

* *Worsaae, Primeval Antiquities, p. v., Intro.,* "British Archæology has suffered very much from the want "of a fixed nomenclature. This has caused a great deal of confusion. The same names and terms have been "used for the most different remains." Worsaae's own nomenclature depends on the division of Stone and Bronze Periods, and is inapplicable to India.

The "finds" in the cairns, as far as intrinsic value is concerned, seem to verify the Badaga proverb, which estimates as follows the value of land in its four *Nâds* (divisions,) "Todanād, 4 annas, Peranganād, 3 annas, Mekanād, 2 annas, Kūndanâd, 1 anna."

The best of the bronzes and weapons have certainly been found in Todanād, and Peranganād ranks next. The result of our researches has had quite the effect of raising or depressing our expectation of a "find" in accordance with the Badaga value of the Nâd in which the cairn is situated.

The cairns are of several forms; one, commonly called the drawwell kind, (*Plate* XXXIV., *fig.* 1,) consists of a dry circular wall; others seem never to have been regularly built up, but the circle is enclosed by a heap of rough loose stones, sometimes built more carefully on the inner side of the circle, or faced inside with larger slabs, but sloping outside into a tumbled heap. (*Plate* XXXIII.) A third kind consists merely of a circle of stones; sometimes of long stones laid round on a sort of ridge sloping inwards, (*Plate* XXXIV., *fig.* 2,) sometimes of common rough stones embedded in the surface soil.

The number of cairns is very great; over forty have been opened in the course of this inquiry, many more had been previously rifled; some, the situations of which are known, are still unopened; and probably a considerable number are not yet discovered, as there are still some ridges which have not been searched.

The following are extracts from the diary kept of the researches.

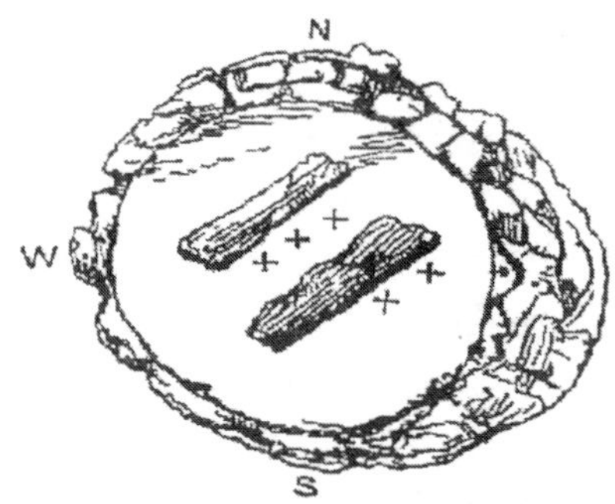

7th July 1871. Cairn near Ebgodū Mand, the enclosed portion overgrown with bushes. Cleared these away, and found two parallel slabs on the ground. Pottery was found at the × × marks, nearly on the surface. We removed the two flat stones, but found nothing beneath. The roots of the trees and shrubs had matted themselves round the slabs and broken the pottery.

Found XXXVI.—Lid of pot with figure of a low country bullock with hump. (*Plate* XXXVII., *fig. b.*)

XXXVII.—Animal, perhaps sheep or goat, hog-backed, with prominent backbone.

XXXVIII.—Two heads, birds, perhaps cocks.

XXXIX.—Animals' heads, perhaps sheep.

XL.—Fragment of pedestal.

Visited this again 13th October. Found that the two stones had lain exactly N.E. by S.W., cleared away the wall to the W., and dug down 2½ feet; at that depth found:—

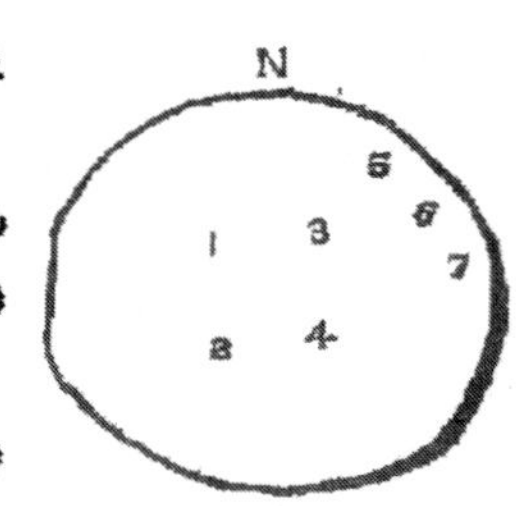

At 1, XL. (*a.*) Vessel of fine pottery of a flattened urn-shape with large lid, containing a few pieces of burnt bone.

At 2, XL. (*b.*) Bronze vase on stand, small, the inside of a beautiful mottled green colour; containing earth and a thin piece of gold wire.

At 3, XL. (*c.*) Another urn of fine pottery, with lid; exactly like XL. (*a.*) (*Plate* XL., *fig. j.*)

At 4, XL. (*d.*) A bronze vase inverted, on a stand, fluted, and very prettily chased inside. (*Plate* XLI., *fig. e.*)

At 5, 6, and 7, fragments of the rough pottery: an elephant's head, part of a man's figure, and a lid with a native stool on it.

August 25th 1871. Opened two cairns on Chiketnavoibetta (mountain with a small slope), near Tūnēri.

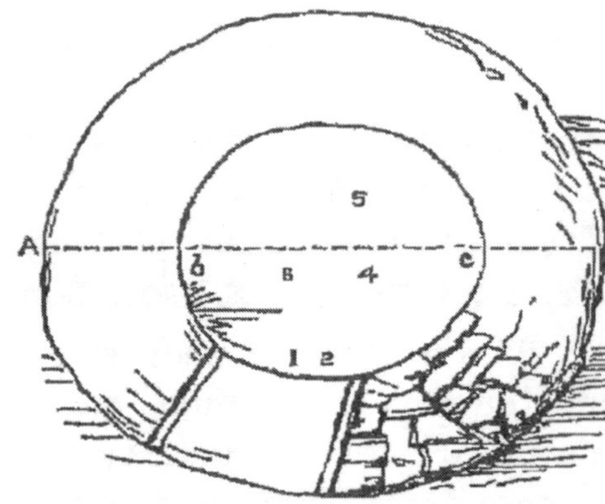

The first cairn at the top of the hill was between 2 and 3 feet high, of loose rubble stones, 23 feet in diameter from A to D, and 10½ feet from b to c. It had evidently been disturbed before, as the large "*Arres*," or slabs, had been removed, and were lying outside the cairn; the soil within the circle had also been disturbed.

The cairn was built on sheet rock, covered with two or three feet of earth. After removing a part of the wall we dug down about two feet, and at that depth found:—

At 1, a beautiful bronze vase (No XLIV.) inverted. It is very solid, in shape a long oval, on a stand, and is chased outside and in, the centre pattern inside representing the lotus or *Padma*. The ornament is done by hand, and shows slight irregularities, but the workmanship is excellent. (*Plate* XLI., *fig. a.*, and XLII., *fig. a.*)

At 2, a smaller bronze basin (XLV.) which had apparently a stand, now missing; it is thinner than XLIV., round, and shallow in shape like the *Puja* vessels used by modern Hindus. (*Plate* XLI., *fig. k.*)

At 3, a large well-shaped iron spear head (XLVI.)
At 4, an iron sickle with a long handle terminating in a knob.
At 5, two razors not very different from the modern Kota razor.
} *See Plate* XLIII.

All over the surface, and from six inches to a foot deep, were scattered broken pieces of pottery, from which Nos. XLIX. to LV., coarse pottery, fragments of animals, were selected.

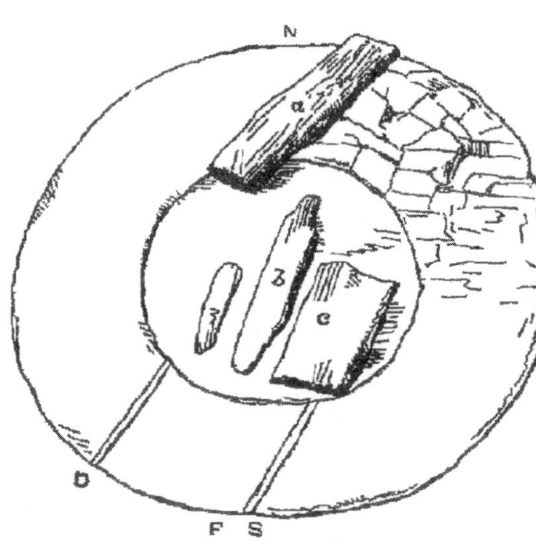

The second cairn was about 20 yards S.W. of the former, and lower down the hill. It resembled the first in construction, but was about 1 foot less in diameter. It had also been disturbed, the slab (*a.*) was lying on the top of the wall, and there were marks of its having formerly lain on the surface to the right of *b.* (*b.*) and (*c.*) lay N.E. by S.W.; *b.* was 6 feet long, *c.* 4 feet. This cairn also stood on sheet rock, the soil being little more than a foot deep. We made an entrance at DE, and carefully removed the soil. Under (*b.*), about the centre, we found a small iron sickle (LVI.), and fragments of broken pottery were scattered in all directions.

Afterwards we went to a hill called Gulicholabetta (hill with a jungle in a ditch) on which were several cairns and a barrow (*see* section below. We opened cairn (*a*) on plan.

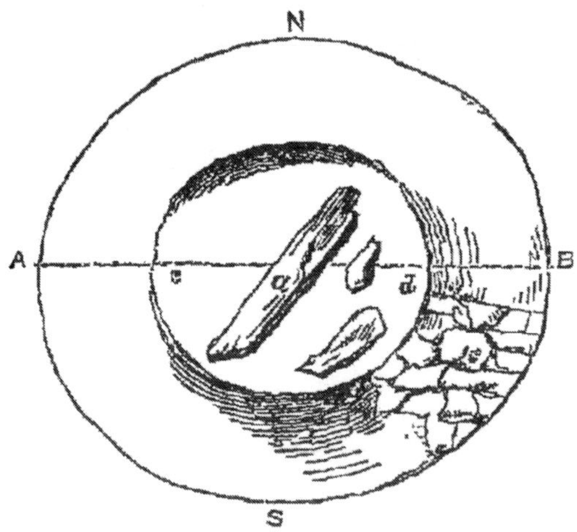

The circle was 4 feet high, and 24 feet in diameter from A to B, and 10½ feet in diameter from *c* to *d*

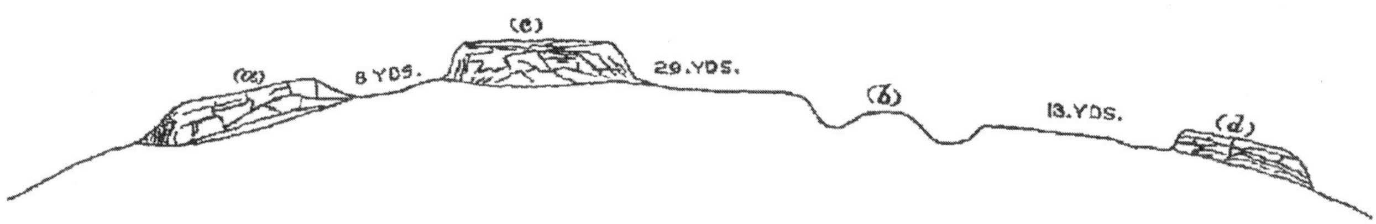

TOP OF GULICHOLABETTA.

(*a*.) Cairn opened 25th August 1871.
(*b*.) Barrow opened 1st September 1871.
(*c*.) and (*d*) Cairns opened 3rd November, but which had been formerly disturbed, only CLIX. and CLXI., small metal vessels perhaps lamps, (*Plate* XLIII.,) and CLX., an iron sickle, were found in them.

One slab (*a*.) about 5 feet long just showed its upper surface above ground, and two broken stones lay to the right; all lay N.E. and S.W. We removed (*a*.) and dug out all the earth, which was full of broken pottery, to a depth of about eighteen inches, when we found two other slabs lying below (*a*.) also pointing N.E. and S.W. These were long narrow slabs lying side by side. We broke them with a crowbar and got them out, and dug about two feet deeper till we came to what appeared to be natural undisturbed earth.* We found nothing but pieces of pottery (LXXXVI. to XCI., fragments of no importance, very rough and coarse).

The second layer of slabs under the first seemed to me strange, but Mr. Metz said he had found it so in several cases.

---

* Mr. Breeks thought that this cairn had not been dug out deep enough. Subsequent experience showed that the cinerary urns were very often sunk in holes in what appeared undisturbed soil, so that they were only detected when actually struck by the pickaxe.—ED.

1st September 1871. At Kunhākkilabetta (hill of small birds) was a cairn containing an old half-decayed tree, which measured 9 ft. 2 ins. in circumference at three

feet from the ground.* Two slabs, lying as usual N.E. and S.W., were exactly under this trunk, their ends peeping out on each side among the roots. We cut down the tree, and attempted to dig out the cairn, but found that the roots of the tree had completely filled it, leaving hardly a square inch unoccupied; fragments of broken pottery were found in every direction, but only one small pot, nearly perfect, which had been jammed between two roots.

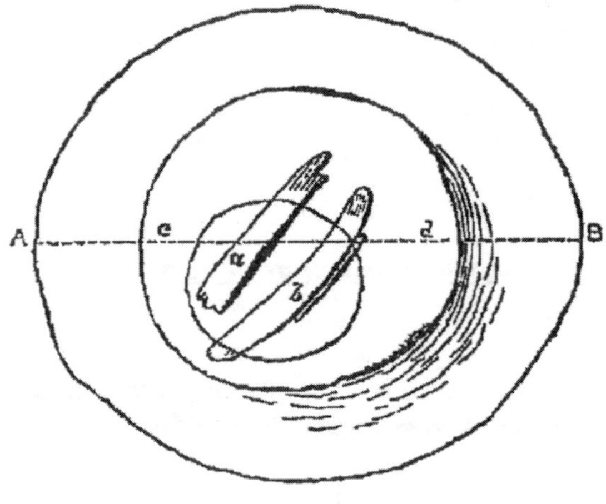

A to B, 36 feet. *c* to *d*, 18 feet.

24th October 1871. Went to Nadubetta, a high hill near Brikpatti Mand.

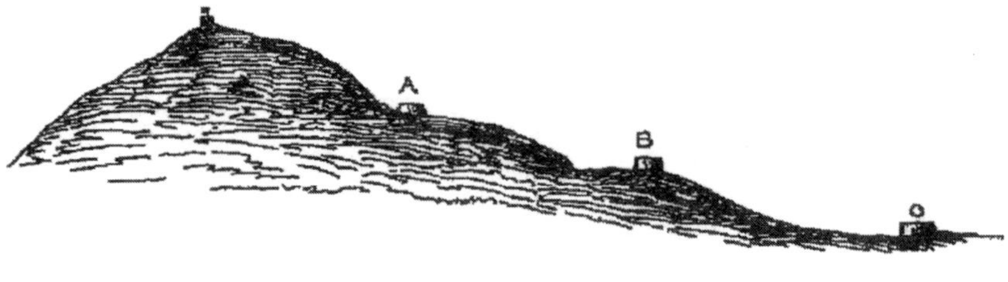

* Considering that the jungle trees of the Nīlagiris are of very slow growth, this must have been very old.

On the top a cairn has been destroyed and a station for flagstaff (Survey) built up. At A was a cairn with two small ones attached.

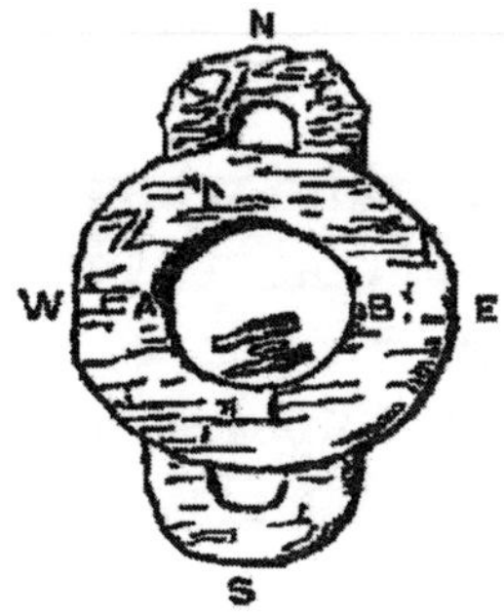

N. to S. 29½ ft. E. to W. 24 ft. A to B 7½ ft.

This triple cairn was built of flat shingly stones on sheet rock where the soil outside was only about two inches deep, inside perhaps six inches. Quantities of fragments of pottery were strewed about the centre of all these circles. The slabs in the centre one had been removed out of place, and one was broken. We removed all the earth, but found nothing but bits of pottery of no value; some one had evidently been before us.

We next opened the cairn at B. The wall was about five feet high, well built of flat stones; inside were trees, with stems as thick as a man's thigh, and shrubs.

There was only one slab lying nearer N. and S. than N.E. and S.W., about six inches below the surface. At this depth, and on the surface, we found several remains of the usual rough clay pots and lids with figures, viz.:

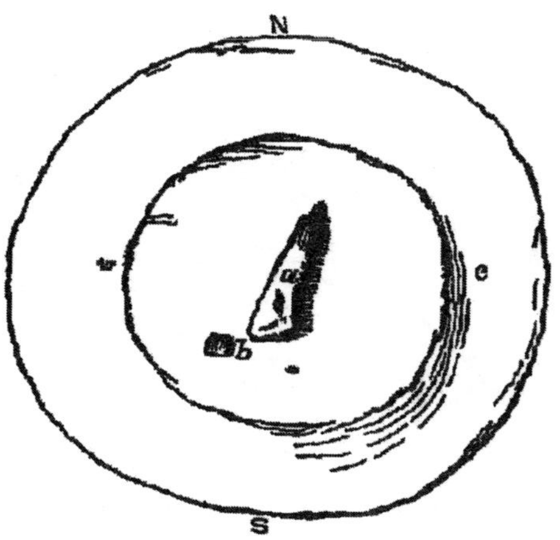

N. to S. 24 ft. *e.* to *w.* 14 ft.

Slab *a*, 3 ft. 9 ins. long; 1 ft. broad; 1 ft. 4 in. thick.
Slab *b*, a small stone about a foot long and 4 inches square, stuck upright in the ground.

CXVII. Pot with pig on the lid. (*Plate* XXXVI., *fig. k.*)

CXVIII. Neck of pot with lid and figure of some animal covered with spots, perhaps leopard. (*Plate* XXXVII., *fig. c.*)

CXIX. Pot and lid with bird. (*Plate* XXXVI., *fig. m.*)

CXX. Neck of pot and lid, with long-tailed bird.

CXXI. Ditto, with bullock. (*Plate* XXXVII., *fig. l.*)

CXXII. Ditto, with jungle cock?

CXXIII. Neck of pot and lid, with sámber.

CXXIV. }
CXXV. } Broken lids and figures.
CXXVI. }

CXXVII. Three human figures of quite a new type, decidedly Buddhist in character. (*Plate* XXXVII., *fig. k.*, and XXXVIII., *fig. h.*) Two have a conical cap, and one of these has very large ears, the lobes hanging nearly to the shoulders. The third appears to have the curly hair characteristic of Buddhist images,* and has also the ears distended.

CXXVIII. }
CXXIX. } Animals.

CXXX. Small shallow pot.

CXXXI. Pot and lid with sunflower? (*Plate* XXXVI., *fig. b.*)

CXXXII. Man riding. (*Plate* XXXVIII., *fig. c.*)

CXXXIII. Pot and lid with sámber. (*Plate* XXXVII., *fig. a.*)

We removed (*a.*) and went down about four feet into the natural soil, and found under (*a.*) an urn of the finer pottery (CXXXIV.) containing a razor with marks of cloth round it, and a small iron implement, bones, and earth. Also a handsome bronze vase on stand, inverted (CXXXV.), with an iron sickle or knife laid round it (CXXXVI.).

4th November 1871. Opened a cairn on Yeresibetta near Kenteri, Todanâd.

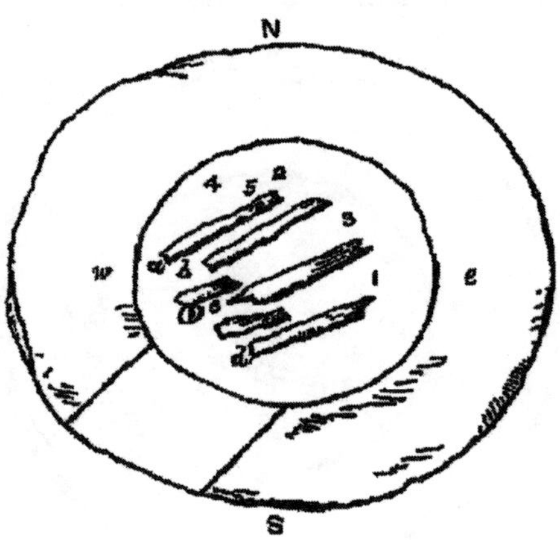

N. to S. 26 ft. *e.* to *w.* 14 ft

a. 3 ft. 4 ins. long;
10 ins. broad;
10 ins. thick.

b. 3 ft. 6 ins. long;
1 ft. 6 ins. broad;
1 ft. thick.

c. 2 ft. 7 ins. long;
9 ins. broad;
1 ft. 1 in. thick.

d. 2 ft. 9 ins. long;
1 ft. 2 ins. broad;
8 ins. thick.

The stone circle to the E. was in a tumble-down state, and much of it had fallen inside, covering the slabs, and filling the cairn with heaps of rough stones. The foundation of the circle was made with immense stones laid evenly and with care.

---

* These figures are unique. No similar ones, nor any objects at all suggesting Buddhism, were ever found again.

We effected an entrance as usual at the S.W., and removed the brushwood and stones from the centre. On the surface we found broken bits of pottery destroyed by the stones and roots (CLXII. to CLXV., lids and figures partly broken). Just below the surface were four large slabs and three small stones, all lying N.E. by S.W. Only one of the three small stones looked at all like a slab.

About a foot below the surface, at 1, found bronze, CLXVI. (*Plate* XLI., *fig. b.*), a large basin-shaped vessel without a stand, covered with dark-green shining rust, containing earth, charcoal, and bone. At the same depth at 2, another bronze, CLXVII. (*Plate* XLI., *fig. c.*), a small saucer, inverted, on a fragment of fine pottery, and surrounded by other fragments, so that it had evidently been inside an urn, and containing some fine earth like snuff, and a small iron implement (CLXVIII.).

At 3, about two feet deep, was an urn, CLXIX. (*Plate* XL., *fig. g.*), containing a shallow bronze vase on a stand, inverted (CLXX.), a spear-head, CLXXI., knife, CLXXII., both much rusted, and another fragment of iron, CLXXIII., rusted to the bottom of the pot; also bone, charcoal, and earth.

At 4, a small thin bronze much rusted and broken, CLXXV., surrounded by fragments of fine pottery, containing earth and bone (CLXXVI.).

At 5, about two feet deep, almost under (*a.*) another bronze, saucer-shaped, covered with bright green rust almost like malachite (CLXXVII., *Plate* XLI., *fig. d.*), inverted, and surrounded by broken pieces of fine pottery, containing earth and bone, CLXXVIII.

Having dug out the earth all round the slabs to the depth of two feet, we removed the slabs one by one and removed the earth under them to the same level. Under (*d.*) we found an iron spear-head and fragments of sickle and knife, CLXXIX. to CLXXXI. A little to the right of *d.* found CLXXXII., an urn of the finer pottery with lid, with a hole in the top and rough pattern scratched round it, full of clear water.

13th January 1872. West of Dunsandle tea plantation, near Sholūr. The circle formed by a low heap of rubble stones, irregular in height and breadth. Outer diameter, 26 ft. 5 ins.; inner, 21 ft. 2 ins. Two small slabs almost due N. and S. *a.*, 2 ft. long; 10 ins. broad; 7 ins. thick. *b.*, 2 ft. long; 1 ft. broad; 9 ins. thick.

Between the slabs, about two feet down, found a razor, CLXXXVI., and sickle, CLXXXVII.; also some bits of thin bronze, and fragments of pottery of no value or interest.

12th January 1872. Well-built cairn near Sholūr, made of small stones, presenting a smooth surface internally. External diameter, 21 ft.; internal, 9 ft. 9 ins. One slab nearly due N. Long, 2 ft.; broad, 7 ins.; thick, 1 ft.

Under the slab, about three feet down, found sickle, CLXXXVIII., and fragment of iron, CLXXXIX.; also some pottery of both kinds, but both coarse of their kind, curiously marked with wavy ridges, some with dark red colour, and trace of glaze (CXC.).

17th and 18th January 1872. Cairn on Kupasingal Hill, W. of Sholūr. A circle of single stones of most irregular size, placed edgewise in the ground.

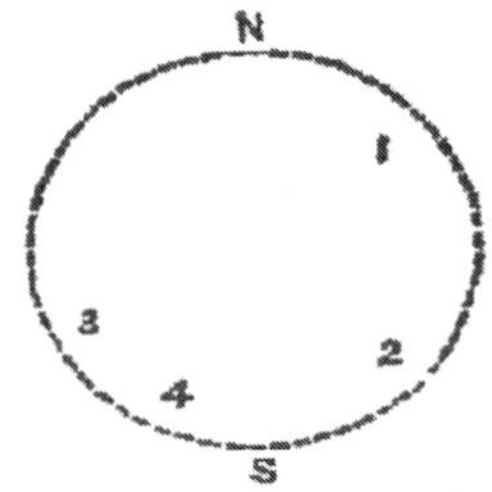

N. to S., 12 ft.

At 1, we found an earthen vessel, CXCIX., a rather coarse pot, shaped exactly like a modern chatty, full of pieces of charred bone.

At 2, 3, and 4, were found fragments of pottery and bones, amongst which were the articles CC., a small pot containing a cylindrical bead of white stone with three lines of black ornament, and some semi-transparent beads,* one or two of which seem to have been fuzed together. Fragments of pottery, CCI., and CCII., broken figures roughly made, were lying on the surface.

18th January 1872. Cairn N. of Tārnāt Mand, drawwell kind; internal face smooth, with large foundation stones.

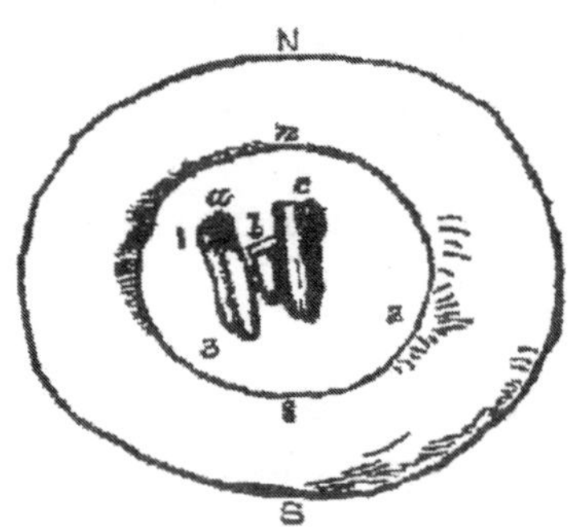

N. to S., 21 ft. n. to s., 6 ft.

Three slabs pointing N.N.W.:—(*a.*) 2 ft. 9 ins. long; 8 ins. broad; 10 ins. thick.
(*b.*) 1 ft. 8 ins. long; 10 ins. broad; 6 ins. thick.
(*c*) 2 ft. 9 ins. long; 1 ft. 4 ins. broad; 9 ins. thick.

About a foot underground, found at 1, pot, CCIII., small, straight sided, of a new shape, containing earth.

At 3, a small pot shaped like a common chatty, CCIV.

At 2, a broken iron bell, CCV., two spear-heads, CCVI., a broken iron pin or style, CCVII., and a fragment of iron, CCVIII. The cairn had been previously

* Pronounced by Dr. Oldham to be "rough blocks of vesicular porous glass, partially worked into beads but abandoned before finishing."

disturbed. Fragments of animals, very clumsy and coarse, CCIX., were found on the surface.

18th January 1872. Cairn ¼ mile N. of the last, drawwell kind.

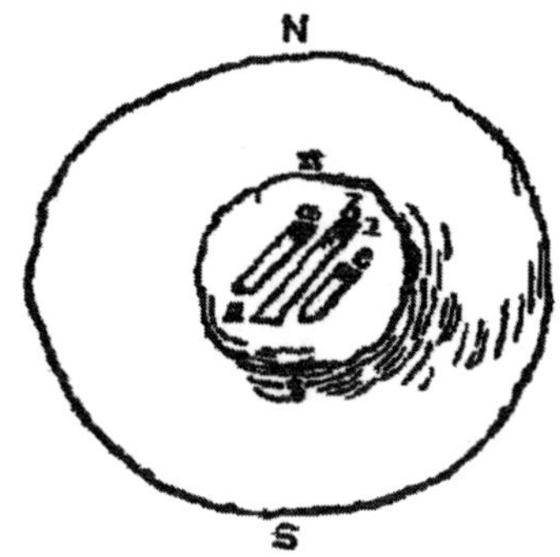

N. to S., 20 ft. n. to s, 6 ft. 6 ins.

Three slabs pointing N.E :—(a.) 8 ft. 8 ins long; 1 ft. 1 in. broad; 5 ins. thick.
(b.) 5 ft. 2 ins. long; 1 ft. 3 ins. broad; 9 ins. thick.
(c.) 3 ft 8 ins. long; 1 ft. 6 ins. broad; 1 ft. 3 ins. thick.

At 1, about a foot below the surface, found a broken bell and chain, CCXII., fragments of razor and sickle, CCXIII., an iron rod or spear handle, CCXIV. Nothing was found under the slabs, which were removed and the earth dug out to four feet and a half deep. On the surface were found fragments of coarse pottery; animals very clumsily shaped.

18th January 1872. Cairn close to the above; an irregular rubble heap.

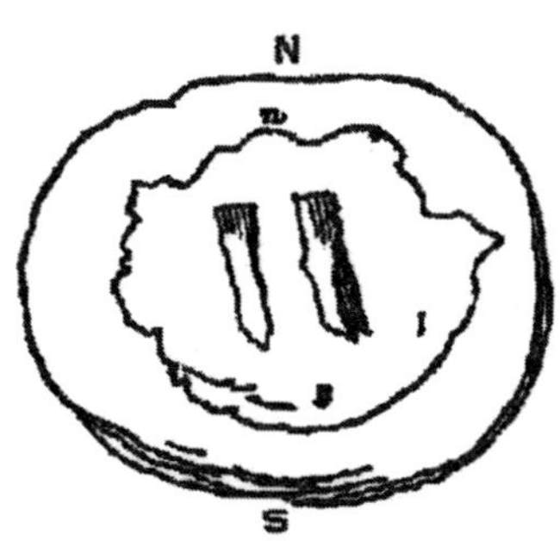

N. to S., 18 ft. n. to s., 12 ft.

Two slabs, N.W..—(a.) 4 ft. long, 10 ins. broad; 10 ins. thick.
(b.) 4 ft. long, 1 ft. 1 in. broad; 1 ft. thick.

At 1, found an earthen pot, much broken, containing earth and bone, and a white substance, CCXIX. (pronounced by Mr. Broughton to be a sort of resin); close beside the pot were a razor, CCXX., a spear-head, CCXXI., and a hone of agate, CCXXII., polished on the inner side as though by use.

The cairn had been previously disturbed. We dug it out to a depth of about five feet.

19th January 1872. Cairn surrounded by six single slabs, placed edgewise, on a hill between Tārnāt Mand and Shōlūr.

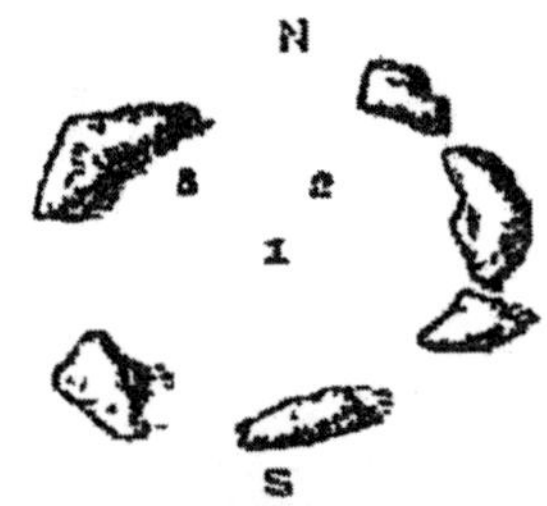

N. to S., 6 ft.

No slab.

At 1, found a large pot, common chatty shape, and rather coarse pottery, CCXXX., containing burnt bones, and a small pot in which were two small pieces of a skull which had also been burnt.* At 2 and 3, other pots were found broken to pieces, and among the débris a number of beads, CCXXXII., mostly of the same rough glass; some of opaque white stone,† and two button-shaped with black marks on them.‡

20th January 1872. Small cairn near Torigōdu Mand, W. of Sholūr. Surrounded by irregular slabs set on end. Diameter 10 ft. One slab, pointing nearly N., 2 ft. 7 ins. long; 1 ft. 1 in. broad; 10 ins. thick.

Underneath the slab was found a pot, CCXXXIV., rough and common, shaped like a modern chatty, full of bones, and containing a small oblong piece of white stone or bone, CCXXXV., and a number of beads, some of the same kinds as CCXXXII., others, nearly three inches long, of agate.§

Along the S.E. side of the cairn were found three small pots, CCXXXVII. to CCXXXIX., rough and coarse, two chatty shaped, and one like a basin.

24th January 1872. Cairn on Konabetta Hill, N. of Kodanâd ūru. Outer diameter 28 ft. 6 in.; inner, 8 ft. 6 in. Cairn previously disturbed. Near the W. wall, two feet underground, found a large pot, chatty shaped, of rough pottery, CCXL., containing a quantity of large bones, and a jaw, and a spear-head, CCXLI. Other broken fragments of pots were found on the western side.

---

* These and other pieces of bone from different cairns were submitted to Mr. Broughton, who reported that they contained only from 3 to 7 °/₀ of organic matter, instead of 35 °/₀ as in ordinary human or animal bones, and added "the conclusion is inevitable that the bones have been burnt."

"The high part of the skull-bone has a sacred character among Buddhist relics. These relics are supposed " to be imperishable and indestructible. They are found among the refuse of ashes after the cremation of any " great saint."—*Travels of Fa-Hian*, p. 41.

† Dr. Oldham says these are "rudely formed bugles of ribboned agate of poor colour. They have been im- " perfectly ground down into a double hexagonal pyramid, each of six faces, very imperfect both as to form and " finish."

‡ These, Dr. Oldham says, are the only specimens which show "even an approach to any advance in art. " The black lines are incised and filled in with black or dark green glass. The material of the disc is white agate- " The finish is not good, but the incising and inlaying with other material shows an advance beyond the " ordinary grinding and polishing of a bead."

§ "Tolerably finished, and shows a nearly true spherically concholdal form, with well polished surface."— (*Dr. Oldham.*)

24th January 1872. Cairn on Konabetta Hill, 10 yards to the E. of above. No slab. Cairn previously disturbed. Long slabs on end lined the inner surface. At 1, was a round stone, 2 feet long, sticking up; half above ground and half below. At 2, a bronze (*Plate* XLI., *fig. f.*) much rusted and broken.

Found also a pair of iron shears, CCXLIII. (*Plate* XLIII.), exactly like modern garden shears but much rusted, a long straight iron tool, CCXLIV., chisel, perhaps, and a bent iron rod, CCXLV.

Over the surface, and down to a foot below, were broken lids, with figures CCXLVI. to CCLI. Amongst them, three figures of men sitting on native stools, (*Plate* XXXVI., *fig. d*,) and a man holding a shield.

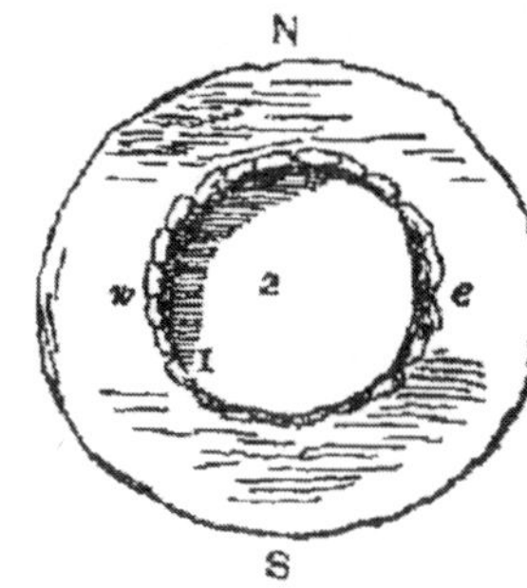

N. to S. 25 ft.; e. to w. 12 ft.

26 January 1872. Cairn S. of Bilikal Hill. Oval. N. to S. 24 ft.; W. to E. 14 ft. Surrounded by irregular slabs on end, sometimes 3 or 4 deep, with rubble at the base outside. About three feet down, at 1, was a pot of the fine micaceous clay, CCLIX., containing bones and bronze, CCLX., with cone-shaped boss at the bottom (*see Plate* XLI., *figs. g, g, g.*) inverted. Under the bronze were two rings, CCLXI., one like a modern gold wedding ring, the other of bronze; and by the side of the bronze, inside the pot, was a piece of pumice, carefully shaped into the segment of a circle, and some iron fragments, CCLXIII.

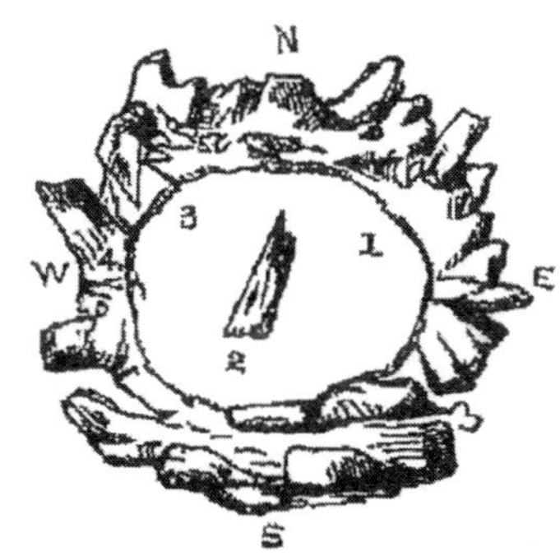

One slab, pointing N., 8 ft. 11 in. long; 1 ft. 6. in. broad, 11 in. thick.

At 2, another fine pot, like XCII. (*see Plate* XL., *fig. m.*), containing bones and earth; bronze, CCLXV., like CCLX., a piece of pumice, CCLXVI., a small bronze cylinder, CCLXVII., and a razor, CCLXIX.

At 3, was a pot broken to pieces.

26th January 1872. Small cairn of the same construction as the last, and about 50 yards N. from it. N. to S. 9 ft.; W. to E. 6 ft. No slab.

About three feet down, rather S. of the middle of the cairn, were 5 small chatties, all in a row from W. to E., of common shape and indifferent pottery, containing only earth and bone.

27th January 1872. Cairn on the S. shoulder of Bilikal Hill. N. to S. 7 ft. 8 in.; E. to W. 9 ft. Surrounded by slabs on end, with rubble at their base. One slab, pointing N.E., 4 ft. 5 in. long; 1 ft. 5 in. broad; 1 ft. 2 in. thick.

Under the slab, about a foot down, found a bronze rusted and broken: directly under it were fragments of the finer earthenware. A little to the left, another small bronze, also broken, and more fragments of earthenware in the same position, also bones, pieces of iron, and bronze, and a bronze ring, CCLXXIII. Alongside these bronzes, but evidently outside the pots which had enclosed them, were fragments of iron razor and other implements, CCLXXIV. A little S.E. of the slab was found a pot, CCLXXV., modern chatty shape, containing, CCLXXVI., bones and earth, a ring, two gold beads, and a small button-shaped piece of gold, two round stone beads,* two gold earrings, one plain and one ringed transversely, a number of small fragments of bronze, looking like pin or nail heads, and bits of an iron collyrium rod.†

27th January 1872. Two cairns near the top of Bilikal Hill; close together; in one, of the drawwell kind, nothing was found. The second was formed of slabs set edgewise like the preceding ones.

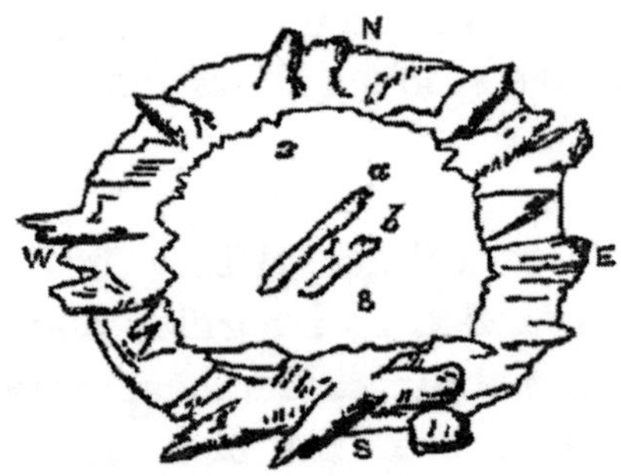

Diameter 13 ft. 2 slabs pointing N.E.
(*a*) 3 ft. 6 in. long; 1 ft. broad; 6 in. thick.
(*b*) 2 ft. 6 in. long; 9 in. broad; 3 in. thick.

At 1, two and a half feet down, found a pot and lid, broken, containing a bronze, CCLXXVIII., with cone-shaped boss like CCLX., containing remnants of cloth, apparently coarse cotton; marks of the same texture are visible on the rust inside. In the bronze were found, CCLXXIX., two collyrium rods, one bronze (*Plate* XLIII., *fig.* 279), one iron; fragments of iron, a gold earring, and a metal or bone cap or ferule (probably), the handle or rod it surmounted having perished. Round the pot outside lay a large sickle, CCLXXX.

At 2, found an earthen vessel, with cover, CCLXXXI. (*Plate* XL., *fig. c.*), containing bones and earth, a bronze, CCLXXXII. (*Plate* XLI., *fig. h.*), small, thick, and rough, without ornament; a bronze or copper ring, and two thin gold earrings, CCLXXXIII., and pumice, CCLXXXIV.

At 3, a large fine pot, like XCII., with cover, containing bones and earth, two pieces of pumice, CCLXXXVIII., a spear-head, CCLXXXIX., a broken razor, CCXC., and a bronze, CCLXXXVI., saucer-shaped, covered with dark green polished rust, in which were a small gold ornament like a *tāli*, a signet ring of bronze? and two fragments of an iron collyrium rod.

---

* Very rude bead of white agate (Dr. Oldham).

† This implement is of frequent occurrence both in bronze and iron (*Plate* XLIII., *fig.* 279). Sir W. Elliot describes apparently a similar article (*Journ. Prehistoric Archæology*) and calls it a collyrium rod, and his authority has been followed. A similar implement, but rather sharper at the ends, is figured by Prinsep, and said to be used for applying soorma to the eyes.

28th February 1872. Enkal Mand hill, W. of Croormand road, near Yenikal Mand. Large cairn, drawwell kind, filled with trees and bushes.

About a foot below the surface were found eleven pots, as marked by figures, of the common rough pottery, and pointed at the bottom, but with unusually wide mouths. (*Plate* XXXIX., *figs. a. a. b*, CCXCI. to CCCI.) Broken pieces of lids, and of figures of very rough shapes, were found on the surface.

Fragments of the finer pottery were found on each side of the slabs.

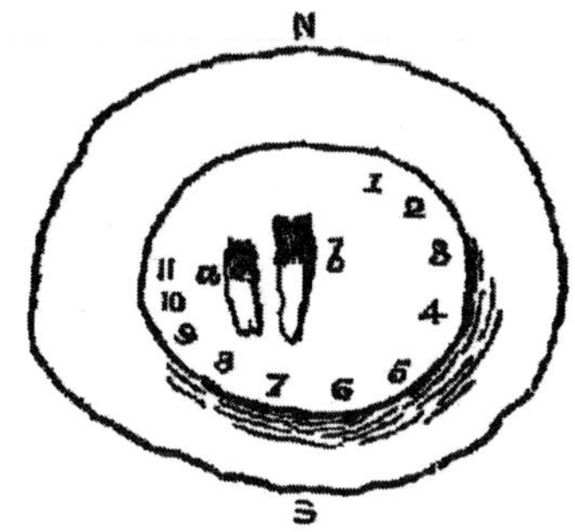

a. 4 ft 6 in long, 1 ft. 6 in broad, 3 in. thick.

b. 6 ft 6 in. long; 1 ft. 3 in. broad, 6 in. thick.

April 24th, 1872. Nidugula, Peranganâd. Cairn of rubble, on a foundation of large stones.

Three slabs pointing N.E.

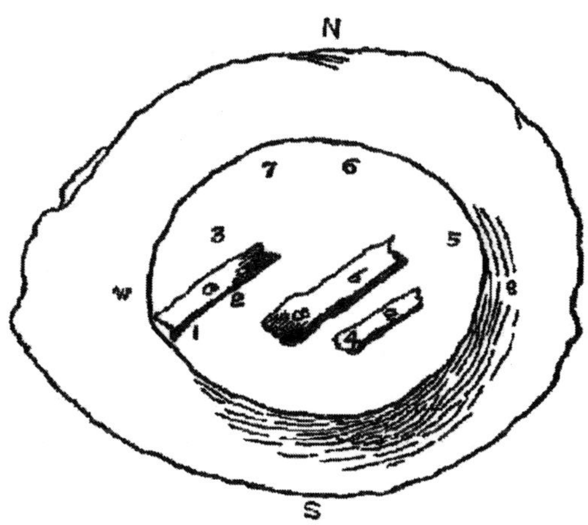

N. to S. 26 ft. *e.* to *w* 10 ft. 11 in.

(*a*) 2 ft. 8 in. long; 1 ft. 3 in broad, 3 in. thick.
(*b*) 3 ft. 9 in. long, 1 ft. 2 in. broad; 5 in thick.
(*c*) 3 ft 8 in. long; 11 in broad; 10 in. thick *

* This was lying on a slope against the wall, and seemed to have been moved out of place.

At 1, found a small pot with lid, CCCXXI., of fine pottery, and a bronze, CCCXXII., inverted over the mouth of the pot, about one and a half feet below the surface. Against the side of the pot lay a razor, knife, spear-head, and fragments of iron, CCCXXIII. to CCCXXVI.

The pot contained pumice, *iron collyrium rod*, CCCXXIX., and some *fragments of a* horn or bone utensil.

At 2, about the same depth, was a large pot, broken, containing earth, and two spear-heads, CCCXXVII.

At 3, what appeared to be a lid, containing earth, and some pieces of iron, CCCXXXV.

At 4, under (*a.*) a large knife, CCCXXXII., and spear-head, CCCXXXIII.

At 5, two feet down, a spear-head, CCCXXXIV.

At 6, two razors, CCCXXXV., and a spear-head, CCCXXXVI.

At 7, a knife, spear-head, chisel, and pin or style, CCCXXXVII. to CCCXL.

At 8, under (*b.*) were two pots, one, CCCXLI., like a lid or dish, with concentric lines outside; the other, CCCXLII., small, with a lid, both of the fine pottery, with mica specks, and containing earth and small pieces of bone. On the surface were some fragments of animals, small and rough, CCCXLIII.

May 9th, 1872. Cairn of rubble stones. Kōdanâd Peranganâd.

Three slabs, pointing N.

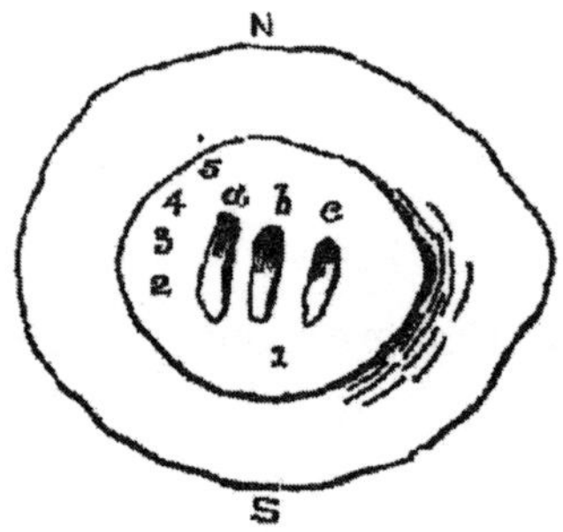

(*a.*) 3 ft. 4 in. long; 1 ft. 4 in. broad; 6 in. thick.
(*b.*) 2 ft. 8 in. long; 1 ft. 2 in. broad; 6 in. thick.
(*c.*) 2 ft. 11 in. long; 1 ft. broad, 9 in. thick.

At 1, two feet down, were fragments of a fine pot, with mica specks, containing pieces of what Mr. Broughton pronounces to be dried orange peel, or the rind of some fruit of the same family. A cylindrical stone like a roller was stuck in the ground over the pot.

At 2, two feet down, was found what appears to be a lid, CCCCVII., inverted, nothing under it.

At 3, two feet down, a small roughly-made pot, broken to pieces in getting out, nothing inside.

At 4, at the same depth, a beautifully made vessel of fine pottery, CCCCVIII., with mica specks, and a trace of glaze,* large lid, having a triangular ornament on the top; fits to the rim of the pot instead of covering it and resting on the sides as is usual; contained a knife, showing marks of a wooden handle, CCCCIX.

At 5, at the same depth, was found a pot, shaped like the ordinary rough pots found on the surface of cairns, and with the figure of a bird on the lid, but beautifully made of very fine pottery,† and containing bone, resin,‡ small gold nose jewel of very neat manufacture, CCCCXII., and razor, CCCCXI.

Close beside this was a basin-shaped bronze, graceful in shape, and prettily ornamented.

* Dr. Hunter (Madras School of Arts) says, that this appearance is not produced by glaze, but by a thin "coating of mica or abracum, ground up into a creamy state with water, and applied uniformly with a wet rag."

† This is unique, the only pot of the high narrow kind with figured lid ever known to contain bones, or to be made of the fine micaceous clay.

‡ A curious white and whitish-yellow substance, pronounced by Mr. Broughton to be "resin, much altered by time." He adds, "It is difficult to identify a special resin so altered by time, but it appears to me to have been the resin of Vateria Indica. It has a pleasant smell when burnt, and may have been used as incense."

10th May 1872. Cairn, smooth inside, rubble outside; outer diameter, 18 feet; inner, 9 feet.

Near the centre, one and a half feet down, found bronze, CCCLXXV., saucer-shaped, irregularly ornamented round the rim by perpendicular lines, in a pot, broken, containing bones, and earth, and bits of an iron rod, CCCLXXIV.

A little N. of this was a small pot, chatty shaped, nearly the roughest of the cinerary urns, containing a small shallow rough pot, CCCLXXIII., inverted over bones, earth, and charcoal.

10th May 1872. Cairn of single stones, diameter, 6 feet; no slabs.

Near the E. side, one and a half feet down, was a chatty-shaped pot, pottery rough, containing earth and bone; N.W. of this, a small pot, broken to pieces, containing nothing but earth.

BARROWS.

Barrow on Gulicholabetta. *See* plan *ante*, with cairn, opened August 25th.

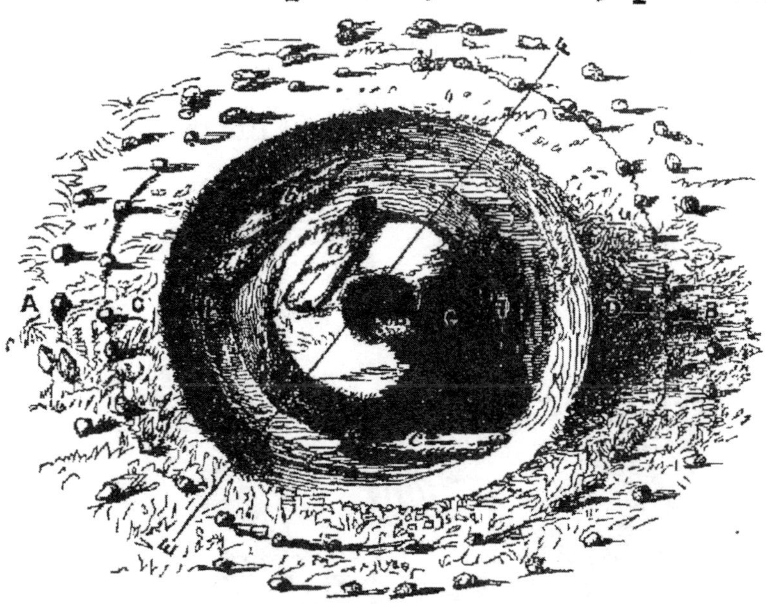

A. to B, 39 ft.; C to D, 20 ft.

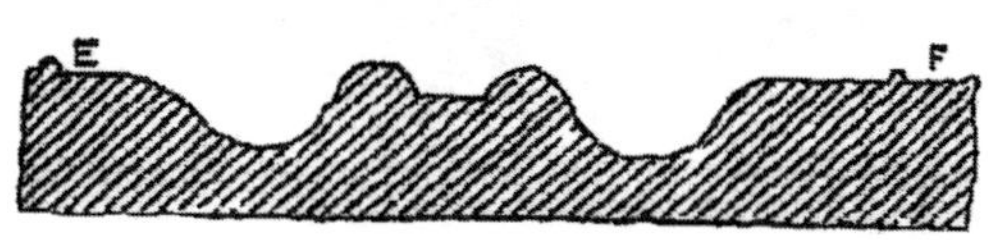

Section through E F.

Section through A B.

a. 5 ft. long; 1 ft. 6 in. broad.
b. 5 ft. long; 1 ft. 5 in. broad.
c. 3 ft. × 1½, and thin like a slab.
d. 3½ × 2, and rather thin.

There was a double row of small stones all round, partly buried and uneven, but quite distinguishable by the most casual observer. Mr. Metz had in former times begun to open the barrow, and had dug away a portion of the central mound at G to the level of the bottom of the central pit, that is, about two feet. He also thinks that he removed stones (*a.*) and (*b.*) out of position; believes they had one end partially in the central pit, as though they had formerly stood upright in the middle.

I found four stones in the position shown in the sketch :—

c. and *d.* were in the ditch, their tops level with the ground. We removed (*a.*), and beginning at H, dug a trench completely across the barrow six feet deep from the top of the mound. We found no sign of anything in the central mound. Below the central pit we came upon virgin soil, compact decomposed granite, but in the ditch at H and K we found bits of pots and figures, so we dug a trench right round, three feet broad and two and a half deep. At about this depth we found pots with figured lids in great numbers; brought away, LXII. to LXXXIV., fragments of men and animals of all sorts, a few complete.

LXII. and LXIII., buffaloes, one with a bell; LXXVII., a bear (*Plate* XXXVIII., *fig. g.*)

15th and 16th September 1871. Barrow near Bilikambe Peranganâd. No circle of stones round it.

A to B, 63 ft. outside of ditch. C to D, 45 ft. inside.

Slab *a*, 5 × 1, 2 × 1.
b, 6 × 1, 1 × 1, 7.

Dug up the ditch for four or five yards long and about three feet deep, at C. and D., but found nothing.

The centre at (*d.*) had been previously opened to the depth of about a foot, and the two stones (*a.*) and (*b.*) rolled out of place.

We dug the whole of the mound one foot deep in some places and three feet in others.

At 1, was a flat stone about a foot in diameter. On taking this up we found the lid of a pot immediately below it ornamented with a vandyked pattern (unfortunately broken). This covered a large urn, xcii., of very fine pottery, and well made (*Plate* xl., *fig. m.*), in which was a bronze, xciii., with a cone-shaped boss in the centre (*see Plate* xli., *figs. g g g*), containing burnt bones and earth, xciv.; crystal, xcv.; pieces of a comb of bone or horn, xcvi. (which have since crumbled away); and some gold beads, xcvii.

Close to this, at 2, was a smaller vessel of fine pottery, xcviii., also enclosing a bronze, xcix., small, neatly made, ornamented with small irregular chasing, which contained earth and bones and an iron collyrium rod, two large oblong cornelian beads, with white lines on them, some small green glass beads, and a small piece of gold, c. to civ.

At 3, we found pieces of two or three broken pots of the finer pottery, with lids of an unusual shape, cv.

At 4, a round stone with a hole through it, cvi. (it is difficult to say what its object may have been).

At 5, eleven feet from the centre of the barrow, was a plain saucer-shaped bronze, cvii., inverted, about half a foot from the surface.

At 6, found another small pot and lid of fine clay, cviii., full of earth, with a spear-head leaning against the rim (*Plate* xl., *fig. o.*).

At 7, was the broken figure of a man with a curiously long narrow head, cix.; and at 8, among the earth, dug out a fragment of bronze, cx.

23rd October 1871. A barrow about two miles N. of Mr. Metz's bungalow at Tūnēri, near a deserted village called Neddilu.

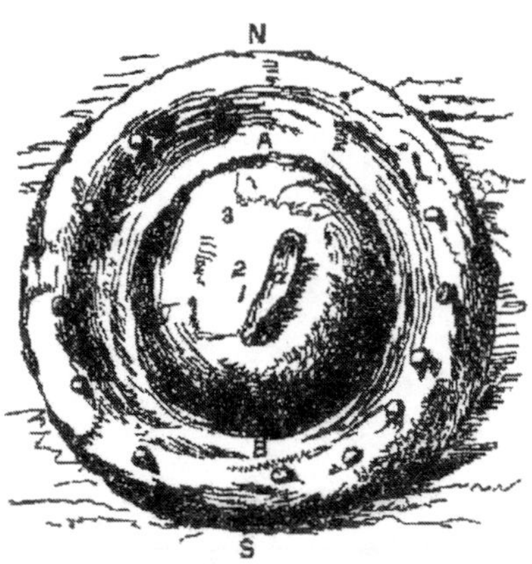

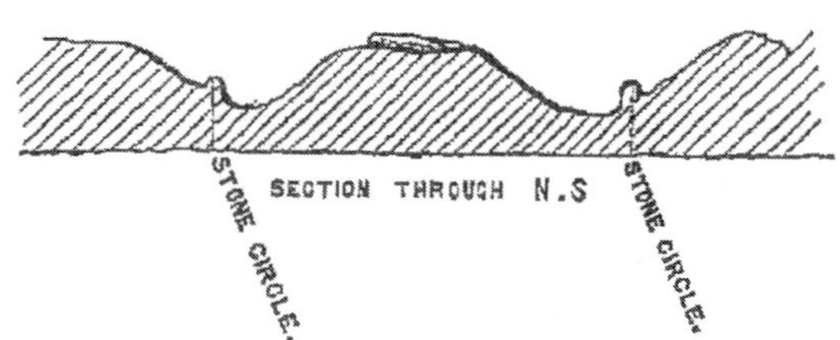

N. to S 40 ft.; A to B, 20 ft. Slab (*a.*) 5 ft. × 2 × 1.

An imperfect circle of stones was perceptible on the outer slope of the ditch.

At 1, about two feet below the surface, we found five spear-heads, cxiv.

At 2, a dagger with the common native double guard, and a handsome hilt elaborately worked in "copper with a slight admixture of tin," cxii. (*Plate* xliii., *fig.* 112): a short broad chisel, cxiii., of bronze, well-shaped and neatly ornamented with raised lines (*Plate* xliii., *fig.* 113); and two iron hollow pointed octagonal implements,

CXI. and CXV., iron pins or styles (*Plate* XLIII., *figs.* 111 and 192). Pieces of charcoal adhered to them, and they seemed to have been burned.

At 3, was a large deposit of black earth, charcoal, and bones, three or three and a half feet deep, as if bodies had been burned on the spot for many years, and the débris raked into a pit.

3rd November 1871. Barrow near Kambhatti Todanâd. No circle of stones.

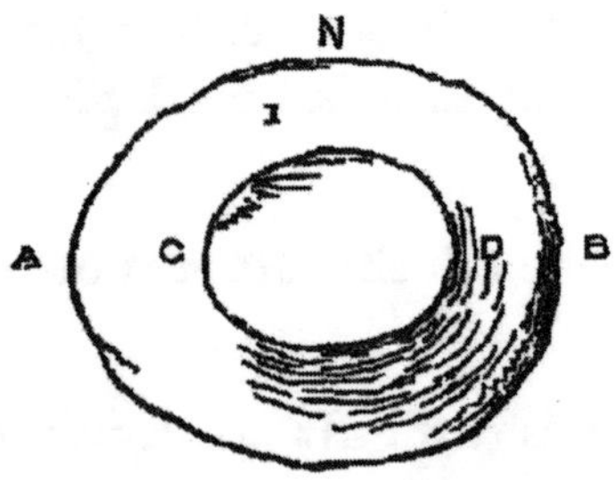

A to B, 24 feet; C to D, 8 feet.

Dug all over the mound to the depth of five feet, but found nothing. We then dug the ditch out to the depth of four feet, and found a number of pots with figures on the lids, unusually perfect.

CXXXVII.—*Plate* XXXVI., *fig. n*, large curious pointed pillar, with knob on one side.

CXXXVIII.—Woman with chatty on her head. *Plate* XXXVI., *fig. o.*

CXXXIX.—*Plate* XXXVI., *fig. c.*

CXL.—*Plate* XXXVI., *fig. f.* Man riding with double-guarded dagger in his belt and double-guarded battle-axe in his hand.

CXLI.—Dog. *Plate* XXXVII., *fig. d.*

CXLII.—Snake. *Plate* XXXVI., *fig. c.*

CXLIV.—Tree. *Plate* XXXVII., *fig. h.*

CXLV.—Buffalo with bell. *Plate* XXXVII., *fig. g.*

CXLVI.—Man with stick. *Plate* XXXVIII., *fig. k.*

CXLVII.—Woman with baby. *Plate* XXXVII., *fig. b.*

CXLVIII.—Man with baby.

CXLIX. and CL.—Buffaloes.

CLI.—Large bird. *Plate* XXXVIII., *fig. e.*

CLIII.—Man making salaam. *Plate* XXXVII., *fig e.*; and other figures (up to CLVII.). Several of the pots contained bits of charcoal.

At 1, about four feet down, was a large rough round stone, about the size of a stable bucket, and under this a quantity of bone and charcoal.

13th January 1872. Barrow on Kovilbetta, W. of Sholûr, surrounded by two rows of stones, the ditch and mound scarcely perceptible. N. to S. 27 ft. 6 in. No slabs. About the middle, at a depth of two feet, was a large straight-sided urn, CXCVIII., of unusual shape, containing fine black earth; no bones to be seen.

19th January 1872. Barrow on Hillava-künde hill, W. of Sholūr. N. to S. 19 ft.; no circle of stones.

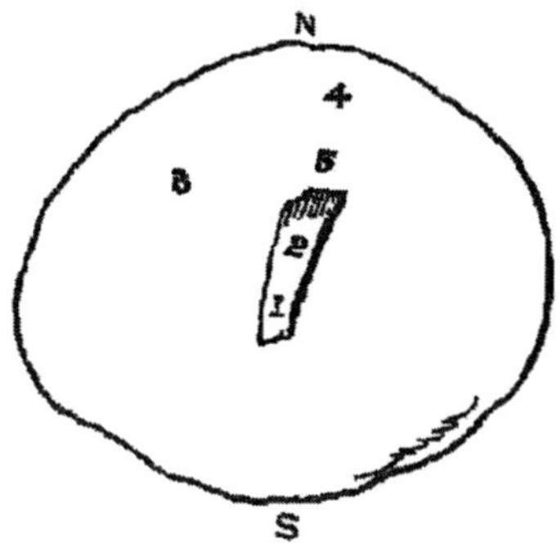

One slab, 3 ft. 4 in. × 0 ft. 11 in. × 1 ft. 3 in. pointing N.

About a foot deep under the slab, at 1, found razor and sickle, CCXXIII.

At 2, a deposit of bone and charcoal, and a small neatly-made spear or javelin head, CCXXIV.

At 3, fragments of a bronze vessel, CCXXV.

At 4, two spear-heads, CCXXVI., one small and well made.

At 5, a broad handsome dagger, CCXXVII. (*Plate* XLIII., *fig.* 227), and broken spear-heads, CCXXVII.

On the surface were fragments of figures, CCXXIX., of no particular interest.

20th January 1872. Barrow near Torigōdu mand, W. of Sholūr. N. to S. 20 ft. No circle of stones. One slab, 2 ft. 11 in. × 1 ft. 3 in. × 0 ft. 10 in. pointing N.

Found only one spear-head, CCXXXIII., one and a half feet deep under the slab.

25th January 1872. Barrow on range of hills E. of Sholūr.

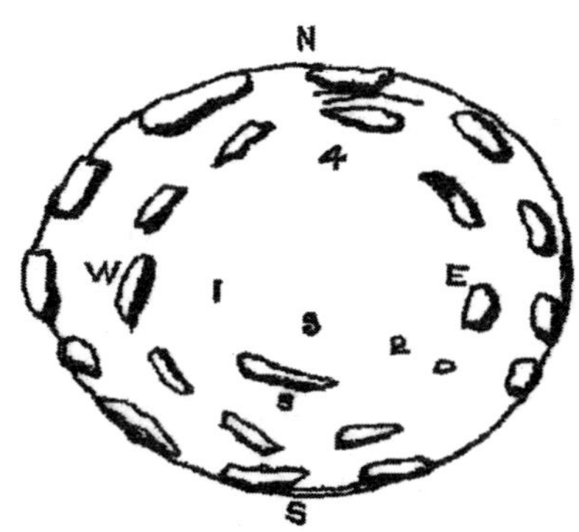

N. to S. 19 ft. E. to W. 18 ft. 9 ins

At 1, about two feet down, found a shallow pot with lid, CCLV., containing bones and a small plain basin-shaped bronze, CCLVI.

At 2, another pot, CCLVII., containing bones and earth, and bronze collyrium rod?

Other vessels were found at 3 and 4, broken to pieces, and containing only earth and bones.

At 5, a great slab 6 ft. × 4 ft. × 0·6 was standing on end, two feet under ground, and four above.

25th April 1872. Barrow, the largest of three on Ponguibetta hill, not far from Kakora Peranganâd (near the road from Kotagherry to Kodanâd).

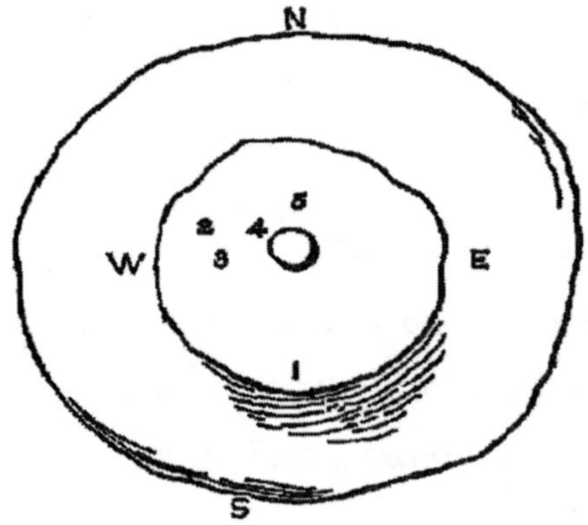

N. to S. 50 ft. W. to E. 25 ft

No circle of stones. An opening had been made in the middle about two feet deep.

Dug out the ditch about three feet, finding only two or three bits of broken pottery; then dug down the central mound.

At 1, found a spear-head, CCCXLIV., in the middle of a deposit of bone and charcoal about a foot from the surface.

At 2, one and a half feet deep, found a pot with earth and bone; broken in getting out.

At 3, pot, CCCXLV., fine pottery, mica glaze, containing bronze, CCCXLVI., saucer-shaped, covered with bright green rust, inverted, and bronze collyrium rod, CCCXLVII., bones and earth.

At 4, a pot of rougher pottery, with longer neck than most of the urns; with lid inverted on the mouth, in shape more like the lids of the deep rough pots, and with marks as if there had once been a figure on the top, CCXLVIII. This was not filled with earth like the others, but contained a small quantity of bones and earth, fragments of iron, a small oblong cornelian bead, CCCL., and a beautiful little bronze bottle, shaped like the bud of a flower, CCCXLIX.

At 5, a large fine pot, with a curious triangular ornament on the lid, with mica glaze, containing a basin-shaped bronze, CCCLIII., iron knife, spears, &c., CCCLIV. to CCCLVII., including a razor, with marks of cloth on it; an iron cap or ferule with traces of the wooden handle which it once contained, CCCLVIII., bones, resin, pieces of a curious dried substance, pronounced by Mr. Broughton to be orange peel, a small piece of metal for the nose, bits of wood, a bronze buckle ring, and minute fragments of silk, rapidly crumbling, but showing the silky texture very plainly, CCCLIX.

25th April 1872. Small barrow, W. of the last.
No circle of stones.
Ditch shallow and rise small.

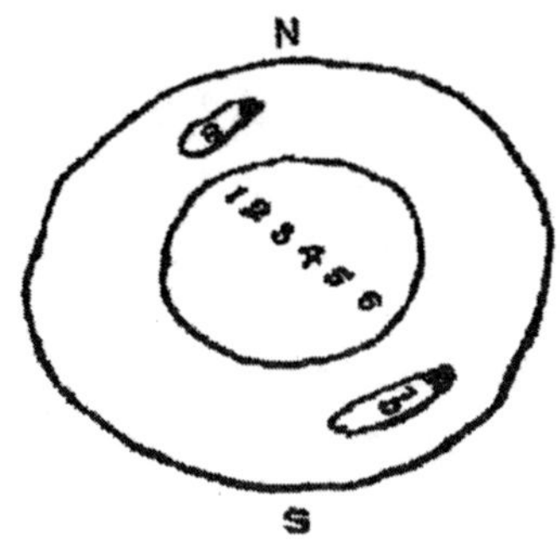

N. to S 21 ft.

Two small slabs, *a* and *b*, in the ditch.

Found six small pots in a row, pointing rather W. of N., a foot below the surface. They were of the ordinary urn shape, with large lid and fairly good pottery.

All contained bones and earth, and one, CCCLX., a spear-head, CCCLXI. Only CCCLX. and CCCLXII. were got out whole.

Nothing was found in the ditch.

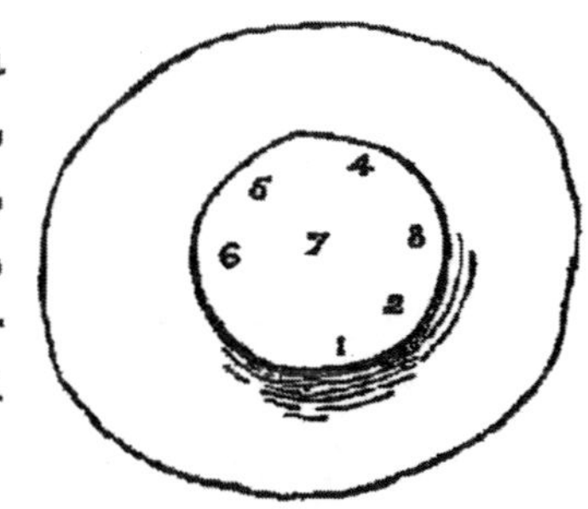

A few yards N. of this was a similar one without slabs, in which, half a foot deep, were found six small pots like CCCLX., CCCLXIII., &c., containing bones and earth, and a smaller one, at 7, two feet deep, containing only earth. One of them, CCCLXVII., had a lip in the rim, as for pouring. Two contained iron implements, one, CCCLXV., being a hollow cylinder, about ¾-inch in diameter, with a flat top.

The above extracts show that the general features of the cairns and barrows vary little. Above and between the slabs, which in a great majority of cases lie N.E. and S.W. exactly as if they had been placed by compass, and round the circle near the surface, lie the rough pots figured in *Plates* XXXVI. to XXXVIII., large deep narrow vessels, pointed at the bottom, so that they cannot stand upright, with rough figures of men and animals on the lid, and empty, or containing only earth, as far as their almost invariably broken state allows us to judge. The number of these is surprising. Baskets full of heads, horns, and tails of buffaloes and other figures may be carried away from some cairns; but in most cases they lie so near the surface penetrated by the roots of trees and bushes that nothing but fragments can be recovered. Below, at depths varying from one to four feet, are the cinerary urns, superior in quality and make.

There does not seem to be any rule as to the arrangement of the actual interments. Sometimes the bones are at the bottom of the urn, sometimes in a bronze vase contained in it, sometimes under the inverted bronze. Often the bronze is not in or near the urn. Some of the urns do not contain bones, but only implements and ornaments, and some only earth. Sometimes the number of interments corresponds with that of the slabs; but this does not occur often enough to prove design.

Most of the urns are filled with earth, several specimens of which were analyzed by Mr. Broughton, who reported that they differed from ordinary soils only by containing oxide of copper. He added: "They were tested for tin, but none was found. It sub-"sequently occurred to me that if the copper should arise from the exposure of bronze "or bell-metal ornaments to heat, the tin might be oxydized to stannic acid, a substance "which is quite insoluble in acids, and which would thus escape detection. In order to "discover this, I fused each specimen of finely powdered soil with potassic hydrate, "in order to bring all constituents into solution. On testing these carefully tin "was in all cases detected. This constituent is of importance, as it shows that bronze "has been heated strongly, continuously, and in contact with air, exactly as ornaments "on a corpse would be heated, otherwise stannic acid could not have been formed."

Mr. Broughton kindly analyzed some bronze from two broken vases found in different cairns, and reports.—

"Its constitution was as follows:

Tin - - -	29·89 per cent.
Copper - - -	70·11 ,,

"The old fragments have a large amount of tin, and approach nearly to speculum "metal.

He adds: "In 1868, I bought in Calicut bazaar some 'brass basins' which like all "such native ware consists really of bronze.

"Its composition is as follows:

Tin - - -	22·87
Copper - - -	77·13

"and a trace of lead, accidental of course.

"I find that Klaproth who analyzed some tom-toms, possibly of Hindu origin, "found 22°/ₒ tin therein."

These Indian bronzes show a considerable excess of tin, as compared with those found in European sepulchral tumuli. Worsaae* gives 10°/ₒ of tin as the average of the latter. An analysis of many English specimens gave 12°/ₒ.†

There are slight, but perceptible, differences which divide the Nīlagiri cairns into three groups. The typical cairn, so to speak, the richest in contents and most regular in arrangement, is found in the central division, the head-quarters of which are about Tunēri. Here the cinerary urns are invariably of the shapes shown in *Plate* XL., *figs. e, o, j, f,* the lids large, plain, and covering loosely the whole top of the urn. The figures on the lids of the deep pots are fairly well-made, of moderate size, and bright red pottery. A line drawn along the Segūr road would form an approximate boundary, west of which the pottery changes character. The figures here are enormously large and heavy, though in many instances hollow, the shapes clumsy and unnatural, and the colour dark and dull. Most of them are in too fragmentary a state for illustration,

* *Primeval Antiquities.*

† *Archæologia,* 19., p. 48. Mr. Broughton says, "In reading Jacobson's 'Chemischtechnisches Reper-"'torium,' (dealing with 1871,) I find that M. Riche in Paris has discovered a malleable bronze, the secret of "which is that it should have the composition 22°/ₒ tin, 78°/ₒ copper. You will see that the discovery "has been anticipated in India. The modern Indian bronze is of course malleable."

Plate XXXVIII., *fig. f*, is a specimen. The cinerary urns are also of inferior make, and their shape varies, sometimes approaching that of the modern chatty; the clay hardly ever shows traces of mica, and is in some cases almost as rough as that of the figures: *Plate* XL., *figs. h, k, b, d, n*. Here also the burning has been less complete, large bones sometimes nearly filling the urn:* Here are found most of the beads, of which Dr. Oldham says, "I have never seen a collection of similar articles giving evidence of "a ruder or less advanced state of the art:" and here the slabs, instead of pointing accurately to the N.E., vary to N. and even N.N.W. On the whole, these are decidedly the roughest of the cairns. On the other hand, the actual stone work in this division is among the best. Many of the cairns are large, regularly built, and often faced with large slabs on the inside.

The Peranganâd cairns, lying between Kotagherry and Kodanâd, differ less from those at Tunēri; the figures are generally smaller and rougher, and the colour darker, but the urns are often very fine, with strong glaze of mica. Here, however, there seems for the first time a certain confusion of plan in the pottery: the lids of the urns often fit to the rim, like those of the figured pots, instead of covering it; they are frequently ornamented with some pattern, sometimes with marks as of a figure broken off, and in one case, the deep pot and the figured lid are imitated in the cinerary urn. This example serves to prove that the figures are contemporary with the interment, and not the votive offerings of a later and ruder generation.

Whether these differences are due to a different date of construction, or simply to the varying habits of rude and isolated families, is not easy to decide. It is, however, remarkable that the rougher remains are found in the division in which lie the two (probably) oldest Toda mands, and the only cairns claimed by the Todas.

The resemblances between these remains and those of similar graves in Europe must strike every one. Mr. Jewitt describes the earthen vessels commonly found in the so-called Celtic grave mounds, as consisting of cinerary urns, food-vessels, drinking-cups, and the mis-named "Incense cups, consisting of diminutive vessels rarely found at all; but which, when they occur, are always *inside* the sepulchral urns, placed on, or among the calcined bones, and frequently themselves also filled with burnt bones."† Except that these were of clay (which exceptionally occurs also on the Nīlagiris) this is an exact description of a good many of our bronzes, while the food-vessels may be represented by the figured pots. The practice of placing some vessels in an inverted position is also a remarkable coincidence. This is exceedingly common in English tumuli, only there it is often the cinerary urn that is inverted, whereas on the Nīlagiris it is always the bronze, and just as often in quite a different part of the cairn from the urn, as over the calcined bones.

Even the mica glazing does not seem to be peculiar, judging by the following quotation from Sir Thomas Browne's "Urn Burial," p. 233. "Some of these urns are

* *Comp. Ten Years' Diggings*, p. 56. "I have frequently observed the difference between Celtic deposits from tumuli and Roman incinerated bones to be most strongly marked; the former are almost uniformly cleanly burnt in pieces sufficiently large to be recognised, and consequently far exceed in quantity the latter, which are as constantly reduced to ashes, and are frequently mixed with sand and other impurities from the embers of the pile." This analogy suggests that the differences between the separate groups of cairns are indications of different dates.

† *Grave mounds and their contents.*

thought to have been silvered over, from sparklings in several pots with small tinsel parcels."

These coincidences at least make the question of the origin of the Nīlagiri cairns more interesting. The investigation here has the advantage of being somewhat narrowed in point of time, because, while the fact that the Badagas, who settled on the Nīlagiris about three hundred years ago, know nothing of the history of the cairns, obliges us to consider them at least four or five centuries old; the articles found do not at all suggest a very remote antiquity.

At one time, they were generally assigned to the Todas; and Colonel Congreve wrote an elaborate essay to prove the Scythian origin of this people and their claim to the cairns. His large theories, and occasionally incorrect facts, discredited his cause rather unduly, and of late years the cairns have been generally attributed either to the Kurumbas or to an extinct race. Those who held these views, however, seem to have been unaware of, or to have overlooked, the significant fact that the Todas even now burn their dead in a circle of stones and bury the ashes there. Now, not only may the circle of stones be called the fundamental idea of cairns and barrows, but some of them consist of insignificant circles of stones, hardly to be distinguished from Toda *Āzārams* except by the trees or bushes which indicate their greater age. Moreover, a reference to the barrows described on pages 86 and 87 reveals the practice of using the same circle for repeated cremation, a plain step in the decline from the sepulchral tumulus to the *Āzāram*.*

The following description of four stone circles, which from their position and contents we supposed to be *Āzārams*, will show how difficult it sometimes is to draw a line between the *Āzārams* and the inferior cairns and barrows:—

26th April 1872. Oval, surrounded with single stones, near Nidigûla, like an *Āzāram*.† Four of these circles lie together, even with the ground. There is a Kêd-mane just below the hill.

N. to S. 11 ft. E. to W. 8 ft. 9 ins.

At 1, a large deposit of charcoal and bones, two feet below the surface, and in the midst eleven brass bracelets,† CCCXCIII.

* It would appear that in England it is chiefly the *barrows* which show traces of cremation without urn burial. Among thirty barrows or earthen tumuli described in Mr. Bateman's Ten Years' Diggings, seventeen contained only burnt earth, charcoal, and charred bones, two urns, and three skeletons, the remainder yielding no results. Skeletons and urns are generally in tumuli wholly or partly of stone.

A rude circle of stones 8 yards in diameter, described in p. 170 of this work, and obviously a burning-place, is not unlike an *Āzāram*.

† It is remarkable that the bracelets, found in the *Āzārams*, not only are a new ornament, but introduce a new metal. Mr. Broughton says,—

" A fragment (of bracelet, CCCXCV.,) was qualitatively examined, and found to consist of copper, zinc, and a " small amount of iron. It was thus brass, and not bronze."

No brass, as far as I know, is found in the cairns or barrows; but the massive armlets worn by the modern Todas are of this metal. Mr. Broughton kindly examined one of these for me.

Two others were exactly the same in the position and nature of the deposits and shape of the enclosure, only varying a foot or so in size; the fourth was more nearly circular (8 ft. 8 by 7 ft. 5); the deposit of charcoal and bone lay a little W. of N., and in it were found three spear-heads, a chisel, knife, and style? CCCXCVI. to CCCXCIX.*

The oval shape of these *Āzārams* is curious, the small modern ones are roughly round.

Some further examination of *Āzārams* would be desirable; at present, judging by the amount of rust on the iron implements exhumed, there seems to be a long interval between the newest cairns and the oldest *Āzārams*. Situation and soil, however, would have much to do with this.

It will be seen that these old *Āzārams*, (supposing them to be *Āzārams*,) shew one or two marked points of approximation to the cairns. 1st. They prove that metal ornaments and objects of value were in old times actually buried by the Todas, instead of being, as now, only offered to the flames and taken away. 2nd. These objects include iron spears, chisels, and styles? at present unused by the Todas, but common in the cairns. The spears were of rather different shape from most of those figured. An old Toda, who had had possession of the spear of Kotēn, but professed to have lost it, told me that it was something like these, but longer. The style is very like some used in Malabar, hollow at the top; one cannot, however, imagine that *writing* was ever a Toda accomplishment; it may have been used for marking pottery. 3rd. The receptacle for the ashes and remains, instead of being indifferently placed at any side of the circle, was, in three cases out of four, at the north-east edge.

Bracelets, however, are *never*† found in the cairns, which is singular, as the human figures on the lids are often represented with bracelets. This fact, together with the frequent occurrence of men on horseback, while the imitation of the horse shews a very limited acquaintance with the animal, suggests that for some reason the cairn builders

---

* Sir A. Arbuthnot has kindly furnished me with the following account of an examination of some Āzārams:

"On the 16th October, I visited, in company with Mr. Metz, an *Āzāram* to the left of the Segūr road. It lay north and south. Its length was sixteen feet, and width ten feet. On digging a depth of about two feet, the following articles were found—

Six spear-heads.
A quantity of bones and charcoal.
Two earthen pots.
Some bits of copper.
A broken copper ring; and
An iron knife handle.

The bones and charcoal were found principally at the north end of the *Āzāram*. Five of the spear-heads were lying at the north end and pointing from north to south, one spear-head pointed from N.N.W. to S.S.E. The two earthen pots were found in the south-east corner, the bits of copper were in two pots. The razor was also at the north end of the *Āzāram*, below the spear heads: the knife handle and the copper ring were at the south-west corner.

Another *Āzāram* immediately adjoining this yielded nothing whatever, nor did five that were opened in the Nanjanâd Valley to the right of the old Avalanche road." Possibly these were not *Āzārams*, which would at any rate have contained charcoal, but circles used at a green funeral. See page 16.—Ed.

† Sir Walter Elliot informs me that he found a child's armlet in one instance.—Ed.

took their neighbours, perhaps their enemies, for models, and not themselves. The iron utensils of the *Āzārams* are very much less rusted than those found in the cairns, and rather different in shape. On the whole, however, the *Āzārams* seem like first cousins to the inferior cairns and barrows, and afford a strong argument for the Todas' claim to the latter. One or two collateral pieces of evidence may be mentioned here.

1st. The cairn builders were clearly familiar with the buffalo. Not only are these by far the most numerous figures found, but while many others are so badly imitated that it is not easy to guess what they are meant to represent, the buffaloes are singularly characteristic and often very spirited, though of course rough.

On the other hand, very few of the human figures at all resemble Todas; the women seem to have the low-country top-knot instead of the Toda curls, and carry chatties on their heads, a domestic occupation to which no modern Toda lady condescends. Moreover, I do not remember that any of the figures wear the characteristic Toda armlet, and the *Pūtkuli* certainly is not represented. The dress of the clay figures generally resembles that found on the sculptured cromlechs (see page 99).

2nd. Besides the bells generally represented as hanging to the buffalo's neck, fragments of iron bells occur occasionally, and small imitations of them in clay frequently. Unless we are to treat *all* the clay figures as idols, which would be to credit the cairn builders with a Pantheon as extensive and varied as the Egyptians', there is hardly anything else in the cairns to which we can assign a religious meaning. In one cairn, indeed, there were two or three figures resembling Buddhist statues, but these are unique. It is needless to say that this is exactly what might be expected in Toda tombs.

3rd. In attempting to decide on the origin of such monuments, one naturally compares them with others existing in India. Now, almost the only *cairns*, properly so called, which I have seen described in detail, (most of the other numerous "rude stone monuments" of southern India, *pandu kulis*, &c., seeming to be more of the nature of kist-vaens), are those examined by Colonel Meadows Taylor in Sorapūr.

These consisted generally of a circle of large boulders surrounding a mound of earth and stones. At one side of the circle were two slabs forming a sort of entrance, and *always* lying N.E. and S.W., and the stone chambers below, containing the interments, followed the same direction (cairn described on page 71 certainly suggests a reminiscence of some similar arrangement). In these chambers lay one or more bodies *laid on their faces*.

I have made many efforts to ascertain whether this position of the body, either in burning or burying, is found among any existing Indian tribes or castes besides the Todas. Mr. Deputy Superintendent Ramiah reports that a pastoral caste of Mahrattas, called Kacha Guligar, are said to bury their dead face downwards, and that in some districts of Mysore unmarried Sudras are so buried; but the position is clearly a very unusual one, and its occurrence in cairns corresponding with those of the Nīlagiris, in such an essential feature as the position of the slabs, is a curious coincidence, especially when we consider how plainly the Toda funeral ritual indicates that their dead were originally buried.

Similar cairns, opened by Colonel Doria in the neighbourhood of Narkailpaki, Nizam's country, contained skeletons laid north and south, and accompanied by jars containing calcined bones. In one a bell was found; another, opened by Sir G. Yule, at Haiat Nagar near Hydrabad, yielded not only a bell, but a lid "surmounted by the figure of a deer or sheep." This was in bronze, however, not clay. Others in the neighbourhood of the first-mentioned contained only cinerary urns. The *Āzārams* seem to exist on a gigantic scale.

At Shahpūr "fifty-six huge rocks enclose a space and tumulus 400 ft. by 260." On driving two levels through the tumulus at right angles, Colonel Taylor "found it to consist of layers of human ashes, charcoal, and pieces of bone. It had in fact been a place of cremation on a large scale, formed of successive layers of burnings, and so had gradually risen."

Against the theory that the cairns belong to the Todas, it has been urged that they do not claim them. This is not strictly correct; they *do*, as has been shewn, claim some. But even if the statement were entirely true, it is not of much consequence with a people like Todas. I have known a Toda, while pointing out the *Āzāram* in which a funeral ceremony then going forward was to terminate, profess entire ignorance of the object of some other stone circles close at hand, obviously old *Āzārams* belonging to the same mand; so that their disclaimer of the cairns carries little weight.

It has been further stated that the cairns contain agricultural implements, and must therefore have belonged to a comparatively civilized people. Except the curious shears, which may have been used for various purposes, the only agricultural implements which have appeared in these investigations, are sickles. These may have been used for cutting grass and bushes, and it is singular that, although the Todas do not now use any tool of the kind, they burn with the dead the *Kăfkatti*, a large curved knife, apparently intended for some such purpose, although, except in one instance, the cairn sickles are of a different shape. The *Kăfkatti*, when committed to the flames, is bound round with cotton cloth, traces of which are often found on the razors in the cairns. On the whole, I think it is more satisfactory to assign the cairns to the Todas than to an unknown race.

Stone circles.—Colonel Congreve lays some stress upon circles, in some instances, surrounding large rocks, which he calls altars. I think I have identified one of his circles pretty plainly with the buffalo kraal at Muttanâd mand, and in others I think he may have taken a deserted kraal for a religious building. There are, however, in two places, circles, which are perhaps neither kraals nor cairns, and both are connected with old Toda funeral mands.

The first were visited on July 17th, 1871. They consist of two or three groups of circles of dry walling, to the right of the Segūr road, opposite Muttanâd mand. One of these first dug out appears to be the kraal referred to in the story of Kotēn.* It is built on sheet rock, in some places quite bare, in others covered only by a thin coating of turf and vegetable soil. Near this were several circles joined together, some large and some small. In one of the latter, about ½ a foot below the surface, were five small stones, about 12 × 6 × 6 ins., laid in this form. Nothing was found between or below the stones.†

* See pp. 36 and 37.

† Mr. Breeks intended to have made further examinations here; the circle was not dug deep enough.—Ed.

Other circles, chiefly in a group, a little way from this, were examined, and found to contain quantities of charcoal. In one, a deposit of charcoal, a piece of bone, and fragment of bronze were found. Another large one seemed to have been a kraal.

The whole hill-side above these last was covered with old *Āzārams;* thirty were counted. The place, therefore, was clearly an old funeral mand; and some of the walled circles were kraals, but whether the others were originally burning-places, and so form another link between the *Āzāram* and the cairns, which the smaller ones closely resemble, or whether they were merely places for cooking and eating, is not certain. In one of them the charcoal lay all around a small circle of stones resembling a fireplace, which suggests the latter purpose. This place would repay careful examination. The neighbouring mand is famous in Toda tradition, and the circles and *Āzārams* are probably old. Both should be carefully dug out to a considerable depth.

The only circle I know, which at all resembles a temple, is one not far from the Paikāra Tiriari. Here, on a hill-side, is a projecting rock surrounded by a circle of single boulders.* No excavation could be made at the time I saw it, but close at hand were one or two *Āzārams*, and traces of a ruined kraal.

Cromlechs. There is apparently no connexion between the cairns and the cromlechs. While the former are scattered over the plateau, occupying mostly the high bare ridges, the cromlechs all lie on the lower levels, and near the ghâts leading from the low country. They are not, as will be shown, sepulchral, but the few objects found in them are quite different from the contents of the cairns, and probably more modern. They do not all face in the same direction, but vary from N.E. to S.S.E. Many of them are made of slabs, carved after the fashion of the *Kollekallu*, very common in Coorg and Mysore, but never, as far as I know, built into cromlechs elsewhere.

The following quotation from Mr. Richter's Manual of Coorg might serve as a general description of the Nīlagiri carvings, except that in the latter hunting adventures take the place of battle scenes :—

" *Monumental Stones* of a more recent date are the *Kollekallu* (from *kollu*, to kill " and *kallu*, stone) tombstones in honour of warriors slain in battle. They are found " along the eastern districts of Coorg. One I saw in Tavalagherigráma in Kiggatnád, " some in Kottcád, six miles to the east of Mercara, and many in Fraserpet and near the " Sómawarpet; the same kind of monuments occur also frequently in the Mysore country, " especially in Nuggur and as far north as Belgaum. In all these localities the stones " show a similar character. A large collection of them may be seen in the town of " Mysore in an open place opposite the graveyard. The slabs are of granite, with rough " facings, about 6 feet high, 4 feet broad, and 9 inches thick, and frequently the lower " half is buried in the ground. The front side is generally divided into three com- " partments, each containing some figures in relief, the background being chiselled " out, so that the figures are level with the frame of the compartments. The objects " represented in the top frame, are one, two, or three central figures, seated in various " postures on low stools such as the Hindus still use, and two female figures standing

* Mr. Breeks intended to have dug out this circle. Unfortunately the place is difficult to find from verbal description. Mr. Metz had seen the circle, but could not find his way to it, and we only discovered it by accident.—Ed.

" by their sides with fans. The central figures are evidently the heroes, they sit sword " in hand with consequential dignity. The second compartment is filled with a " string of three, five, or seven figures, alternately males and females, the latter " preponderating and in most lively attitudes, the male figures extending the arms " and resting their hands on the shoulders of the females, who support their partners' " arms near the elbows. The extreme figures, who are always females, hold fans (or " *guitars ?) in their hands.** The third frame encloses a battle scene in which warriors " on foot and armed with bows and arrows, sword and shields, are engaged in combat, " one man lying dead on the ground. In the right corner there is a warrior on " horseback with sword in hand making gestures of command or encouragement, and " in the left corner one or two bulls are represented. The figures are in grotesque " attitude, but remarkably well grouped, and closely resemble the sculptured reliefs " of Halibíd.

" In the top compartment there is occasionally a lamp and a *Linga*, both on " pedestals, and these insignia, together with the *Basavas* in the third frame, evidently " denote the heroes as Linga worshippers and aliens from the present Coorgs, who " know nothing about them; the Canarese Gaudas, in whose countries they are chiefly " found, claim them as relics of their ancestors, and annually present before these stones " offerings of cakes and fruit. The dresses of all the figures represented are not in the " Coorg, but in the costume of Hindus of the scantiest clothing. Colonel Wilks, in " his *History of Mysore*, Vol. I., p. 15, explains the sculptured representations in the " three compartments thus: 'The lowest describes a battle in which the hero was " 'slain; the centre compartment represents him in the act of being conveyed to " 'heaven between two celestial nymphs; in the uppermost he has arrived at the " 'regions of bliss and is delineated as seated before the peculiar emblem of his religion " '—generally the lingum—for the practice of erecting monuments seems chiefly to " 'belong to the sect of Síva.'"

Plates XLIV. (*a*) and (*b*) are plans of groups.

Plate XLV. represents a group of cromlechs at Sholūr.†

The photographing of the carvings involved some labour. The covering slabs had to be removed, and the side slabs arranged on a line. After the photographs had been made, the cromlechs were built up again.

Plates XLVI. to XLVIII. represent separate slabs from the Sholūr cromlechs. In XLVI. the upper frame of the right-hand stone contains the Basava‡ kneeling before what is probably intended for a lingam, the usual sun and moon in one corner, and behind the Basava, a human figure, somewhat defaced, apparently the *Pūjāri*. As the central figure in the third frame is on horseback, and holds a sword, it may be presumed that war, and not sport, is here commemorated.

The women's coiffure, with a large knob on one side, is peculiar, and on the second stone, men and women wear the large earrings common on the west coast. Both the

* Water-bottles, I should say, from the Nīlagiri specimens.

† The notes of the excavation of these cromlechs are brief. They contained a good many *deva-kotta kallu* (water-worn stones), but nothing else, except (I think) some large bones on the surface, belonging to some animal, and probably dragged in by a jackal.—ED.

‡ The sacred bull of Siva. Basava was the founder of a Saiva sect, and supposed to be an incarnation of the bull, which in the South of India goes generally by this name.

figures on the cromlechs, and those found in the cairns, are naked above the waist, as on the west coast.

The men are armed with spears, and one has a bow and arrows, the quiver fastened behind the left shoulder by a strap across the breast. The other sculptures represented in *Plates* XLVII. and XLVIII. agree on the whole with Mr. Richter's "second compartment."

Plate XLIX. represents the principal group of cromlechs below Mēlūr, remarkable as containing the only inscription on the Nīlagiris. This is on the stone at the back of the large cromlech and is shown in *Plate* LI.

The stone is thus described by Sir W. Elliot, to whom a photograph was sent:—
"The subject of the carving is a memorial *virgal** and *māstikkal;* a record of a man killed, "in this case, by a tiger; whose wives performed *sati* at his funeral. The *māstikkal* "(quære, *mahá sati kal* †) is known by the figure of a woman holding up the right hand "with a lime or something round in it.‡ In many instances, the hand and arm alone "are sculptured attached to a pillar. When the husband has met with a violent death, "the whole scene is carved as in this instance."

The inscription, which Dr. Pope has kindly deciphered as far as possible, does not throw much light on the history of the cromlechs. It is, he says, "in Tamil, not at all "old, the letters being rudely fashioned, but not essentially differing from those in "common use. But the writer was a very ignorant person, and the spelling is "barbarous. The end of each line has been broken off, and it is thus impossible to "give a connected translation.

"It reads thus:—'In the Vegudânya year of the month Sittirai (April—May) in "the Aswini Nakshêtra, the 42nd cycle of the Saka year 1518 (the character which "I suppose to be 5 is ഌ, which as a numeral is unknown) . . . . . . for a gift " . . . . for a tiger . . . . this writing.' . . .

"I have tried to piece together the rest, but can hit upon nothing that commends "itself to my own mind."

This appears to be the record of a grant, but throws no light on the origin of the cromlechs. To whom was the grant made? Saka 1518, *i.e.*, A.D. 1596, is late enough for the Badagas, but they do not seem to know anything of the cromlechs, and were, or professed to be, ignorant even of the existence of the second group which was hidden among some bushes. *Plate* L. shows a small curiously-shaped pot found in the cromlechs overgrown with brushwood.

The other sculptures present nothing remarkable. Dr. Pope says:—"The dress "is that which appears to have been common throughout the south of India before "the advent of Europeans, but after that of the Musalmans; all are naked to the "waist; all have necklaces, hair gathered up into a knot on the right side of the head,§ "the lobe of the ears artificially lengthened, large bangles on the arms, on the wrists,

---

* *Virgal* or *bira kal*, hero stone.

† *Mahā*, great, *kal*, stone; great *sati* stone.

‡ Possibly from the fact that the sati frequently distributes limes, flowers, &c., to the by-standers, who venerate them as sacred relics. *See* Dubois.

§ In the Doddūru, Achenna, and H'lai ūru cromlechs, the men have mostly the knot on the top of the head, or none at all.

" and at the ankles. All are bareheaded and barefooted. The men have quilted and " padded drawers. The weapons are those in use among the Poligars."

The *sati* figure is repeated on the upper stone in *Plate* LIII., and in *Plate* LIV. a figure spearing a samber suggests that a hunting party occasioned the death of the hero; LIV. also shows some of the *Deva-kotta-kallu*, as the Badagas call the water-worn stones found in most of the Nīlagiri cromlechs. Nothing else was found but a few broken bits of pottery in one cromlech. The second group, consisting of two cromlechs, (*Plate* LVI.,) was hidden among bushes; a little way off was another (*Plate* LVIII.), and in the middle of the three groups was a circular enclosure, containing what seemed to be a small barrow, the only instance I know on the Nīlagiris of a barrow in proximity to cromlechs.* The carving on the centre slab of the larger cromlech in this group (*Plate* LVII.) is the best specimen on the Nīlagiris. It seems intended to commemorate the same event as *Plate* LI., but the dress of the principal figure is more elaborate. He wears a turban with a curled projection on the left side, and a knob on the top, large earrings distending the lobes of the ears, and an elaborate sword-belt and dagger. A horse is in the left-hand corner, two little figures under the hero's foot seem to be imploring his help, three *Apsaras*† are over the heads of the chief figures, and above the horse a figure stands behind two posts, the object of which does not appear. The carving is in much better preservation than most.

The horse reappears under the feet of two figures in *Plate* LVII.: the roughness of these figures is a great contrast to those on the larger slab.

Plate LX. shows the principal cromlechs at Doddūru, two or three miles from Kotagherry.

They are in considerable numbers here, close to the remains of a large village, which is overgrown with jungle, and only traceable by lines and heaps of rough stones. Only one cromlech is sculptured; the slabs are represented in *Plates* LXI. and LXII. The Basava and other objects of worship in the upper compartment, *Plate* LXI., are the same as at Sholūr, the *Pūjāri* is more distinct, and seems to have a bell in one hand. The figures are so obscured and defaced that it is not easy to make out whether the women with uplifted hands hold a lime or not, but as two women occupy the post of honour in the second slab (*Plate* LXII.), the object may be to commemorate a double *sati*. One of the lower figures seems to be spearing some nondescript animal. All the cromlechs contained numbers of *Deva-kotta-kallu*, some very large.

The cromlech at Jakata Kambē is interesting, as being the place of the yearly sacrifice performed for the Badagas of the Jakanēri Grāma by their Kāni Kurumba. It stands quite alone, a mile or so from the Doddūru remains.‡ The sculptures, *Plates* LXIV. and LXV.,§ do not differ much from the others, except that two figures in the two top compartments hold something between their two hands like a pot or basket.

---

* Mr. Breeks intended to have opened this. It should be examined, for not only is its situation with regard to the cromlechs unique, but it appears by a pencil note that the single slab lay E. and W., corresponding in this respect with the kistvaens and chambered tumuli of the plains, but not with any other Nīlagiri barrow.—ED.

† Hindu angels.

‡ The name Kambē suggests that there must have have been a Kurumba village near. I do not know whether there is one now or not.

§ Plate LXV. has not been printed. It was unimportant, and very badly photographed.—ED.

About a mile from Jakata Kambē, is Achenna, and here, built into the wall of the village kraal and used as calf pens, are some of the finest cromlechs on the Hills (*Plate* LXVI.) The slab figured in *Plate* LXVII. appears at first sight to record any number of *satis*, as no less than eleven women's figures hold up one hand with the lime in it. A closer inspection, however, suggests that the four figures in each of the two lower lines are identical, and that the third line represents their beatification, want of space having reduced the sculptor to curtail the head-dress of the fourth *sati*, and put the lime only in the left hand that hangs by her side. The circular head-dress is new, and as it is only given to the *satis*, may have some symbolical meaning, it looks almost like the halo of Christian pictures. The right-hand figure in the lower line, and left-hand in the third, do not seem to be so decorated. The conical cap of the principal man is also new. The right-hand figures at the top appear to be the *Basava* and *Pūjāri* with bell or some other implement. The men's figures are in warlike attitudes, and in the next slab, *Plate* LXVIII., in which three of the *satis* reappear, there are two men on horseback, brandishing swords. The sun and moon are above as usual; in the middle compartment, a man is spearing what seems like a horse—, the only spear in these slabs: the rest have all apparently short swords or daggers, except the single figure at the bottom of the slab in *Plate* LXVII., who has a long curved weapon, either a scimitar or battle-axe.

Plates LXIX. to LXXII. represent cromlechs at H'lai ūru, which lies low on the slopes between Kotagherry and Kodanâd. This is again a hunting memorial; three figures in the different slabs are spearing bears and tigers, and two women hold limes (*Plate* LXXI. right-hand bottom, and LXXII. top of left-hand slab), while four sportsmen and one woman share the glorified repose of the upper compartment. The man spearing a bear wears a cap or top knot with two ribbons hanging from it, which is peculiar. The most remarkable feature of these slabs, however, is a rough but unmistakeable snake, which is carved on the top of the slab in *Plate* LXXI. on a level with the sun and moon. This is the more remarkable as there are no traces of serpent worship now on the hills. The Badagas will not kill a snake or pass near a dead one, but this is simply a superstition, such as exists in some parts of England, and I do not know that the other tribes have even such scruples; the Todas certainly have not. The snake does not appear to be a *Nāga*, and its position close to the sun suggests that it might record an eclipse, which, as is well known, is in India attributed to the capture of the sun by a great serpent.

Plates LXXIII. and LXXIV. represent two cromlechs at Kakusi, six miles from Kotagherry. These face east; the three stones of the left-hand one were sculptured, but the sculptures have no particular interest. The sun and moon, *lingam*, and *Pujāri* are at the top of one; the figures seem to have both swords and spears, and there does not seem to be a *sati*, but they are not easy to make out. No *Deva-kotta-kallu* were found here, but a small earthen lamp, No. 11, was in the corner of one, about a foot underground. Besides these, there are carved cromlechs in Major Sweet's plantation beyond Kārtēri. These were not photographed. The sculptures, besides the usual *Basavas*, sun and moon, man spearing animal, women holding fan, &c., have a horse caparisoned, but not mounted, and a figure on horseback with an umbrella held over him. These cromlechs yielded, besides *Deva-kotta-kallu*, a number of iron and bronze armlets, sickles, rings, two small iron hatchet heads, and a small rough common chatty, but no bones or charcoal. The iron was much less rusted than in the cairns.

Another sculptured cromlech at Mēlkūndah is surrounded, as usual, by smaller ones unsculptured. The sculptures were of the usual type, but the large cromlech was full of hundreds of *Deva-kotta-kallu*, reaching from two feet underground to the covering slab. Such a mass could only be the accumulation of generations, and is difficult to account for, except by some such custom as that of the Kurumbas, who place a stone in a cromlech after every death. These stones must have been brought some little distance from the bed of a stream.

The Badagas would seem to have usually selected the neighbourhood of these cromlechs for their temples, as for example, at Melūr,* Kakūsi, H'lāiuru, Tudūr, and Jakatāda.

At Achenna (*Plate* LXVI.) they have made them serve the purpose of a wall to the village kraal, with the advantage of each cromlech forming a separate pen for the calves.

The cromlechs at Doddūru (*Plate* LX.) are in a jungle in the midst of a heap of ruins of what appears to have once been a considerable village.

The Badagas and Kotas about Tēnad claim the unsculptured cromlechs as the work of their ancestors, but say they do not know who made the sculptured ones. I think, however, that if their forefathers had really been the builders of any, the Badagas would have retained some more definite tradition of the fact, as their original stories and songs go back at least a century and a half. Some of them are from low country legends probably very much older, and they have distinct ideas as to their migration from the plains, which none of the other tribes have. It is hardly necessary to point out the connection between the stones found in these cromlechs and the existing funeral rites of the Kurumbas.† It is more important to note the light which these throw on Colonel Taylor's discoveries in Sorapūr. He found kistvaens and cromlechs together, the former containing ashes, bones, &c., the latter always empty. Mr. Fergusson inclines to the idea that they had been rifled, and insists that they must have been sepulchral; but the practice of the Kurumbas leads us to suppose that they may have been purely memorial, and have contained only perishable offerings of rice, &c., such as are made by the Kurumbas and by the Kols of Chota Nagpore.

Plates LXXVII. to LXXIX. show the utensils and ornaments of the Kotas, Kurumbas, and Irulas; and LXXX. to LXXXII. some scratches on the sides of a cave on the eastern slopes, of no great interest, which were photographed because they are mentioned by Capt. Congreve.‡

---

* The Badaga temple at Melūr is shown in Plate LXXV. The ceremony of walking through fire takes place there once a year.

† A similar custom exists among the Travancore hill tribes (*Rude Stone Monuments*, p. 479). "The Mala "Arryians are a race of men living in dense jungles and hills, cromlechs are common among them, and they "worship the spirits of their ancestors, to whom they make annual offerings. At the present day they take "corpses into the sacred groves, and after making offerings of arrack, &c. to the departed spirit, a small stone is "placed in a model box or vault, formed of small slabs, and it is covered over." These Mala Arryians are evidently the Malē Arasu Kurumbas or Malsars.

‡ *Mad. Jour.* vol. XIV.

Kistvaens. There remain only the kistvaens, *Plate* LXXVI., to be described. These have as yet been found only in one locality, near the ruined fort of Udirāya, on the slopes below Kotagherry (Udirāya is too modern, and too well known to the Badagas, to be connected in any way with these kists, which they know nothing of, and call *Moriaru mane*).

They are all so much alike in construction, that a description of the one photographed will be sufficient. It was surrounded by a circle of single stones 18 feet in diameter. Four large slabs were standing edgewise in the ground, (natural soil, not vegetable earth or refuse,) their tops just level with the surface of the ground; another large slab lay at the bottom. The covering slab had been removed and was lying outside the circle.

The earth inside the kist was mixed with charcoal, and was loose vegetable soil; the outside undisturbed, as if a square hole had been dug and the slabs put in.

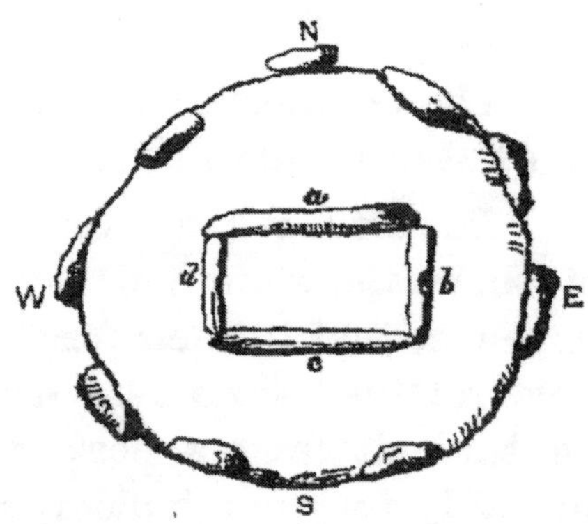

The kist measured 3 ft. 6 ins. from E. to W., and 2 ft. 6. ins. from N. to S. In the middle of the eastern slab was a round hole, varying in different instances from 12 to 15 ins. in diameter. The kistvaens had all been rifled; we dug round some of them, inside the stone circle, and found a broken dagger, CCCXIX., and some fragments of pottery, thick and highly glazed, quite different from that of the cairns.

Nothing, therefore, exists on the Nīlagiris to give us any clue as to the authorship of these remains, or to connect them with the cromlechs. For presumptive evidence of their relationship, we must turn to Colonel Meadows Taylor's discoveries at Rajan Kolūr and Haggeritgi, where, as mentioned above, he found cromlechs and kistvaens of various sizes side by side, the latter only being sepulchral.

The scanty records left by explorers in the plains, and their indiscriminate use of the terms cairn, cromlech, &c., make it difficult in many cases to ascertain what class of monument is described. Many of the so-called Druidic remains in southern India are kistvaens* and cromlechs, the former sometimes surrounded by a tumulus and a circle of stones, sometimes only by a circle, sometimes apparently standing alone. They are found in the Nizam's country, about the Godavery, in the Bellary district, in Coorg, Mysore, Wainâd, in north and south Arcot, Chingleput, Coimbatore, &c., and in all cases seem to present much the same features. (The *kodē kals* of Malabar are a distinct variety.) In some places the kistvaens go by the name of *Moriaru mane*, in others, they are called *Pāndu kuli*, *Panta curzi*, *Vedar kudi*, *Kurumba kudi*, &c. The two first names are the commonest.

Those in Bellary are classified as follows in a Report furnished to Mr. Pelly for Colonel Meadows Taylor.

1. Having a slab of stones on each of three sides as walls, and one above as roof, leaving one side open.

* Comp. *Archæologia* 35., pp. 233, 234.

2. Having a slab on each of four sides as walls, and one at the top as roof, one of the side slabs having an aperture in the centre.

3. Ditto without the aperture.

4. Compounds, or enclosures built of stones enclosing dwellings of this description.

Three other classes are the same as the first three, but without the covering slabs. The total number in the seven classes is said to be 2,120. Mr. Boswell describes kistvaens in Palnâd, in the Krishna district. These were often divided into two or four compartments, and contained burnt bones, accompanied by vases of different coloured pottery, generally inverted. In one tomb was part of a *bracelet*.

Mr. Boswell says, "In one of the sides there is often a sort of entrance left." It is not clear from this whether one side is entirely open or not. He does not allude to the round hole often found in kistvaens, as is clear by the context.

Captain Cole found many kistvaens in Coorg and Mysore, all with the orifice to the east, and often surrounded by one or two circles of stones; some were buried, leaving the top slab level with the ground, and contained cinerary urns and other remains, others stood on rock and were empty. It does not appear whether these were cromlechs or kistvaens.

Mr. Minchin tells me that some large kistvaens are to be seen on the road between Gudalur and Tippukādu.

In those opened at Oossoor by Sir W. Denison,* the kistvaen seems to have been covered by a tumulus, with a double ring of stones, while the urns examined by Mr. Kearns† in Tinnevelly are said to have been "closely surrounded by a chamber of unhewn stones, boulders such as are at present procurable in the bed of the adjoining river," a description which leaves it doubtful whether they are cairns or kistvaens. The traditions translated by Mr. Taylor about the *pāndu-kulies* in Tondamandalam ‡ are vague as to description, but fortunately Captain Newbold has supplied the deficiency by his description of the sepulchres of Pānduvaram Dēval near Chittoor.§ Here are numbers of kistvaens with the usual circular aperture, not always, however, in the eastern slab. One which was opened, contained a sarcophagus of terra-cotta six and a half feet long, in which a body had apparently been laid, and some other small vases. To this, or some similar burying ground, the following tradition appears to refer:—

Of the old Caves at Paduvūr. (*Mad. Journ. Vol.* XIV., *pt. ii., p.* 89.)‖

"Anciently men wearing tufted hair, Curumbars, and various others of the Jaina "credence, dwelt in this town. They were the aboriginal residents, those beings from

* *Eth. Jour., vol.* I., *No.* 2. † *Mad. Jour., vol.* V., *N.S., No.* IX.

‡ Said to exist in Paduvūr, Vallam, Manuvur, Anamur, Cannatūr, Avātthūr, Kuvathūr, Vayavūr, Koluttūr, Chittamūr, Uttramelūr, Ayarpakam, in the Chittūr country about Gingi, in the Bhavāni district, &c.; some near Puralūr are mentioned by Sir W. Elliot and Captain Newbold. Colonel Congreve has described one at Pulicondah.

§ *Journal R.A.S.. vol.* XIII., *Part* 1.

‖ In other MSS. translated by Mr. Taylor, these excavations, called *Pantu curzihal*, are said to be constructed with large slabs under ground, some built like a fort, some round, some four-sided, some covered at the top, some not. Sometimes the relations after the death of the old people buried alive, "shut up the cavern "and covered it with earth";—this evidently refers to the tumuli round kistvaens.

"very old times were ruled by Jaina kings. By a Jaina king, named Pāndyadever, * "this town was given to a Jaina-basti. . . . There is here an inscription on stone, . . . "Paduvūr and its entire precincts are given in full and perpetual grant to the aforesaid "temple. This full endowment for a length of time pertained to the Jaina-basti. "Afterwards, in the days of Adondai-Cholan, when, by the advice of the Brahmans, "he destroyed the Jainas, it was added to the common revenue.

"Anciently in this town they did not keep the very old people till death, but "seeing the time approach, they put them into very strongly-made earthen jars, "together with food suitable for them. Such was the practice in this Paduvur. Such "kind of earthen jars are called *Matamaccachāl;* even now many such *chāls* are to "be seen. Human bones and drinking vessels which had been placed therein have "been taken out and buried. In this way the anciently pleasant suburbs the towns-"people turned into a half desert, and having placed these *Matamaccachāl,* they "returned. The posterity of the Pandavas and other wealthy people having built "sepulchres, placed the people of their race there. To the east of Paduvūr, there "are seventy-five of these ancient pits or caves, to the north there are sixty ancient "excavations."

Mr. Fraser† thus describes the "cromlechs" and "tumuli" of Coimbatore.

"The cromlechs in this district are formed of carefully-selected flat stones, placed "on edge, so as to form a chamber nearly square, and nearly completely enclosed.‡

"Of unmistakeable cromlechs, I have not seen more than six. Four of these are "in the valleys of the Bhawāni and Moyār rivers, and two in the valley of the Noyel "or the Bolamampatti valley. These two are remarkable for having in a stone forming "one side of the chamber an oval-shaped hole 10 or 12 inches in diameter. Major "Hamilton, when he visited the higher ranges of the Ānamalais, discovered a cromlech "precisely similar to those of the Bolamampatti valley.

Sepulchral tumuli.

"These are found in every part of the district. In the cultivated plains around "the base of the Ānamalais, in the deep gorges at the foot of the Nīlagiris, and in the "now untrodden, unhealthy jungles in the valleys of the Bhawāni and Moyār, I have "found these tumuli, with their kistvaens, cinerary urns, &c.

"These tumuli are not generally found isolated or singly, here and there; in "some places 10 or 12 acres are covered with them; and these burial places are so "close to each other that it is impossible to resist the belief that the whole of the "country must at one time have been thickly peopled; it is scarcely possible that these "could be the results of the occasional visits of a few wandering tribes.

"By far the finest specimens of these remains are in Moyār valley.

---

* Comp. *Pānduvaram Dēval of Capt. Newbold.*

† *Mad. Jour., vol.* VI., *N.S., No.* XI.

‡ Mr. Fraser also mentions "numerous small buildings of this type formed with dressed stones and generally "having one or two figures of Hindu deities carved upon them," but does not give their localities. Further description of these would be desirable.

"Generally the tumuli are not much raised above the surface of the land. Along "the Moyār, many of them are raised eight or nine feet, and each tumulus is surrounded "by a stone circle.

"In some places one tumulus is much larger than the rest, and surrounded by a "larger circle of flat stones standing on edge, and about three feet above the ground. "In every instance there is a large flat stone on the top of the tumulus; in a few cases "I have seen two within one circle, and I presume each covered a kistvaen, as was "the case in all (perhaps 100,) that I have seen open.

"The kistvaens are generally from four to five feet in length, and two to three "in width; they are all, as far as I have seen, placed east and west. I opened one "of the tumuli in the valley of the Moyār; it contained the usual cinerary urns of "baked clay, with portions of calcined and uncalcined human bones. The cinerary "urns are of various shapes, and vary in size from two or three feet to four or five "inches in diameter. Of the origin of these tumuli the same tradition is found in "every part of the district, that they are the houses of a race of pigmies called Pandura, "who were punished by fire rained upon them from heaven, that they sought protection "in their houses, and pulled these huge stones over them. The people have no "veneration for these remains; not even the Erulars and Kurumbars."

General Cunningham says that some cromlechs and circles are found "in the "hilly districts of Northern India, in Mirzapur, Delhi, and Rajputana. The Delhi "remains are small cromlechs."

Colonel Congreve says that some such remains exist in Orissa, (I have not found any other mention of these,) and mentions cairns and cromlechs near Palipaliam, in the Salem district, and at Peri Sūndram, in Mysore. Whether these are what I have called cairns, or tumuli surrounding kistvaens, I cannot say, in the absence of plans or descriptions. These are all the notices I have been able to find.

It will be seen by this summary, how much accurate and detailed information is wanted.*

I cannot find that any excavations have been made in the Bellary district, nor, except in Captain Newbold's paper, are there records of any in Tondamandalam, which, as the stronghold of the Kurumbas, deserves particular attention. The rude stone circles near Amravati noticed by Mr. Fergusson,† would probably repay careful examination. I would suggest that, in any future researches, special attention should be paid to the following points:

1st. Are the monuments examined, cairns, in which the stone circle or heap is the principal feature (or barrows, in which the tumulus is composed entirely of earth, without a chamber,) or are they cromlechs and kistvaens, in which the stone chamber is the main object, and the tumulus or circle is accessary, and are the two classes of monuments found together or in quite distinct localities?

2nd. Are cromlechs generally found with kistvaens, as at Rajan Kolūr?

---

* This is very obvious to any reader of the Indian chapter of Mr. Fergusson's *Rude Stone Monuments*.

† Mr. Boswell (*Proceedings of Mad. Govt.*, 7*th Nov.* 1870) says that these "have always yielded cinerary "urns, burnt bones, and other indications of being burning places." I have not met with any more detailed account of excavations there.

3rd. Do cromlechs, especially in Tondamandalam, ever contain round water-worn stones,* and are bones, charcoal, &c. found in them or only in the kistvaens? Plans and sections should always accompany descriptions, and the orientation should be noted. Certain resemblances in the shape of urns and other remains† exist between the two classes of monuments; and the tumuli of Oossoor and Coimbatore, surrounded by one or more circles of stone, may not be readily distinguishable from Colonel Meadows Taylor's cairns. It must be remarked, however, that the orientation is different, the slabs or chambers in the cairns lying N. and S. or N.E. and S.W., while the great majority of the kistvaens lie E. and W.; and this is an important point, and in our present state of knowledge, I think, warrants the distinction drawn.

It would be interesting also to note whether, in other parts of India, bracelets are ever found in cairns or barrows, and of what metal.‡ Thus the indications afforded by the Nīlagiri excavations, slight as they are, may serve to suggest more detailed inquiries, inasmuch as they give us some grounds, not only for distinguishing broadly between two kinds of monuments, but for connecting these two distinct classes with the two pastoral tribes, though the evidence as regards the Kurumbas is very small.

No general theory as to the origin of either class of remains can be fairly started in our present state of knowledge, or rather ignorance, but it can do no harm to note such scattered hints as are afforded us by the habits of the Todas and Kurumbas, the Male Aryas of Travancore, and the shepherds of the Dekhan.

---

* In a note to No. 4 of Mr Pelly's tables it is mentioned that "a smooth long stone" was found in "one "of these dwellings." In Mr. Taylor's account of the *Pāndu-kulies*, round stones are enumerated in the list of contents. In the course of Dr. Honigberger's researches among the topes of Kabul he found, in a small wooden case, among a quantity of ashes and earth, a little silver box containing a coin of Kadfises together with "a blackish "stone in the form of an egg (Nerastra)" with some small bones, apparently those of a child. The connection between the Buddhist topes, with their single or double rail, and the kistvaens and cromlechs, &c., with their stone circles has often formed the subject of speculation. Both appear to be sometimes reliquaries rather than sepulchres.

† Captain Cole describes an oblong cornelian bead from the Mysore kistvaens which seems to have resembled those found in the Nilagiri cairns, and the urns in different places are often similar; the clay figures, however, seem to be peculiar to the Nilagiris.

‡ See p. 90. It would appear that on the Nīlagiris the introduction of bracelets and of brass marks the transition from cairns to *Āzārams*. An examination of the coins and ornaments of known ages in Southern India might enable us to fix the date of the introduction of brass.

Since the above was written a report on some tumuli in the Salem district by the Rev. M. Phillips has been published in the Indian Antiquary (vol. II., page 223). These tumuli are of three different kinds, which Mr. Phillips describes as "cromlechs" or "tumuli," the inside of which is formed by four perpendicular stone slabs in the shape "of a cist or box;" "cairns," having no internal lining of stone, but divided into two classes, one in which the chamber is surrounded by large urns containing bones, small urns, and ornaments, and one which apparently contains no urns and only very insignificant fragments of bone. All seems to have a large covering stone; "in the case of cromlechs the entrance is from the east." Unluckily, Mr. Phillips does not explain what he means by the *entrance*. Is one side open, or partially so, or is there a hole in the eastern slab? No plans accompany the paper, and the direction of the covering stone in the case of cairns is not mentioned. The tumuli are often surrounded by circles of stones. No clay figures seem to have been found; the urns had a slight glaze, said to be produced by rubbing with the juice of a tree.

Mr. Phillips remarks that the cromlechs yield very little. "In some of them nothing is found, in others only "small urns with small bits of iron, and small pieces of bone which look like the remnants of cremation." The large bones are always found in the large urns contained in the first class of cairns; it does not appear certain whether they have been burnt or not. The second class, without chambers or urns, may have been only burning places, but it does not appear whether any deposits of charcoal are found in them.

APPENDIX A.

VOCABULARY OF NILAGIRI TRIBES.

TABLE of LETTERS used.

Vowels.

a like a in *America.*

ā „ a in *father.*

ă „ a in English *what.*

â „ a in English *all*

ĕ „ e in English *get.*

ê „ e in French *mère.*

e „ second e in German *gehe* and e in *end.*

ē „ first e in German *gehe* and ay in *way.*

i „ i in English *pin.*

ī „ i in *pique* and in French *abîme.*

o „ o in *opinion* and in German *Gott.*

ō „ o in *opium.*

ŏ „ o in German *können.*

ô „ o in German *könig.*

u „ u in English *full.*

ū „ u in English *rule.*

ŭ „ u in French *du.*

û „ u in French *fûmes.*

ei „ ei in English *height.*

Consonants.

(With their respective nasals.)

Gutturals.

k like ck in English *look.*
g „ g in *go.*
kh „ ch in Scotch *loch.*
dh

Palatals.

ch like ch in English *church.*
j „ j in English *jail.*

Cerebrals.

ṭ, ḍ, and ḷ.

Dentals.

t like t in English *tin.*
d „ d in English *day.*
th „ th in English *theft.*

Labials.

b like b in English *belt.*
p „ p in English *pin.*
f „ English f.

Liquids.

y like y in English *yes.*
r }
rzh }
v like v in English *river.*
l „ l in *light.*
s as in English *sin.*
sh as sh in English *shot.*
m.
n.

" The system of pronunciation is almost the same as that of Sir W. Jones, which is now used " nearly everywhere.

" The Tamil rzh (ழ) is also acknowledged by linguists, and kh for the German ch (like the " Scotch in loch) is not much out of the way. F. M."

The acute accent is used to mark the emphasis.

VOCABULARY.

The words given are those selected by Dr. Hunter for his Comparative Dictionary of the Non-Aryan Languages.

English.	Toda.	Kota.	Kurumba.	Irula.	Badaga.
One	vodd	vodde	vondu	vondu	vondu
Two	ŏd	yede	yeraḍu	rendu	yeraḍu
Three	mūd	mūnḍe	mūḍu	mūru	mūru
Four	nânk	nāke	nālku	nālku	nālku
Five	ŭjj	anche	eidu	eindu	eidu
Six	âr	āre	āru	āru	āru
Seven	ôḷ	yeye	yeḷu	eḷu	eḷu
Eight	eṭṭ	yeṭṭe	yettu	yeṭṭu	yettu
Nine	onpath	vompade	vompattu	vompadu	vompattu
Ten	path	pade	hattu	padu	hattu
Twenty	evvath	irvade	ibbattu	irvadu	ibbattu
Thirty	mupath	mūvate	mūvattu	mūbadu	mūvattu
Forty	nārzhpath	nālvate	nālvattu	nābadu	nālvattu
Fifty	ēbath	eivate	eivattu	eivadu	eivattu
One hundred	nūr, voddnūr	nūre	nūru	nūru	nūru
I	ân	āne	nānu	nānu	nānu
Thou	nī	nīne	nīnu	nīnu	nīnu
He, she, it	atham	avane, avaḷe, ade	avanu, avaḷu, adu	as Kurumba	ava, avla, adu
We	*âm, ēm	angḷe, yengḷe*	angla, yengḷa*	nāvu	angḷa, yengḷa*
You	nīv	ninglẹ	ningḷa	nīvu	ninglu
They	atham	avare	avaru	athuru	avaku
Mine	yendathd	yennade	yennadu	yennadu	yennadu
Thine	nindathd	ninnade	ninnadu	ninnadu	ninnadu
His	andathd	avanadu	avanadu	avanadu	avanadu
Ours	nammadu, yemmadu*	nangade, yengade*	nammadu, yengadu*	nammadu, yengadu*	angadu, yengadu*
Yours	nimmadu	ningade	ningadu	nimmadu	ningadu
Theirs	athamd	avarade	avaradu	avaradu	avakaradu
This	itham	ivane	ivanu	ivanu	iva
That	atham	avane, ade	avanu, adu	avanu, adu	avanu, adu
Which (relative)	*caret*	*caret*	*caret*	*caret*	*caret*
Who	âr	āre	yāru	āru	āru, yāru
Which?	ennu	yēde	yāvadu	yēdu	yeadu
What	ennu	yēne	yēnu	yenna	yēnu
Any-body-thing	*caret*	*caret*	*caret*	*caret*	*caret*
Above	mok	mēle	mēle	mēle, moke	mēle, vodega
And	ū	ū	ū	ū	ū
As	iggei	henge	henge	henge	henge, hānge, māke
Below	erk, nerahk	kḷiage	kiḷe	kelage	kḷia
Between	narthkāshi	nadḷe	naḍuve	naḍuve	naḍuve
Far	padthchi	dūrame	dūra	dūra	dūra

* The form in â, a, is used when the pronoun includes the person addressed, that in e when he is excluded.

English.	Toda.	Kota.	Kurumba.	Irula.	Badaga.
By or from (ablative case).	edd, ind, ārzh	inde	inda	irinda, inda	inda
Here	it	iyane	illi	inge	itte, illi
How much	yet	yēje	yēsaga	yetani	yēja, yesaga
In	ulch, uḷg	vollage	voḷlage	voḷle	voḷlage
Little	yeddi, kinud	kuna, konje	vōsı	kanja	kanje, jogi
Much	upām	yettāme	apara	tumba	apara, tumba
Near	kekhuri	vottle	pakkaru	kitṭa	vottura, hattara, sāre
No	âkh	ille	illa	illei	illa
Not	âkhadi, âti	vēda	bēda	bōḍa	bēda
Now	ēni	innāle	iga	ipo	iga
Of (genitive case)	*caret*	na, ra*	na, ra*	na, ra*	na, ra*
On	mok	mēle	mēle	mēle	mēle
Or	innân	illave	illave, *or*	illadhōle, *or*	innadhōle
Outside	pormutkh	porenche	horrage	volli	horrasu, horrage
So	ate, angeta	ate	hāge	ipadi	hāgeta
Then	ani, etvan	ānāle	āga	apōḷe	āgale
There	at, ang	alle	alli	arge	alli, at
Thus	ite, ing	inge	hīge	ipadi	it, hīge, ite
To (dative case)	g or k	ge, ke	ge, ke	ge, ke, ku	ga, ke
To-day	eddu, eni	inde	indu	indu	indu
To-morrow	măkâl, belkāshk†	nālke	nāle	nāle	nāle
When	etvan	yēnāle	yēga	yēpa	yēgva
Where	et	yeye	yelli	yenge	yet, yelli
Why	êd	yenḍea	yēka	yennake	yēke
With	vōḍi	sengaḍa	sangada	kūḍa	kōḍa
Within	ulg	ulule	voḷlage	uḷḷe	voḷlage
Without	illade	illade	illade	illade	illade
Yes	hâ	hā	hâ, handu	hâma	hâ, handu
Yesterday	ennêr	nēr	ninne	nēṭṭu	ninne
Air	kâṭṭu	gāle	gāli	kāṭṭu	glai
Ant	erb	irbe	irupu	irumbu	irupu
Arrow	âbbu	ambe	ambu	ambu	ambu
Bird	pilṭi	pakki	hakkilu	pakki	hakkilu
Blood	bôkh	netra	netra	latta	netra
Boat	aragilu	dhōni	dhōni	dhōni	dhōni
Buffalo	ēr	erume, yemme	erume	erumei	yemme
Cat	kotti	pīse	kotti	pūne	kottu
Crow	kāk	kāke	kāke	kāke	kāke
Cow	dănăm	āve	dana	mādu	dana
Day	nâl, păkal	nāle	dina	nālu	dina, jina
Dog	nâi	nāi	nāi	nāi	nāi
Ear	kevvi	kive	kive	kādu	kive

* Na singular, re plural.

† This means to-morrow morning.

English.	Toda.	Kota.	Kurumba.	Irula.	Badaga.
Earth	būmi, mănn	būmi, manu	bumi, manu	bumi, manu	bumi, manu
Egg	muṭch	moṭṭe	moṭṭe	moṭṭe	moṭṭe
Elephant	ān	āne	āne	āne	āne
Eye	kănn	kanne	kannu	kannu	kannu
Fire	nebb, dilth	dije	kichu	tû	kichu
Fish	mīn	mīne	mīnu	mīnu	mīnu
Flower	pūf	pūve	hūvu	pū	hūvu
Foot	kâl	kāle	kālu	kālu	kālu
Goat	âḍu	āḍu	āḍu	āḍu	āḍu
Hair	mīr	mīre	kūḍalu	meiru	kūḍalu
Hand	kei	kei	kei	kei	kei
Head	modd	mande	mande	tele	mande, tale
Hog	pandi	panje	handi	panni	handi
Horn	kuor	kōbe	kombu	kombu	kōdu, kombu
Horse	kadare	kudure	kudure	kudure	kudure
House	ārzh, koat*	pei	mane	kure	mane, āle†
Hunger	bīr erthchi‡	peṭṭi, hoje	hasu	pasi	hasu
Iron	kabbuṇ	ibbe	kabbuṇa	irumbu	kabbuṇa
Leaf	erzh	yelle	yelle	yelle	yelle
Light	veḷak	beḷaku	dīpa	velaku	dīvige, beḷaku
Man	âḷ	āḷe, manijan	manisha	manisha, āḷu	manija, āḷu
Monkey	tūruni, kōḍan§	kōḍe	korangu	korangu	korangu
Moon	tiggal	tiggale	chandra, tingḷa	nālavu	chandra, tingḷa
Mosquito	kusugu	jikkaṭu	sugane	jolle	jikkaṭu
Mother	aff	avve	avve	avve	avve
Mountain	diṭṭu	veṭṭume	beṭṭu	malo	male, beṭṭu
Mouth	bâi	vāi	bāi	vāi	bāi
Name	pēr	pēre	hesaru	hesaru	hesaru, pēru
Night	iruṭ, kaggār	kāval	iru	irutu	kalale
Oil	enne	yenne	yenna	enne	yenne
Plantain	bāvom	vākanne	bālehannu	bālepambu	bālehannu
River	pā	peyi	nīru	palla	halla, holle
Road	âlâr	ālāre	dāri	1 vai, 2 doḍḍa‖	1 dari, 2 doḍḍa
Salt	uppu	uppu	uppu	uppu	uppu
Sky	bân	vāname	bāna	vānu	bānu
Skin	tuvarzh	tûval	tōlu	tōlu	tōlu, toggalu
Snake	pâb	pābe	hāvu	pāmbu	hāvu, pāmbu
Star	mīn	mīne	mīnu	vānu, mīnu	mīnu
Stone	karzh	kalle	kallu	kallu	kallu
Sun	bīrzh	potte	hottu	poddu	hottu
Thirst	nīr-kāschi¶	artoje	arupu	veke	arupu
Tiger	pūrzh	pujje	huli	puli	huli
Tree	mên**	marame	mara	mara	mara
Tooth	parzh	palle	hallu	pallu	hallu

* A bungalow or English house † A Toda house ‡ Bīr, belly; erthchu, I have.

§ Tūruni for the black monkey, kōdan for the brown. ‖ 1 road, 2 path.

¶ Again a compound, as in hunger. Toda seems incapable of abstract terms.

** This should properly be spelt with an "a" as the derivation is no doubt from maram, but none of the four "a" sounds given will represent it, and it seemed unnecessary to make a fifth for this word.

English.	Toda.	Kota.	Kurumba.	Irula.	Badaga.
Badaga village	haṭṭi, ūr	paṭṭi	haṭṭi	haṭṭi	haṭṭi, ūru
Toda do	mădd	mand	mand	mand	mand
Kota do	kŏkāl	kokeal (kotagiri)	kotagiri	kotagiri	kotagiri
Kurumba and Irula do.*	moṭṭa	moṭṭa	moṭṭa	moṭṭa, ūru	moṭṭa
Water	nīr	nīre	nīru	dani	nīru
Weariness	kâl ārthchi †	jalupe	jalupu	jalupu	jalupu
Bad	ollada	polla	keṭṭa	polla	keṭṭa, holla
Bitter	kaṭhchi ‡	kāju	kabi	kesape	kabi, kasapu
Black	karthchi, kappu	kari	kappu	kari	kari, kappu
Cold	kuarthchi, perthchi	jalli	jayi	jalli	jalli, koravu
Crooked	balug	kenke	gokke	kokke	gokke
Fat	pekhiti	porāle	kobbu	kolupu	kobbu
Good	vuḷḷi, voḷḷi	volle	voḷḷe	naḷḷu	voḷḷe
Great	etud	doḍḍa	doḍḍa	peria	doḍḍa
Green	paj	paje	hase	pase	hase
Handsome	nārzhchi	pasane	singāra	alagu	singāra
Hot	kāschi	uri	bisse	kāja	bisse
Long	nerigiti	uddane	udda	udda	udda
Red	kenthti	kempu	kempu	jevve	keppu
Round	uḍḍi, uruṭ	mudde	uruṭu	ruṭse	uruṭu
Short	kurud	modāḷe§	kūle āḷu§	kūle manisha§	kūle, mone
Small	kinud	kuna	kuna	chinna	kuna
Sour	pūlthchi	pulsa	huli	puli	huli
Straight	edduru	neṭṭu	neṭṭage	neṭṭe	neṭṭage
Sweet	dūjati (it is sweet)	se	si	ruse	si
Tall	nirigiâl§	uddaman	uddava	udda manishâl§	uddava
Thin	kinud	vottale	melle	vodoge	melle
Ugly	âdadi	māse	holla	polla	holla
White	belthchi	veḷape	boḷe	veḷe	biḷapu
Awake	edderzh	mēkiku	yecharikeāgu	yeḷ	yecharikeagu
Bring	tar	kod	tar	tar	tar
Come	var	vă	bă	bă	bă
Drink	ūṭ	ūn	kuḍi	kuḍi	kudi, uṭ (suck)
Eat	tin	tin	tin	tin	tin
Give	kor	koḍu	koḍu	koḍu	koḍu
Go	fo	hōgu	hōgu	pō	hōgu
Hear	keḷ, voraṭ (listen)	voraṭ	kēḷ	kêṭ	kêḷ
Kill	besht	tavar	koll	koll	koll
Laugh	karzh	kars	nagu	jirike	nage

* Some are called kambē; thus, like the Badaga ūru, applies, I think, to the more important. The Badaga ūru contains a temple, and is generally, I believe, the mother village

† Kâl = foot; ārthchi = it pains or rises.

‡ To this and a good many adjectives the verb seems always appended—"it is bitter, black, &c."

§ It seems that the noun is always used with these adjectives

Lift up	tūkh	tūk, yettu	tūk, yettu	tūk	tūk, yettu
Move	nade	nade	naḍe	naḍe	naḍe
Run	vōḍ	vōd	vōd	vōd	vōḍ
Be silent	pokkir	pokkir	summaniru	summaniru	japaniru
Sit down	neshkir	kūsir	kūtir	kūk	kuli
Sleep	vorg	vorag	vorag	rombu	vorag
Stand	nirzh	nillu	nillu	nillu	nillu
Strike	puith	puia	huia	adi	hui
Take	yett	veḍe	tegi	tege, bāngu	tegi
Take away	yettfo	ett hōgu	yettiunḍhogu	eḍedu, kondupo	yettiunḍhōgu
Tell	êrzh	peid	hēlu	sollu	hḷêgu
Understand	arth	arsi	aria	aria	aria
Weep	ârzh } *	alu	aḷu	aḷu	alu
Play	ārzh }				
Speak	êrzh	mans	nuḍi	pēsh	mātadu, nudi

As the proofs were corrected in England, there has been no opportunity of rectifying any mistakes in copying; and some inaccuracies may have crept in which would have been corrected if reference to Mr Metz or the natives had been possible.—Ed.

The difference between Toda and all the other dialects will be at once perceptible. The two most nearly allied are Kurumba and Badaga, which are mere varieties of Canarese. These have 138 words in common† out of 172.

Irula, which is nearer to Tamil, agrees with the two former in only 60. Allowing for a difference of terminal letter, which in Kota is generally e, where the others have a or u, this dialect has 57 words in common with Irula and 67 with Kurumba. On the other hand, it constantly retains the Tamil initial p where the Canarese has h.

Toda is identical with Badaga in 33 words, with Irula in 29. The Kotas seem to have adopted some Toda words, but their pronunciation quite disguises the relationship. The deep pectoral voice of the Todas always suggests an imitation of their own buffaloes, while the Kotas snarl like jackals, a comparison which cannot fail to occur to anyone who has seen them squabbling over a carcase.

---

* The two words are hardly distinguishable in Toda

† I have throughout only reckoned those words which are absolutely identical or differ only in the terminal letter, of course many more differ very slightly.

APPENDIX B.

DESCRIPTIVE CATALOGUE of ORNAMENTS, IMPLEMENTS, &c. of NĪLAGIRI TRIBES.

TODAS.

No. I.—*Pútkuli,* worn by men and women. *See* Report. The cloth purchased from weavers who come to the Hills from Serumugē in Coimbatore. Rupees 4.

No. II.—*Tharp.* Waistcloth worn by men. Purchased from Serumugē merchants. Rupees 1.

No. III.—*Konu* (కోను) Langooty. Procured from Serumugē merchants. 2 annas.

No. IV.—*Kāng* (కాంX), worn round the waist over No. II. by men who take a part in the funeral ceremonies. Procured from Calicut. Rupees 4.

No V.—*Mekari* (మెక్కరి). Four baskets, of sizes, to hold grain, made by Todas and Kotas of bamboo and ratan. Annas 10.

No. VI.—*Pon* (పొన్న). Two milk vessels, of sizes, for milk and curds, made by Todas and Badagas from bamboo joints, with handle and binding of ratan. 8 annas.

No. VII.—*Wāk* (వాకా). Drinking vessel size of a pint, made by Todas and Badagas of small bamboos and bound with ratan. 1 anna.

No. VIII.—*Kuarsh.* Walking sticks, two of bamboo, two of jungle wood.

No. IX.—Four pairs of rings worn by Toda men and women. Rings made by Kotas Rupees 4, 10 annas.

No. X.—*Sticks* and "*Cat*" used in the game *Ilāta*. *See* page 7. Made by Toda men. *Gratis.*

No. XI.—Toda club (ornamented as used at a funeral ceremony). *See* Plate XI. Made by the Todas of the Hâli tree. Rupee 1.

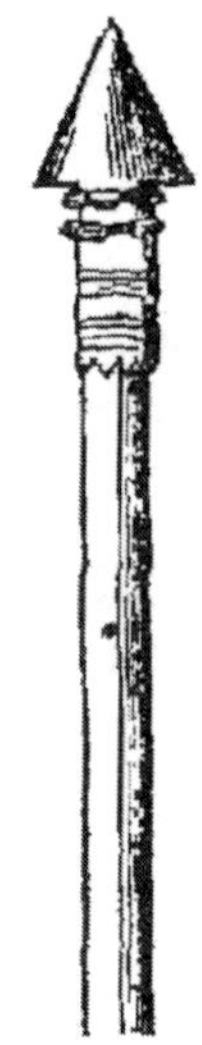

No. XII.—Gold earrings. Worn generally by men and sometimes by women. Made by Kotas. Gold procured from Malabar in the shape of sovereigns. Rupees 12, 8 annas.

No. XIII.—Silver box, end opening with a screw. Used for small gold coins. Worn round the waist over the *tharp* with a string, or sometimes a silver chain. Silver, got from silver coins. Made by low country smiths, and bought in its present shape by the Todas. Rupees 6.

No. XIV.—*Tŏlwădi.* Brass armlet worn by women above the elbow; big ones weigh each 2¼ lbs., small ones 1 lb. Made by Kotas of brass brought up by low country merchants. An armlet made of Nilagiri nettle fibre, bound with cotton thread, with a coarse tassel, is worn as a sort of buffer between the brass armlets. A woman will sometimes wear two of the big brass armlets, and two of the small ones on each arm. Girls of ten years old will begin to wear the small ones, and three or four years after the big ones. The armlets are never taken off except for repairs. Rupees 12, 8 annas.

No. XV.—Two necklaces worn and made by Toda women. Beads purchased in Bazaar. The beads are strung upon thread made of the Nilagiri nettle. Black beaded necklaces called *Keehwad.* Red beaded necklaces called *Nerballi.* Annas 4.

No. XVI.—*Kyțthwodiwâri.* Tied round the elbow of a female corpse, and burnt with the body. Made by Toda women.

Tiffiri (తిప్పరి) The bag or lump at the end contains the flower and leaf of * 6 pice.

No. XVII.—*Tegh.* Cocoa-nut drinking vessel, used by women for milk and *tyre.* Made by Todas out of cocoa-nuts brought from the low country. *Gratis.*

No XVIII.—*En.* Cloth tied round the waist of a female corpse, and burnt with the body. Cloth made by Badagas in Jakanēri in this district The same villagers make the Pâlâl's cloths (Tunni). *See* page 16. Rupee 1.

No. XIX.—*Kafthriath* (కఫధ్రథ). Silver earrings worn by women in each ear. Made by Kotas. Rupees 5.

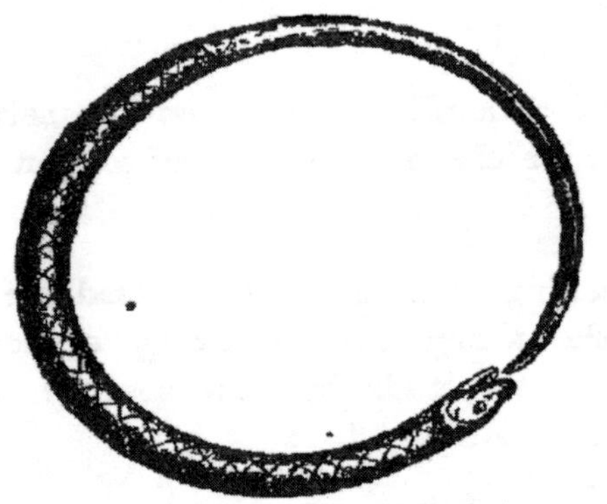

No. XX.—*Hibbal* (హిబ్బళ). Iron bracelets worn by women on the left wrist. Made by Kotas. 12 annas.

No. XXI.—*Hebbu* (హెబ్బు).—Two small iron rings worn by women on the first finger of the left hand; they usually wear two, sometimes four. Made by Kotas. *Gratis.*

---

* This was left blank, probably till the botanical name could be ascertained. I do not know what tree is referred to.—ED.

No. XXII.—*Tharig* (థరగ్). Dish of bell metal made in the low country, used by Todas to eat out of. Four or five sizes will be found in each house. Rupees 3, 12 annas.

No. XXIII.—"Pútkuli." Same as No. I., but worn by women so as to hang down to the feet, and not thrown so much over the left shoulder. Rupees 3.

No. XXIV.—*Tharp* (థర్ప్.) Waistcloth worn by women high up over the breasts. The female "tharp" is larger than the man's "tharp" Procured from Serumuge. 10 annas

No. XXV.—*Bilthagār*. Necklace, made by Kotas. The chain of silver, the tassels of cowries. When worn, the tassels hang down behind. Rupees 3.

No XXVI.—*Tinnigáni* (టిన్నిగాని). Purse made by Toda women. At funerals it is put into the pouch of the Pútkuli and burnt with the corpse. Made of coloured cotton thread. *Gratis.*

No. XXVII.—*Káṭṭshíram.* Ordinary purse worn by Todas Made in the low country and bought by Todas from traders who came to the Hills. *Gratis.*

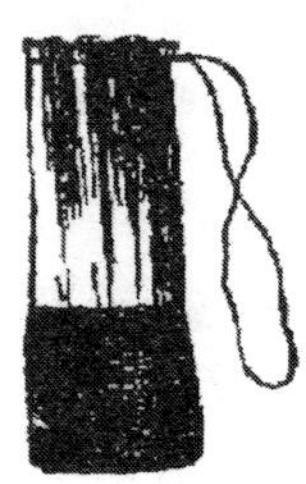

No. XXVIII.—*Pénnār* (పెంనార్.) Made of black and white cotton by Toda women. Tied round the waist of the corpse and burnt at funerals. Ends done up with cowries. Sometimes eight or ten are burnt at one time. *Gratis.*

No. XXIX.—*Kévilth* (కేవిల్థ). Necklace made by Kotas. Worn generally by women; burnt with the body at funerals. 30 rupees.

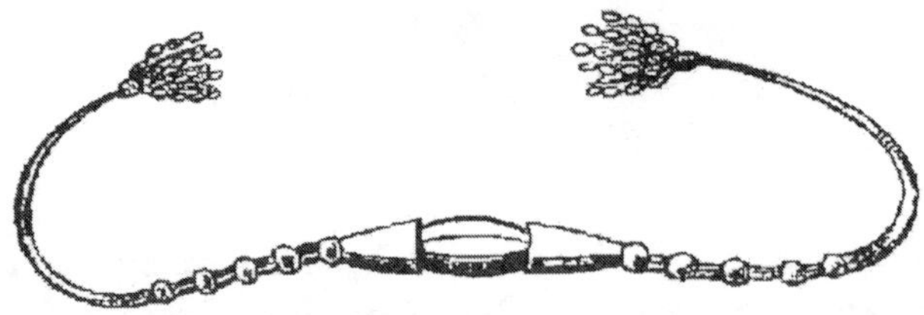

No. XXX.—*Billvall* (బిల్వల్లు). Worn by women on the right wrist. Made by Malabar jewellers. Small silver beads rattle inside. Rupees 5, 8 annas.

No. XXXI.—*Thaggár* (థగ్గార). Brass chain worn by women round their waist next to the skin. Made at Kota village. Rupees 1, 4 annas.

No. XXXII.—Módara (మోదర). Silver ring worn by men and women on the small finger of either hand; a coin often forms the seal of the ring. Made by Tamil smiths. Rupees 3, 4 annas.

No. XXXIII.—*Pitteh.* Worn by males and females on the third finger of the right hand, and made by Tamil smiths. Rupees 4, 8 annas.

No. XXXIV.—*Kvelth* (క్వెల్థ). Bamboo for blowing up fires. Made by Todas.

No. XXXV.—*Paṭṭi.* A square basket covered with cloth and cotton, and ornamented with cowries; at dry funeral for a female, 15 or 18 will be burnt, each containing a piece of jaggery, garlic, safron, sandalwood, and some nār (fibre) for sewing thread, the latter prepared by Toda women; the basket is made by the Kurumbas.

No. XXXVI.—*Kuttkuelth* (కుట్టుక్వెల్థ). Burnt at the dry funeral of a female. Made by Kotas.

No. XXXVII.—*Bugúri* (బుగూరి). Musical instrument, a sort of flute. Made by the Todas, and played by them and by Badagas.

No. XXXVIII.—*Put* (ಪುಟ್). Wooden implement, used in cooking to stir the rice. Made by Todas.

No. XXXIX.—*Nirzh.* Dry sticks which produce fire by friction. *See* page 13. Every mand has some of these sticks.

No. XL.—*Ohidi* (ಓಡಿ). Spoon of cocoa-nut, and bamboo handle. Made by Todas.

KOTAS

PLATES LXXVII, LXXIX.

The Kotas wear the same cloths as the Todas, *Plate* LXXVII., Nos. I. to IV.

The *putkuli* (I.) is called in Kota language *vevād.* The *tharp* (II.) is called *mund,* and the *kōnu* (III) is called *kōsal* or *jalladam.* No. IV. is not generally worn by Kotas.

V.—Three baskets of sizes used and made by Kota men :—

(*a.*) *kik* or *kikoluk.*

(*b.*) *ambām chik.*

(*c.*) *moram.*

VI.—Bamboo milk vessel, not in common use, as Kotas do not keep cows or drink milk.

VII.—Two ordinary clay drinking vessels used and made by Kota women.

VIII.—Sticks; not generally used.

IX.—Two silver rings (Kota, *madaram*), made by Kotas, and worn on third and fourth fingers of right hand by men and women.

IX.—Two bell-metal toe rings (Kota, *kākojī*), made by low country men, worn by Kota women on second toe of right foot.

X.—Red and black beaded necklaces (Kota, *koiavila* and *karg*), worn by Kota women; purchased from low country traders.

They wear also the *hebbal,* No. XX. in the Toda list.

XI.—Purse (Kota, *chingan seruma*), worn by Kotas; purchased from low country traders.

XII.—Clarionet (Kota, *kola*), made and played upon by the men.

XIII.—Drum (Kota, *parē*), made and played upon by the men, beaten by the hands.

XIV.—Tambourine (Kota, *tapatē*), made and played upon by the men, beaten by two sticks.

XV.—Horn, played upon by Kota men; purchased in the low country.

Kotas play also upon the *bugari,* No. XXXVII. of Toda list.

XVI.—Two copper wristlets (Kota, *tebugan*), worn by Kota women on the right wrist; purchased in the low country.

XVII.—Two bell-metal wristlets (Kota, *vodshalle*), worn by women on the left wrist; procured from the low country.

XVIII.—(*a.*) Bellows (Kota, *tithi*), used in Kota forges, and made by themselves.

(*b.*) Bellows mouthpiece (Kota, *mork*), made by Kotas of clay.

XIX.—Ordinary pots, made by Kota women on a wooden wheel turned by the hand (Kota, (*a.*) *arāt,* and (*b.*) *kodam*).

XX.—Big hammer (Kota, *tabita*), made by Kotas from iron brought from Coimbatore.

XXI.—Small hammer (Kota, *matige*), made by Kotas from iron brought from Coimbatore.

They now use English anvils, but formerly a piece of iron fixed in a wooden block.

XXII.—Hatchet (Kota, *iruvāl*), made by Kotas for cutting brushwood.

XXIII.—Sickle (Kota, *kanaket*), made by Kotas for cutting grass.

XXIV.—Hook (Kota, *mava*), made by Kotas for forking straw.

XXV.—Poker (Kota, *shedigol*), made by Kotas for their forges.

XXVI.—Two pincers (Kota, (*a.*) *kodikilla*, (*b.*) *kaikilla*), made by Kotas for their forges.

XXVII.—Axe (Kota, *madat*), for chopping wood, made by Kotas.

XXVIII.—Mamoty (Kota, *kudai*) and hoe (Kota, kala kudai), made by Kotas.

XXIX.—Plough and share, made by Kotas.

XXX.—Iron (Kota, *hibbi* or cutter), as purchased from low country traders.

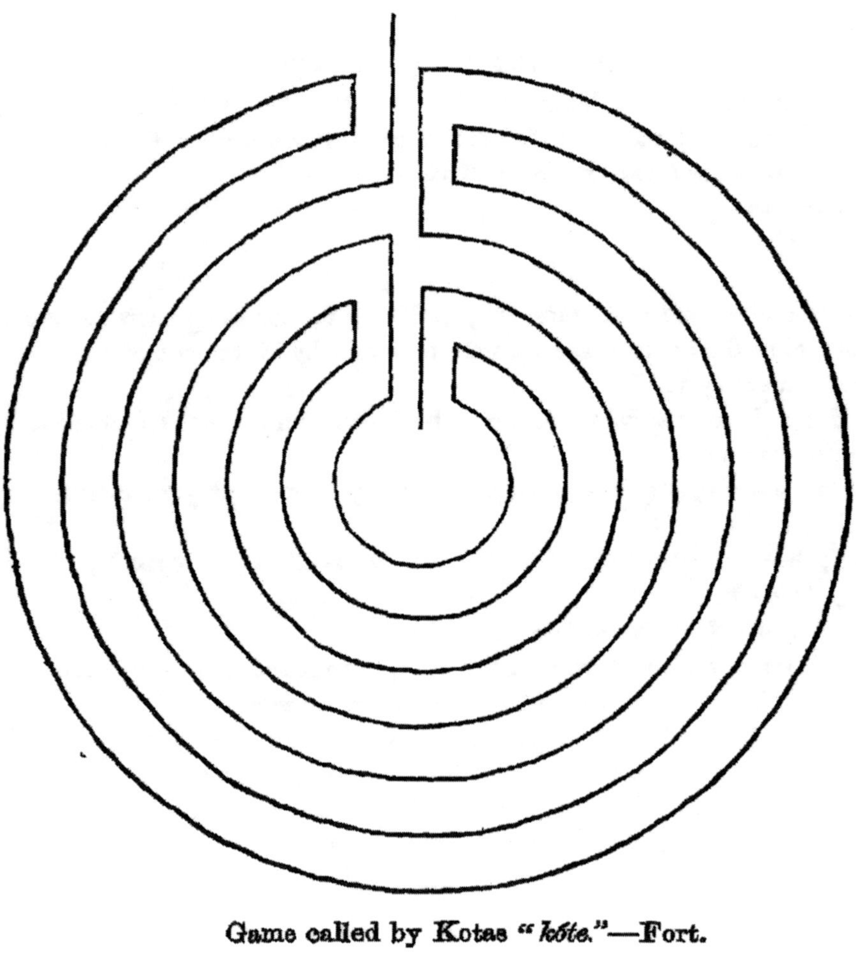

Game called by Kotas "*kōte.*"—Fort.

KURUMBAS and IRULAS, *Plate* LXXVIII.

I.—A brass wristlet, worn by Irulas (men) on the left hand, called in Irula, *tōvandi* (தோவந்தி). Low country manufacture.

II.—A silver wristlet, worn by Irula men on the right hand, called *kārē* (காரே). Low country manufacture.

III.—A brass earring, worn by Irula men on the fleshy lower part of the ear, called *kaduku* (கடுகு). Low country manufacture.

IV.—A brass earring, worn by Irula men on the upper part of the left ear, called *patta-mētti* (பட்டமெட்டி). Low country manufacture.

V.—Bead necklace, called *kallē* (கல்லே), consisting of red, white, blue, and black beads; the number of each kind worn by women is indefinite. The beads are bought of the low country traders.

VI.—A brass earring, worn by women on the fleshy part of both ears, called *olē* (ஓலே).

VII.—A brass wire earring, worn by women on the upper part of the left ear called *uruttei-mētti* (உருட்டைமெட்டி). Low country manufacture.

VIII.—A brass nose ornament (gilt), worn hooked into the left nostril, called *mūkkutti* (மூக்குத்தி). Low country manufacture.

IX.—A brass finger ring, worn by women on all the fingers of the left hand, thumb included, four or five rings on each finger, called *keimōdiram* (கைமோதிரம்). Low country manufacture.

X.—An iron wristlet, worn by women on the right wrist, called *tunde* (துண்டே). Low country manufacture.

XI.—A brass wristlet, worn by women on the right wrist, called *himbala*. Low country manufacture. As many as thirty or forty are worn at a time.

XII.—Glass wristlets, some red, some black, worn by women in large numbers on the left wrist, called *valē* (வளே).

XIII.—A toe ring, made of bell-metal, called *kanju* (கஞ்சு), worn on the third and fourth toes of both feet. Low country manufacture.

The Kurumbas wear the same ornaments as the Irulas, only the brass wristlet, No. XI, is worn on both hands. The Kurumba men wear also,

XIV.—An iron and a copper finger ring, the former on the fourth finger of the left hand, and the latter on the little finger of the right hand, called *ungira* (உங்கிர).

XV.—A gourd bottle, used by Irulas, called *kūmmē* (கூம்மே), for water; grown and manufactured by themselves.

XVI.—A large net, used by Irulas principally to catch jungle sheep, called *korūngū vallē* (கொரூங்குவல்லே).

XVII.—A small net, used to catch jungle fowl, called *koli-vallē* (கோழிவல்லே).

XVIII.—An Irula umbrella, manufactured by themselves, called *kodē* (கொடே).

XIX.—A basket, made by Irula men, called *kūdē* (கூடே).

XX.—A spear, called *īdi* (ஈடி), the iron head made by Kotas, the handle of *salamara* wood, used to stick jungle sheep when caught in the net.

XXI.—A primitive rat trap, used by Kurumbas, called *yelī kattiri* (எலிகத்திரி).

APPENDIX C.

DESCRIPTIVE CATALOGUE of objects discovered in the CAIRNS, CROMLECHS, &c.

From Kambhatti, Todanád.

I. Part of a woman's figure, carrying a chatty on her head; bangles on her arm, and rings on fingers; hair in the usual low country knot. No dress above the waist, but marks as of necklaces.

II. Pot and lid, with man on horseback; conical head-dress or hair-knot, short beard. Waist-cloth, in which is a dagger with double guard; left hand rests on the horse's ear; legs gone.

III. Man with conical head-dress and long beard; legs wanting.

IV. Buffalo.

V. to IX. Fragments of men and animals; horse, buffalo, and deer or sheep.

X. Buffalo bell, in pottery.

XI. Six iron spear-heads, one barbed.

XII. Upper part of woman.

XIII. Bird with a crest and wide wings; legs represented only by a solid pedestal, and a few scratches for claws.

XIV. A curious monkey or satyr figure, without head; seems to have a girdle of leaves on; legs with something like claws at the end.

From Tirichigiri, near Kotagherry.

XV. to XIX. Fragments of animals, chiefly heads; some nondescript, others like sheep and camels.

XX. Women's figures; upper part naked to the waist; bracelets and bangles.

From Adikarhatti Mekanád.

XXI., XXII Human heads and figures; some very animal-like. One has a square-topped head-dress, like one figured by Colonel Congreve.

XXIII. Pieces of swords and daggers.

From Hukupoliam Todanád.

XXIV. Snake and pieces

XXV. Fabulous animal; two heads and necks covered with spots on a centre pedestal.

XXVI. and XXVII. Animals; one without a head.

From Italāru Mekanād.

XXVIII. to XXX. Fragments of animals, chiefly buffaloes.

From Kalamaē Kotagiri, Mekanád.

XXXI. Cylindrical pedestal; conical at the top, with a row of projections round it.

From Nidikādu, Mēkanād.

XXXII. Pot with a spout, neatly made.

From Tirichigiri, Todanád.

XXXIV. Pots and lids.

From Adikarhatti, Mēkanād.

XXXV. Cornelian bead; oblong; plain.

From Ebgōdu.

XXXVI. Lid, and figure of low-country bullock, with hump.

XXXVII. Animal; hog-backed, with prominent notched spine.

XXXVIII., XXXIX. Animals' and birds' heads.

XL. Pedestal.

XL. (*a.*) Urn; small, flat, with large lid covering the top loosely.

XL. (*b.*) Bronze vase, on stand, small, well-made; ornamented with a few concentric lines, and covered inside with dark green mottled shining rust

XL. (*c.*) Urn like XL. (*a.*), containing two iron implements (*Plate* XL., *fig. j.*)

XL. (*d.*) Bronze vessel, on stand; large, round, fluted, chased with a pretty pattern in the centre. (*Plate* XLI., *fig. e*)

XL. (*e.*) Native stool, man on lid.

XL. (*f.*) Elephant's head.

XL. (*g*) Part of man.

XLI. Animal's head, perhaps jungle sheep

From Stone circles by Segur road.

XLII. Pieces of bone, charcoal, and metal (copper alloyed with small quantity of tin).

From Seven Cairn Hill.

XLIII. Bird; legs wanting.

From Chiketnaoribetta, near Tuneri.

XLIV. Bronze, on stand; long, oval vase; fluted, and chased very prettily round the edge, inside a lotus pattern. (*Plate* XLI, *fig. a.* and XLII.) Very solid and heavy.

XLV. Bronze vase; stand missing; round and shallow; resembles "puja" vessels now used by Hindus.

XLVI. Large well-shaped spear-head; rib up the middle.

XLVII. Sickle, with long handle ending in a knob.

XLVIII. Two razors.

XLIX. Fragments of pottery, showing varieties of ornament.

L. to LV. Fragments of animals.

LVI. Small sickle.

From Kunhakkilabetta Tūnēri.

LVII. Apparently a fabulous animal, with a head at each end. *Plate* XXXVII., *fig. g.*

LVIII. to LXI. Fragments of animals.

From Gulicholabetta Tūnēri.

LXII. Lid, with buffalo and bell round neck.

LXIII. Pot and lid, with buffalo.

LXIV. Figure on horseback; horse seems to have been in a sitting posture, but hind quarters are gone.

From Gulicholabetta.

LXVI. Animal with spots.

LXVII., LXVIII. Three human figures; one has a conical, one square head-dress; one is a woman with very large nose.

LXIX. to LXXI. Animals and fragments of arms; hatchet and shield.

LXXII Woman.

LXXIII. to LXXVI. Pots and fragments, pedestals, sword; animal's head.

LXXVII. Pot and lid, with bear

LXXVIII. Pot and lid, with buffalo.

LXXIX. to LXXXIII Animals of various sorts; heads and bodies

LXXXIV. Men and women; one with a turban.

From Kunhakkilabetta.

LXXXV. Broken pot.

From Gulicholabetta

LXXXVI to XCI Fragments of figures.

From Barrow.—Bilikambe, near Kotagherry.

XCII. Urn; large, flattened, round shape; fine pottery. *Plate* XL, *fig. m.*

XCIII Bronze basin; fluted. (*Plate* XLI, *fig g*) With cone in the middle.

XCIV. Earth contained in bronze.

XCV. to XCVII. Comb*; crystal; bone; gold ornaments contained in bronze.

From Barrow.—Bilikambe.

XCVIII. Urn; fine pottery; much broken.

XCIX. Small bronze, neatly made.

C. and CI. Earth and bones from bronze.

CII. Iron collyrium rod.

CIII. Two cornelian beads.

CIV Green glass and gold beads.

CV. Lids of urns; fine pottery.

CVI. Round stone with a hole in the centre; perhaps hammer.

CVII. Bronze saucer.

CVIII. Urn like XL. (*a.*); contains earth and a spear.

CIX. Part of man's figure; long narrow head; no top-knot or turban.

CX. Fragment of bronze.

From Barrow between Tūnēri and HebbanAd.

CXI. Iron style? Hollow; octagonal.

CXII. Dagger, iron, with double guard; hilt of copper, very much carved.

CXIII Broad bronze chisel; neatly ornamented.

CXIV. Five iron spear-heads.

CXV. Iron implement.

CXVI Charcoal, bones, and earth.

---

* This has crumbled away.

From Cairn.—Nādubetta.

CXVII. Pot; rather like a goglet; with lines of ornament round neck; lid with pig? on it.

CXVIII. Neck of pot and lid with leopard?

CXIX. Pot like CXVII.; bird on lid, hawk; very well made, but without head.

CXX. Neck of pot and lid with a long-tailed bird.

CXXI. Do. with bullock; long tail resting on the lid.

CXXII. Pot and lid, with jungle cock flying.

CXXIII Neck of pot and lid, with sambre; well made.

CXXIV. to CXXVI. Lids and fragments; one with snake, one with bullock.

CXXVII. Three human figures of quite a new type; two with conical head-dress, one with what seems meant for curly hair, one seems to have been riding, but has lost legs and animal; one has the lobes of the ears hanging to the shoulders, and seems to have been in the sitting posture common in Buddhist statues; both these have the oblique Mongolian eye, and strongly resemble Buddhist images.

CXXVIII. Three birds.

CXXIX. Animals, one like a sheep with bell round neck; one is a small buffalo.

CXXX. Small shallow chatty.

CXXXI. Pot and lid, with sunflower.

CXXXII. Man riding; feet resting on lid

CXXXIII Pot and lid, with sambre.

CXXXIV. Urn and lid; fine pottery; contains earth and bones, small iron implement and razor, with marks of cloth on it.

CXXXV. Round bronze vase, on stand; very prettily chased round the rim and at the bottom.

CXXXVI. Iron sickle; found round the bronze.

CXXXVII. Pot and lid with large obelisk, pointed at the top; a row of projections about an inch from the top, and below these a curious knob on one side.

From Barrow—Kambhatti, Todanád.

CXXXVIII. Pot and lid, with woman carrying chatty on her head, short petticoat.

CXXXIX Do, with leopard?

CXL. Do, with man riding a spotted animal, horse, perhaps; man has conical head-dress; cloth round waist with double guarded dagger stuck in it; his right hand holds a battle-axe resting on his shoulder, also with double guard.

CXLI. Pot and lid, with dog.

CXLII. Do. Snake coiled up.

CXLIII. Lid, with man.

CXLIV. Pot and lid, with what appears to be the stump of a tree.

CXLV Lid, with buffalo; bell round neck.

CXLVI. Lid, with man naked, holding a stick.

CXLVII. Woman nursing baby.

CXLVIII. Lid with a ridge round it; man on it with short beard, holding baby; has a short petticoat reaching to his knees.

CXLIX. Lid with buffalo; bell round neck; perfect.

CL. Do. without bell; one horn wanting.

CLI. Lid, with large bird; legs as usual represented by a large round pedestal, and some scratches for claws; a smaller one seems to have stood beside it, and a hand or claw broken off is on the pedestal.

CLII. Lid, with animal, possibly pig.

CLIII. Lid, and man with short beard, making salaam; short petticoat.

CLIV. Lid, with man riding, what may be either a bullock or elephant; the head wanting; man has square head-dress, and short beard; arms and one leg wanting.

CLV. Man; naked; conical head-dress; left hand before mouth.

CLVI. Two animals' heads; one with tusks like a boar, but has something like a bridle on; other has a sort of collar.

CLVII., CLVIII. Bone and charcoal, and fragments of pottery.

From Cairns—Gulicholabetta.

CLIX. Bronze lamp? or censer; small; neatly made, and well finished, with fragments of chain.

CLX. Iron sickle.

CLXI. Iron square lamp? with fragments of chain.

From Cairn.—Yeresibetta, Kentorre, Todanâd.

CLXII. Lid, with small animal; head wanting.

CLXIII to CLXV. Lids, with figures, more or less broken.

CLXVI. Large bronze basin; no stand; covered with dark green shining rust; ornamented only with a few concentric lines.

CLXVII. Small bronze saucer; concentric lines round bottom; contained earth, &c.

CLXVIII. Small iron implement; broken.

CLXIX. Urn; fine pottery; much broken; contained:

CLXX. Shallow bronze vase, on stand; only ornamented with one or two concentric lines; and

CLXXI. Large iron knife or bill-hook, much rusted; and

CLXXII. Iron spear-head; and

CLXXIII. Do. Broken, and rusted to the side of the pot; and

CLXXIV. Bone, charcoal, and earth.

CLXXV. Fragments of bronze vessel, much rusted and broken; contained·

CLXXVI. Earth and bone.

CLXXVII. Bronze saucer: no stand; bright green polished rust; contained:

CLXXVIII. Earth and bone.

CLXXIX. Iron spear-head.

CLXXX. Fragment of sickle.

CLXXXI. Fragment of knife.

CLXXXII. Urn; fine pottery; with a hole in the top of the lid, round which a sort of pattern has been roughly scratched.

CLXXXIII. Iron bell; tongue wanting.

CLXXXIV. Spear-head; square at the bottom.

From Seven-Cairn-hill, Segür road.

CLXXXV. Fragments of animals; very rough and clumsy; and pieces of pots.

From Cairn, near Sholür.

CLXXXVI. Iron razor.

CLXXXVII. Iron sickle.

CLXXXVIII. Iron implement; flat; widening at both ends.

CLXXXVIII. Iron sickle.

CLXXXIX. Iron implement; broken.

CXC. Fragments of pottery of both kinds, but inferior; new marking with raised wavy lines some dark red colour; with traces of glaze.

From Cairn, near Sholūr.

CXCI Bronze saucer; much rusted and broken.

CXCII. Soil, with fragments of rusted bronze.

CXCIII. Iron style? or pin? hollow.

CXCIV. Broken urn; moderate pottery.

CXCV. Urn; pottery rather less good.

CXCVI. Iron razor.

CXCVII. Iron style or pin.

From Barrow, near Sholūr.

CXCVIII. Urn of unusual shape; straight-sided; indifferent pottery.

From Cairn, near Sholūr.

CXCIX. Urn; coarse pottery; shaped like a modern chatty, and full of charred bones.

CC. Fragment of small pot, containing a cylindrical bead of white stone, with three lines of black ornament, and some semi-transparent beads of rough glass, some of which seem partly fused together.

CCI. Broken figure? stag's horn or stump of a tree.

CCII. Small animal; very rough; like cow lying down.

From Cairns N. of Tarnāt Mand.

CCIII. Small urn; straight-sided; ornamented with raised lines; containing earth.

CCIV. Small rough chatty.

CCV. Iron bell; broken.

CCVI. Two iron spear-heads.

CCVII. Fragment of iron style.

CCVIII Fragments of iron.

CCIX. Broken figures; clumsy and coarse.

CCX. Earth and charred bone.

CCXI. Hollow-pointed piece of iron, like a modern arrow-head.

CCXII. Iron bell and chain, in pieces.

CCXIII. Fragments of razor and sickle.

CCXIV. Iron rod or spear handle.

CCXV. Two spear-heads.

CCXVI. Lid, with long-legged animal of the clumsy sort; head and tail wanting.

CCXVII. and CCXVIII. Animals, clumsy, and pieces of coarse pottery.

CCXIX. White substance, probably resin.

CCXX. Broad iron razor or knife.

CCXXI. Spear-head.

CCXXII. A hone of agate or some striped stone.

From Barrow, near Sholūr.

CCXXIII. Two razors.

CCXXIV. Very small javelin or arrow-head; neatly made, and ornamented with two sharply-cut converging ridges near the handle.

CCXXV. Fragments of bronze vessel.

CCXXVI. Leaf-shaped arrow or javelin head, and spear-head of the same shape.

CCXXVII. Broad handsome dagger.

CCXXVIII. Feagments of spear-heads.

CCXXIX. Fragments of animals.

From Cairn between Tarnāt Mand and Sholūr.

CCXXX. Urn; chatty-shaped; indifferent pottery; containing a quantity of burnt bones, and

CCXXXI. Small chatty, with two bits of a skull.

CCXXXII. A number of beads, chiefly of rough glass, but one or two are of white agate, and two are button-shaped and inlaid with black.

From Barrow near Sholūr.

CCXXXIII. Small narrow spear-head.

From Cairn near Sholūr

CCXXXIV. Urn; chatty shape; inferior pottery; full of large bones.

CCXXXV. A flat, oblong piece of white substance, apparently bone; pierced with five holes.

CCXXXVI. Beads; some long double cones of agate, well made; the ends blunt; pierced longitudinally; others of the same kind as CCXXXII.

CCXXXVII. Small urn; very coarse and rough; chatty shaped, with a lid.

CCXXXVIII. Do. without lid.

CCXXXIX. Do. basin shaped

From Cairn near Kodanâd ūru.

CCXL. Urn; chatty shaped; indifferent pottery; full of large pieces of bone; amongst others, part of a jaw.

CCXLI. Small iron spear-head.

CCXLII. Large round bronze vase, on stand, like XL. (*d*), but rusted and broken. *Plate* XLI., *fig. f.*

CCXLIII. Pair of iron shears, with bent spring like small garden shears. *Plate* XLIII.

CCXLIV. Long straight piece of iron; chisel?

CCXLV. Pieces of iron rod or hook.

CCXLVI. Pot and lid, with man sitting on native sofa.

CCXLVII. Do. do. with head badly shaped, and retreating forehead and large ears.

CCXLVIII. Do. do. something broken on one arm.

CCXLIX. Man; conical head; holding shield.

CCL. and CCLI. Fragments of pottery.

CCLII Iron razor.

CCLIII. Pot and lid, with buffalo; rather different from the ordinary type.

CCLIV. Fragment of large bird and neck of pot

From Barrow near Kodanâd ūru.

CCLV. Shallow pot.

CCLVI. Small basin-shaped bronze; dark colour.

CCLVII. Urn, containing bone, earth, &c.

CCLVIII. Bronze collyrium rod.

From Cairn S. of Bilikal Hill.

CCLIX. Fragments of urn; fine pottery; containing bone, and

CCLX. Bronze basin, with cone inside; dark colour; *Plate* XLI., *fig. g*, and

CCLXI. Two rings; one gold, plain and thin, one of bronze; and

CCLXII. Piece of pumice, shaped as if moulded in a saucer; and

CCLXIII. Pointed piece of iron, and bits of collyrium rod.

CCLXIV. Urn; fine pottery; like XCII., containing

CCLXV. Bronze, with cone at the bottom; *Plate* XLI., *fig. g.*, and

CCLXVI Pumice; segment of oval; and

CCLXVII. Bronze cylinder open at the top; ornamented with rings; bottom flat; and

CCLXIX. Razor.

CCLXX. Small urn; inferior pottery.

CCLXXI. Bronze; bottom rusted out.

CCLXXII. Small bronze; dark colour.

From Cairn on Bilikal Hill, S. shoulder.

CCLXXIII. Lid of urn; fine pottery; containing bone, bits of iron and bronze, and pieces of bronze ring

CCLXXIV. Large fragments of iron sickles, razors, &c., much rusted and broken.

CCLXXV. Urn; chatty shaped; contained bones; and

CCLXXVI Bronze ring, fragments of collyrium rod, two gold beads and a gold button or knob, two round stone beads, two gold earrings, one plain, one ringed, and a number of small fragments of bronze like nail or pin heads.

From Cairn.—Bilikal Hill.

CCLXXVIII. Bronze, with cone at the bottom, containing fragments of coarse cotton cloth, some of which adhere to the side, and have left marks on the rust of the bronze, contained:

CCLXXIX. Bronze collyrium rod? iron do. and fragment, gold earring, ferule or cap of some staff or weapon.

CCLXXX. Sickle.

CCLXXXI. Urn like modern chatty, but with large round lid; containing—

CCLXXXII. Bronze; small, thick, and rough; without ornament; basin shape; and

CCLXXXIII. Bronze ring, well made, and two thin gold earrings; and

CCLXXXIV. Pumice.

CCLXXXV Urn; fine pottery; flattened; globe shape, like XCII.; contained bones and two bits of skull, and

CCLXXXVI. Bronze saucer; dark green rust outside, and

CCLXXXVII. Bits of collyrium rod? bronze signet ring, and gold ornament like tali, and

CCLXXXVIII. Pumice.

CCLXXXIX. Spear-head, small.

CCXC. Broken razor.

From Cairn.—Enkal Mand Hill.

CCXCI. to CCXCIV. Pots; mouths unusually large and wide; lids wanting.

CCXCV. Urn-shaped pot, small; rough pottery.

CCXCVI. to CCCI. Like CCXCI. to CCXCIV.

From Small Cairn E. of Enkal Mand Hill.

CCCII. to CCCIV. Similar, but with rather smaller mouths; CCCIII. has a lid with curiously marked pillar, with two hooked projections.

CCCV. (*a.*) Small iron knife, like bill-hook.

CCCV (*b.*) Broad knife with round handle.

CCCV. (*c.*) Large animal's head; indescribable.

From Natanēri Hill.

CCCVI. Bronze vase; stand missing; fluted with pretty pattern inside.

CCCVII. Two very pretty gold earrings; the ring formed by a kind of plait which passes over a shield-shaped piece of gold, with three rows of small balls.

From Seven-Cairn-Hill, Kilkotagiri.

CCCVIII. Small pot.
CCCIX. Lamp or censer, like CLXI.
CCCX. Spear-head.
CCCXI., CCCXII. Two bells in pottery
CCCXIII Enormous stag's horn?
CCCXIV. Body of large bird; head wanting.
CCCXV. Pillar; conical top.
CCCXVI. Do. or tree.
CCCXVII. Fragment of do
CCCXVIII. Small urn; fine pottery; mica specks and glaze.

From Kistvaens.—Udrāya kote.

CCCXIX. Iron dagger; handle wanting.
CCCXX. Fragments of thick pottery very highly glazed

From Cairn near Nidugula, Perangandd.

CCCXXI. Small urn with flat lid; fine pottery.
CCCXXII. Bronze basin; broken.
CCCXXIII. Razor.
CCCXXIV. Knife.
CCCXXV. Spear-head.
CCCXXVI. Three pins or styles.
CCCXXVII. Two spear-heads
CCCXXVIII. Pumice.
CCCXXIX. Small iron collyrium rod.
CCCXXX. Fragments of some horn or bone implement.
CCCXXXI Lid containing broken collyrium rod.
CCCXXXII. Knife or sickle.
CCCXXXIII. to CCCXXXVIII. Spear-heads, razors, and a knife or sickle.
CCCXXXIX. Iron chisel.
CCCXL. Pin or style.
CCCXLI. Shallow urn, like a lid reversed; fine pottery; mica glaze; contained earth and a little bone.
CCCXLII. Small urn; lid broken; fine pottery, contained earth and a little bone.
CCCXLIII. Fragments of rough pottery; deep pot broken; small animals and birds.

From Barrow.—Ponguibetta, near Kakora, Perangandd.

CCCXLIV. Small spear-head; well shaped.
CCCXLV. Urn, broken; fine pottery; mica glaze; contained:
CCCXLVI. Bronze saucer with bright green rust; and
CCCXLVII. Bronze collyrium rod.
CCCXLVIII. Urn; chatty shaped; small lid inverted; seems to have had a figure on it; pottery indifferent; no glaze; contained—
CCCXLIX. Bronze bottle; very pretty; shaped like a flower bud; no stopper; and
CCCL. Small oblong cornelian bead; and
CCCLI. Iron and fragments.

CCCLII. Large urn; fine pottery, with mica glaze; lid fits to the rim, and has a small ornament at the top, of three bars from one centre; contained:

CCCLIII. Bronze basin, ornamented with a few plain lines; and

CCCLIV. Iron knife; much rusted; and

CCCLV. Iron razor, with remains of cloth round it; and

CCCLVI. Small iron spear-head; leaf shaped; and

CCCLVII. Fragments of iron; and

CCCLVIII. Iron ferule or cap, with traces of wooden handle; and

CCCLIX. Bits of resin, dried pieces of orange peel, a small piece of metal for one side of the nose, a bronze ornament, perhaps part of a buckle, bits of wood, and minute pieces of silk, bone, &c.

From Second Barrow, same hill.

CCCLX. Small urn, with large lid; medium pottery; contained:

CCCLXI. Iron spear-head.

CCCLXII. Urn, like CCCLX

From Third Barrow, same hill.

CCCLXIII. Urn; lid very small.

CCCLXIV. Do large lid; broken.

CCCLXV. Iron cylinder with flat top

CCCLXVI. Iron collyrium rod?

CCCLXVII. Urn, with channel in the rim for pouring; lid broken.

CCCLXVIII Urn, like CCCLX.; lid broken.

CCCLXIX. Bone, and bronze collyrium rod.

From Cairn near Kodanâd.

CCCLXX. Urn; fine pottery; the lid fits closely to the rim, and seems to have had a figure on the top.

CCCLXXI. Spear or javelin head; iron; leaf-shaped.

From Cairn near Banganni.

CCCLXXII. Small urn, chatty shaped; coarse pottery; roughly ornamented; one of the roughest of the cinerary urns; contained earth, bone, and charcoal, &c.

CCCLXXIII. Small pot; very coarse; shallow and broken; contained:

CCCLXXIV. Bones and earth, and broken iron rod; and

CCCLXXV. Bronze saucer; irregularly ornamented round rim with perpendicular lines.

CCCLXXVI. Large iron razor.

CCCLXXVII. Small, narrow spear-head; broken.

CCCLXXVIII. Piece of sickle.

CCCLXXIX. Long razor.

CCCLXXX. Small spear-head.

CCCLXXXI. Small knife; broken.

CCCLXXXII. Fragments of rough pottery; small rough figures, men sitting; one looks like a woman in long petticoats, sitting; one might be a cobra; but all are much defaced.

CCCLXXXIII. Urn; chatty-shaped; inferior pottery.

From Cairn near Banganni, top of conical hill.

CCCLXXXIV. Fine urn; large, with several lines of ornament; mica glaze.

CCCLXXXV. Razor.

CCCLXXXVI. Small sickle.

CCCLXXXVII. Chisel; broken.

CCCLXXXVIII. Small piece of iron for nose.

CCCLXXXIX. Urn, with broad rim turned inwards and projecting; moderate pottery.

CCCXC. Sickle, with long handle.

CCCXCI. Small urn; lid fitting to the rim; neatly finished and ornamented; rising to a point in the middle; pottery fair; traces of glaze.

CCCXCII. Resin.

From Azārams near Nidugūla.

CCCXCIII. Charcoal, and eleven bronze bracelets, some ribbed across, some plain.

CCCXCIV. Ditto. two or three bracelets and fragments.

CCCXCV. Bracelet and fragments, and two bronze rings.

CCCXCVI. Three spear-heads; iron; very little rusted; square at bottom, like CLXXXIV., but larger.

CCCXCVII. Long and broad chisel.

CCCXCVIII. Knife.

CCCXCIX. Iron implement, something like Malabar style; differs from cairn styles in having a hollow tapering cylinder on the top of a solid one.

CCCC. Charcoal and bone.

From Cairn near Kodanād.

CCCCI. Fragments of figures; small; rather defaced; men and women; double-headed monster, men with big heads and idiotic faces; dog?

CCCCII. Razor.

CCCCIII. Spear-head; long; well-shaped.

CCCCIV. Knife; something like Kāfkutti, but smaller

CCCCV. Fragments of figures; snake; sitting figure; man riding on headless animal; all small and defaced.

CCCCVI. Orange peel.

CCCCVII. Lid, flat; good pottery.

CCCCVIII. Fine urn; very good pottery and mica glaze; lid with triangular ornament like CCCLII., fitting to the broad rim, which is marked by two or three lines.

CCCCIX. Knife, with long tongue, which still retains the marks of the wooden handle into which it has been stuck.

CCCCX. Urn; containing bones; beautifully made; of the finest pottery, with mica glaze, but shaped exactly like the common pots, deep and narrow, and with figure of a bird on the lid.

CCCCXI. Razor.

CCCCXII. Small nose jewel of gold wire, neatly made; like a small bunch of grapes.

CCCCXIII. Small bronze basin; graceful shape and prettily ornamented round the outer edge; chasing, however, rather irregular.

CCCCXIV. Bronze basin, like CCCLXXV.

FOUND in CROMLECHS.

From Major Sweet's plantation near Kolakambē, Chennapatna tada.

1. Rings, iron and bronze.
2. Ankle bells.
3. Iron and bronze bangles; thinner than those found in Azārams.
4. Broken earrings.
5. Pickles.
6. Iron and bronze bracelets, rather thicker.
7. Small sickles.
8. Small hoes.
9. Deva-kotta-kal; small.
10. Small, thick, common chatty.

From Kakūsi.

11. Small lamp; thick pottery.

Major Sweet's plantation.

12. Bits of bone.
13. Signet rings.
14. Nondescript ornaments.

From Mēlūr.

15. Chatty; small; with two strange knobs or horns on one side.